ON THE ELEMENTS

BIJDRAGEN TOT DE FILOSOFIE

onder redactie van prof. dr. ir. H. van Riessen,
prof. dr. J. van der Hoeven en prof. dr. mr. C. A. van Peursen,
in samenwerking met de centrale interfaculteit van
de Vrije Universiteit, Amsterdam

1 Dr. ir. E. Schuurman, *Techniek en toekomst*
Confrontatie met wijsgerige beschouwingen

2 B. H. Son, Ph. D., *Science and person*
A study on the idea of "Philosophy as Rigorous Science" in Kant and Husserl

3 A. P. Bos, Ph. D., *On the Elements*
Aristotle's Early Cosmology

A. P. BOS, Ph. D.

ON THE ELEMENTS

ARISTOTLE'S EARLY COSMOLOGY

VAN GORCUM & COMP. B.V., ASSEN, 1973

The translation of the Dutch manuscript as well as the publication of this book was made possible through a grant from the Netherlands Organization for the Advancement of Pure Research (Z.W.O.)

Translation by J. N. Kraay, Toronto

Printed in The Netherlands by Van Gorcum Assen

TABLE OF CONTENTS

INTRODUCTION   1

CHAPTER ONE. ARISTOTLE'S *DE CAELO* AND MODERN STUDIES   5

A. The Introduction of the Genetic Method by Werner Jaeger (1923) . .   5
B. H. Von Arnim on the Theology of Aristotle (1931) 10
C. W. K. C. Guthrie on the Development of Aristotle's Thought (1933) . 12
D. Some Editions and Translations of *De Caelo* 14
E. The Work of Paul Moraux 16
F. A Commentary on *De Caelo* by L. Elders (1966) 18

CHAPTER TWO. A RENEWED STUDY OF *DE CAELO:* THE COMPOSITION . . . 23

A. The Two Prologues of *De Caelo* III 23
B. *De Caelo* I, c.1-3 and III in Their Relation to the Remainder of the
   Treatise 25

CHAPTER THREE. THE REFERENCES IN *DE CAELO* I, c.1-3 & III 27

1. Introductory Methodological Notes 27
2. Aids Towards Chronological Determination 28
3. The Internal References 28

CHAPTER FOUR. THE CONTENT OF *DE CAELO* I, c.1-3 & III 33

A. Aristotle's Starting-Point (I, c.1) 33
   1. The *Soma* as Central Theme 33
   2. The Basic Principle Posited, Not Demonstrated 34
   3. No *Metabasis eis allo genos* 34
   4. Does *Protrepticus* B33 Provide a Counter-argument? 44
   5. The Physical is Irreducible 45
B. The Doctrine of Motion (I, c.2, 268b11-26) 46
   1. Aristotle's New View of Motion 47
   2. No A-somatic *Psyche* 48
   3. The Same Doctrine of Motion in *De Philosophia* 48
C. The Method of Division in *De Caelo* I, c.1-3 & III 49
   1. The Basic Division 49
   2. *Diaeresis* 50
   3. The Role of the Number Three 51

D. The Theory of the First Element (I, c.2-3) 54
   1. Introduction 54
   2. The Proof for the Existence of the First Element 55
   3. Characteristics of the First Element 55
   4. The Intention Behind the Introduction of the First Element . . . 56
   5. Two Kinds of *Ousia* 58
   6. First or Fifth Element? 60
   7. The First Element Moves by Virtue of Its Own Nature 60
   8. The Interpretation of *De Philosophia* fragment 21b (R) 62
   9. The Home of the Gods 65
E. The Realm of Becoming and Passing-away (Book III) 66
   1. The Sublunar Bodies 66
   2. A Critical Attitude Towards the Eleatic Philosophers 67
   3. The Chronological Relation of Book III to *De Philosophia* 68
   4. A Further Criticism of Plato 69
   5. Motion in the Realm of the Four Elements 69
   6. Genesis 70
   7. The Components of the Physical World 71
   8. The Intent of Book III is not Exclusively Critical 72
   9. A Connection Between III, c.8 and I, c.3, 270a32 74
F. The Physis-concept in *De Caelo* I, c.1-3 & III 75
   Excursus: Aristotle on 'First Philosophy' 79
G. The Theory of Knowledge 82
   1. Rejection of the Platonic Doctrine of the Intelligible World . . . 82
   2. Aristotle's Scientific Method 83
   3. A Difficulty in this Method 86

CHAPTER FIVE. EVALUATION OF THE SYSTEMATIC VIEW IN *DE CAELO* I,
   c.1-3 & III 87

A. No Hylomorphism 87
B. The Term ἐντελέχεια is Not Used 88
C. The Theory of an Unmoved Mover Does Not Occur 89
D. The Discussion is Still Limited to the Presocratics and Plato 91
E. *De Philosophia* is Not Cited 92
F. *Kinesis* and *Metabole* 93
G. Aristotle's Teaching on the Motion of the Stars 95
H. Determination of *De Caelo* I, c.1-3 & III, Continued 98
   1. The Early Date of Its Cosmology 98
   2. The Philosophical View of *De Caelo* I, c.1-3 & III 99
   3. A Correction to the View of W. Jaeger 100
J. The Original Title of *De Caelo* I, c.1-3 & III 101
   1. The Opening Lines of I, c.1 101
   2. The Subject-matter of *De Caelo* I, c.1-3 & III as a Whole 102
   3. Similarity with *Physics* I, c.1 103
   4. A Work 'De Natura' in Three Parts 103

CHAPTER SIX. THE RELATION OF SOME WORKS OF ARISTOTLE TO
DE CAELO I, c.1-3 & III 108

A. 'De Principiis' (*Physics* I) 108
  1. The References 109
  2. The Composition 110
  3. The Principles Constitute a Triad 110
  4. Aristotle's Criticism of Plato's Theory of Principles 111
  5. Becoming, Non-being and the Void 113
  6. Does the Conception of *Physics* I allow a Fifth Element? 113
  7. The Terminology of *Physics* I 114
  8. The Distinct Kinds of Genesis 114
  9. *Physis* Identical with Truth 115
B. 'De Causis' (*Physics* II) 115
  1. Two Theories of Causes 115
  2. The Theory of the Four Causes Does Not Stem From Aristotle's
    Early Period 117
  3. Self-movement in *Physics* II, c.1, 193a29-b21 121
C. The *Protrepticus* 122
  1. The *Protrepticus* and the *De Philosophia* in Relation to the *Physics*
    and *De Caelo* 122
  2. The *Protrepticus* and *De Philosophia* 123
  3. Are There Traces of the Theory of Ideas in the *Protrepticus*? . . . 124
  4. *Physis* in the *Protrepticus* 125
  5. Plato's *Laws* X, 888e ff. 126
  6. Τὰ πρῶτα 127
  7. Knowledge of Nature and Ethics 128
  8. 'Here' and 'Hereafter' 129
D. *De Philosophia* 129
  1. The Chronology 129
  2. Aristotle's Theory of Principles Compared to That of His Predecessors 132
  3. The Highest Deity 133
  4. The Fifth Element in the Psychology of *De Philosophia* 138

CONCLUSION 141

BIBLIOGRAPHY 142

INDEX OF NAMES 151

INTRODUCTION

Books and articles devoted to the philosophy of Aristotle in recent decades display two opposing approaches. One group of writers attempts as much as possible to fuse all of the conceptions attributed to Aristotle into one closed, coherent system, the basic pattern of which was developed during the early years and came to expression with ever increasing clarity. By reason of the problems this method calls forth it sometimes looks as if the representatives of this group are trying to fit too large a balloon into too small a box: the moment the lid is almost closed on one side the balloon bulges out at the other. Their opponents eagerly point out such lumps as being out of place in a supposedly harmoniously constructed philosophical system. They consider it unthinkable that a philosopher of Aristotle's stature should, simultaneously and at a comparable level of exposition, have maintained incompatible theories. After Werner Jaeger's trailblazing work in this area such considerations have persuaded many to accept the idea of evolution in the insights Aristotle developed over the years with respect to the area of theology (H. Von Arnim, W. K. C. Guthrie), the teaching concerning the soul (F. Nuyens), the theory of substance (W. D. Ross), etc. The main objection that may in turn be levelled at their position is that it is far from easy for them to point to clear incisions in the preserved works of Aristotle, evident boundaries between parts out of an earlier period and sections of later date. Just as the Sceptics used the existence of different 'dogmatic' philosophies against the truth of any systematic philosophy at all, so the mutually quite divergent results offered by adherents of the evolution-hypothesis, such as W. Jaeger, P. Gohlke, H. Von Arnim, F. Nuyens, D. H. Th. Vollenhoven and others, provided their opponents with ready arguments against the correctness of either their view or their method, or both.

This criticism was justified to the extent that the 'evolutionists' tended to base their results on criteria with insufficient scope, or frequently neglected significant characteristics of the *Corpus Aristotelicum*. But this criticism overstates its case when it claims that

1

every development-hypothesis leads to conclusions different from the results of every preceding one. On some issues at least those in the 'evolutionist' camp are pretty well agreed, as, for example, the fundamental difference between Aristotle's approach to psychology in the dialogues and in his later study *De Anima*. The possibility remains, therefore, that on other issues the differences among the results are to be charged to the condition of the text of Aristotle's work, particularly to the circumstance that the preserved treatises are the outcome of the philosopher's teaching activity, and that he re-used the one year's notes as the basis for later lectures, meanwhile not hesitating to provide them with additions and corrections. Moreover, it is not impossible that larger units, such as the *Politica*, the *Metaphysics* and the *Physics*, are composed of parts from different periods, joined because of similar or relevant content, just as Porphyry did not edit Plotinus' writings in the *Enneads* according to chronological but to systematic criteria.

It is therefore not a lack of respect regarding the philosopher Aristotle that induces me to seek once again for the characteristics of his earliest philosophical conception in contrast to the later one. It is not impiety which leads me, on the basis of this study, to conclude that within the text of *De Caelo* one must distinguish an earlier and a later stratum. After all, 'respect for the text' of a philosopher is not a quest to prove the literary unity of his writings, but rather to think through his intentions and to search out the motives of his insights. Intensive examination of the texts repeatedly confronts one with difficulties that force one to pose questions regarding development in Aristotle's philosophy during the forty years of his theoretical activity, and of Greek philosophy as a whole, within the context of which the appearance of Aristotle marked an important turning-point.[1]

In view of the leading position classical Greek philosophy accords to cosmology, I have directed myself particularly to it. In addition, from among the writings with cosmological import, I have taken the liberty to pick *De Caelo* to serve as the point of departure for this study. With O. Longo[2] I suspect that in this work an earlier core of

---

[1] Cf. O. Gigon, 'Aristoteles-Studien I', p. 114: 'Wir kennen bisher die Nuancen wie die ursprünglichen Entwürfe des Aristotelischen Denkens immer noch zu wenig. Daher wird es auch kommen, dasz uns die geschichtliche Stellung des Aristoteles immer noch zu wenig klar ist.'
[2] *Aristotele, De Caelo*, p. xxxi, (note 3).

Aristotle's philosophizing on the constituent parts of the cosmos is traceable. I have thought it desirable to check the conclusions of my study of *De Caelo* against *Physics* I and II and the *Protrepticus*, and to compare it with the remnants of the most important lost work of Aristotle, the dialogue *De Philosophia*. One of the reasons why admirers of Greek philosophy eagerly await the development of a method to render charred bookrolls legible is that it may enable us to find the text of this dialogue among the remains of the libraries of Herculanum and Pompeii. The significance of this work has been enormous and the problems occasioned by its loss are many. Next to Plato's *Timaeus* this lost work has had the greatest influence on the cosmologies and theologies of countless later theologians and philosophers. But, whereas in the case of Plato's dialogue there is 'merely' the problem of interpretation, to gauge the influence of Aristotle we must first reconstruct the very work. Unlike most authors who have busied themselves with this part of Aristotle's *oeuvre*, it seems to me that the conception of *De Philosophia* may not be dissociated from the earlier parts of *De Caelo*, and that the cosmology preserved in *De Caelo* I, c. 1-3 & III was also the core of the dialogue, which was composed somewhat later. I will explicate my arguments for this view below.

In the course of a study such as this, one should constantly bear in mind that the search is for lines of evolution in a philosopher's work, that is to say, the search is for the course of development of thought. To be sure, in the case of Aristotle, who made expert use of language, this process would result in a development of his terminology; nevertheless, not every innovation in his thinking comes to expression in his words. Often the words he uses remain unchanged (such as φύσις, οὐσία, ὕλη, ἀρχὴ κινήσεως), while their meaning shifts gradually. Better insight into the cosmological notions of Aristotle at the beginning of his career seems to me attainable only when a complex of them can reasonably be demonstrated to occur in Aristotle's earliest works and when, further, it is indicated how in this conception Aristotle seeks to answer problems which he considers occasioned or neglected by his teacher's dialogues, particularly the *Timaeus*. A complete picture of Aristotle's development would finally require investigation of how difficulties or unsatisfactory solutions in his new approach compelled him to go further in the direction of the 'Aristotelian system' as we know it. To great, original thinkers philosophizing is not mere 'adherence to a tenet or membership of a church or party.

3

It is exploration.' Hence, the question is not: 'Did Aristotle grow', but 'What was the course of his philosophical growth?'[3] Only the method indicated will, I believe, do justice to the historical aspect of a philosopher's thought. The method combines a 'problem-historic' approach with a 'person-historic' one. An historical study which directs itself exclusively to the history of philosophical problems is just as one-sidedly inadequate and abstract as one that would rest content to describe the philosopher as a unique individual, meanwhile not reckoning with the fact that it is the problems of predecessors and teachers for which a thinker seeks new and if possible, better solutions.

Outlining this program does not mean that the realization of this ideal is to be expected as the result of this study. In Aristotle's works all sorts of problems form veritable knots of questions so that the preliminary analysis requires a disproportionate amount of time and paper relative to the achieved results. I merely hope to show that in addition to and apart from the fragments of the dialogues there are ways to get closer to Aristotle's early cosmology.

[3] G. Ryle, *Plato's Progress*, p. 10 (in connection with Plato's philosophy).

4

CHAPTER ONE

ARISTOTLE'S *DE CAELO* AND MODERN STUDIES

A. THE INTRODUCTION OF THE GENETIC METHOD BY WERNER JAEGER (1923)

The aim of this study is to investigate a specific phase in the development of Aristotle's thought. As indicated in the Introduction, I hold it to be meaningful to study the works of this thinker on the hypothesis that in the course of years profound changes occurred in his views. As to this important point I readily join Werner Jaeger whose well-known researches gave this viewpoint currency.[1]

While the nineteenth-century classical scholars had long concluded to distinct conceptions within the whole of Plato's writings, and had based on it a chronology of the dialogues accepted by most, it is remarkable that a break-through towards an historical approach to the works of his pupil did not occur before 1923. It was Jaeger who removed the dust of the unifying interpretations from the *Corpus Aristotelicum* by calling attention to the earlier materials it contains. In addition, by his new way of putting the question he achieved important results with respect to the fragments of Aristotle's lost writings.

The significance of Jaeger's book and the renewal of Aristotle-study it engendered are sufficiently known and consequently need not be described in detail here.[2] I would briefly summarize his view

---

[1] W. Jaeger, *Aristotle, Fundamentals of the History of His Development*. On the preparatory studies to this work see A. Mansion, 'La genèse de l'oeuvre d' Aristote d'après les travaux récents'. The early Aristotle-article by T. Case in the Eleventh Edition of the *Encyclopaedia Britannica* is left out of consideration, since my aim is not to present a general historical review, but rather to indicate certain points relevant for this study in works published during the last forty years (this period is somewhat arbitrary, as any incision in a continuity must be). For a brief account of nineteenth-century studies see E. Berti, *La Filosofia del primo Aristotele*, pp. 9-33.

[2] Cf. for instance the introductions by F. Nuyens, *Ontwikkelingsmomenten in de Zielkunde van Aristoteles* pp. 1-23, and H. E. Runner, *The Development of Aristotle Illustrated from the Earliest Books of the Physics*, pp. 14-25; E. Berti, *Filosofia*, pp. 9, 34 ff.

on the work of Aristotle which is the topic of this study and on a number of related problems that will be dealt with in subsequent chapters.

Jaeger's surest gain is that he insistently called attention to the fragments of the works of Aristotle not handed down in the *Corpus*, and to their dissimilarity compared to the generally accepted Aristotelian doctrine. These differences led him to posit a Platonic period (367-347 B.C.) in Aristotle's development, during which nearly all the dialogues that are listed in the bibliographies[3] were supposedly written. In an extensive treatment of the remnants of the *Eudemus* and the *Protrepticus* the whole of Jaeger's argument is meant to indicate a virtually complete philosophical agreement between Plato and his brilliant pupil; even the doctrine of the Ideas was supposedly completely shared by Aristotle in his early years.[4] To be sure, Jaeger does notice that the affinity of the fragments with the Platonic dialogues is primarily literary, but 'it would be strange if the influence of his model had been confined to the choice of subject-matter, and to details of style and content, while the general attitude to Plato was one of rejection, as it later became.'[5]

Notwithstanding the wide acclaim Jaeger's work received from all sides, there were repeated objections, especially relative to his treatment of the lost works mentioned.

a. Jaeger placed great emphasis on the literary ties between Plato's *Phaedo* and the *Eudemus*, even though the *Phaedo* was written approximately thirty years earlier. Yet it was Jaeger who had expressly called attention to the fact that Aristotle only knew Plato during the master's last years in the Academy (from 367).[6]

Jaeger's interpretation of εἶδός τι, *Eudemus* fr. 7, 8, in the sense of

---

[3] Excepting *On Philosophy* and the *Alexander*; *Aristotle*, pp. 24, 125. The *Protrepticus* was, according to Jaeger, not a dialogue (p. 55), but belonged to the Platonic period as well.

[4] *Aristotle*, pp. 22, 37-38, 81, 84, 86. In agreement with this view are A. Mansion, 'La genèse', p. 318 ff.; P. Wilpert, *Zwei aristotelische Frühschriften über die Ideenlehre*, p. 52; D. J. Allan, *The Philosophy of Aristotle*, p. 8, (note 1), and many others. (In the preface to the second edition, 1970, however, Allan writes 'today those who believe this definitely find themselves in a minority', p. vi.)

[5] W. Jaeger, *Aristotle*, p. 31.

[6] G. E. L. Owen, 'The Platonism of Aristotle', p. 127 ff., clearly exposes the anachronistic character of Jaeger's treatment of the *Eudemus*; cf. also E. Berti, *Filosofia*, pp. 416-417.

'an Idea or something of the nature of an Idea' has drawn increasing criticism.[7]

A number of commentators have connected the thesis that the soul has no opposite *Eudemus* fr. 7a (R)) with Aristotle's doctrine of the Categories or with his theory in *De Caelo* I, c.2, which state that the first element has no opposite.[8] It is difficult to take either of these statements as being Platonic.

On p. 48 Jaeger translates τὸ μὴ γενέσθαι, *Eudemus* fr. 6 (R): 'not to enter into becoming' and considers the thought behind it to be the same as Plato's *Philebus* 53 ff. But in my chapter IV, D and E it will become clear that the domain of the fifth element in *De Caelo* I, c. 1-3 & III is placed over against the world of genesis in just the same way as in Plato the intelligible world. It seems possible to ask, therefore, whether the fragments of the *Eudemus* may be explicable in terms of a conception on the part of the early Aristotle which cannot be identified with a Platonic one.

b. Jaeger's interpretation of the *Protrepticus* as being virtually entirely Platonic rests especially on fr. 13 (R). I. Düring, however, argues in many places – as for instance in his edition of the fragments of this work – that fr. 13 does not rest on Plato's doctrine of the Ideas, but derives from Aristotle's own view and implies a rejection of the opinion of Plato.[9] After discussing *De Caelo* I, c. 1-3 & III I will try to indicate to what extent those sections agree with the fragments of the *Protrepticus*. A comparison of the dialogue with those early parts of *De Caelo* is surely as likely as is the comparison with *Metaphysics* A and the *Analytics*, to which Jaeger (p. 91) refers.

---

[7] W. Jaeger, *Aristotle*, p. 46; Cf. J. Pépin, *Théologie cosmique et théologie chrétienne*, p. 233, (note 3). The edition of Aristotle-fragments used in this study is W. D. Ross, *Aristotelis Fragmenta Selecta*, Oxford: 1955.

[8] Cf. J. Moreau, *L'Ame du monde de Platon aux Stoiciens*, p. 121; J. Pépin, *Théologie cosmique*, p. 233, (note 3); p. 245.

[9] I. Düring, *Aristotle's Protrepticus, An Attempt at Reconstruction*, pp. 205, 212-222; (in a discussion with C. J. de Vogel): 'Did Aristotle ever accept Plato's Theory of Transcendent Ideas?', pp. 312 ff.; 'Aristotle on Ultimate Principles from 'Nature and Reality', pp. 38-40; 'Aristotle in the *Protrepticus*', pp. 91-92; 'Problems in Aristotle's *Protrepticus*', p. 141; *Aristoteles*, p. 47. In the same spirit also E. Frank, 'The Fundamental Opposition of Plato and Aristotle'. Cf. quite early W. Theiler, *Zur Geschichte der teleologisches Naturbetrachtung bis auf Aristoteles*, (1924), pp. 86-88, who concludes that in the *Protrepticus* an immanent teleological view of nature is present, and who therefore dates the work later, even subsequent to *De Philosophia*.

c. The *pièce de résistance* of Jaeger's book is his treatment of *De Philosophia*. He holds that in this work Aristotle, shortly after Plato's death[10], published his own views as an independent thinker, departing from his master on important points. In the remaining fragments of this dialogue Jaeger discovers a systematic critique of the doctrine of the Ideas, and believes that the existence of a transcendent unmoved mover, the ether theory and the imperishability of the cosmos are posited. But, in spite of these important differences relative to the views of Plato, Jaeger still takes the positive expositions in this dialogue to be 'completely Platonic'.[11] This is mainly connected with Jaeger's opinion that Aristotle still subscribes to the psychology of the *Laws*, in which the *physis* plays but a subordinate role, i.e. that of the realm of the four elements subject to the world-soul.[12] In *De Caelo* I Aristotle is finally supposed to have brought the heavenly *soma*, the ether he himself introduced, within the realm of the *physis*. But, as appears from the quotations from *De Philosophia* pointed out by Jaeger, this entire book must then have been written after the dialogue, that is, after 347.[13] Yet Jaeger suspects, on account of the self-assured tenor that he takes to be audible in *De Caelo* I, c. 2-3, that the theory of the five elements had already been treated prior to *De Philosophia* in an earlier version of those sections which, shortly after the writing of the dialogue, were supposedly rewritten on the basis of a mechanistic conception.[14]

Provisionally I would make the following comments on these

[10] The fact that Aristotle did not voice his criticism of Plato until he was more than 37 years old remains unexplained. W. Jaeger, *Aristotle*, p. 125, considers it to be 'apriori probable' that his independent position in Assos led Aristotle to develop his own views. But it may not be forgotten that Aristotle already lectured on rhetoric in the Piraeus as early as about 360 BC. Although *De Philosophia* may have been composed after 347 BC, it seems to me that the possibility of earlier criticism of Plato should not be excluded a priori. P. Wilpert, *Frühschriften*, pp. 10, 23, has already demonstrated this with respect to *De Ideis*.

[11] W. Jaeger, *Aristotle*, p. 140.

[12] *Aristotle*, pp. 151 ff. The interpretation of *De Philosophia* fragment 21b (R) is decisive here.

[13] *Aristotle*, pp. 153 ff.

[14] *Aristotle*, pp. 299 ff. Cf. A. Mansion, 'La genèse', p. 425. Their introduction is supposedly occasioned by the computation of the volumes of the various layers of elements around the earth, as discussed in *Meteor.* I, c.3, 339b2 ff., especially in 340a1. W. Jaeger, *Aristotle*, p. 154.

views of Jaeger: in *De Philosophia* also the *physis* is the origin of motion.[15] This seems to be in disagreement with the *physis*-conception in Plato's *Laws* X.

How would Aristotle, in the original version of *De Caelo* I, c. 2-3 – supposedly written before *De Philosophia* – have proved the existence of a fifth element? Is it correct to derive an argument from *Meteorologica* I, c. 3 – considered to be later by Jaeger himself[16] – for the introduction of this *soma*, even though in *De Caelo* Aristotle felt no need to make use of that argument, not even as additional proof? Why did the theory of the unmoved mover, if defended in *De Philosophia*, not influence the Stoa, although as a whole this dialogue was very highly regarded by the adherents of this school?[17]

To determine the chronological order of the writings of the *Corpus* their relation to *De Philosophia* is of great importance to Jaeger.[18] It may be mentioned that Jaeger places *Metaphysics* Λ in the period of Aristotle's stay in Assos, shortly after *De Philosophia*, because he holds that the theory of the unmoved transcendent mover expounded in the former is present also in the latter, and because a number of passages in book Λ display a higher livel of style and hence hint at their first use in a dialogue. Jaeger holds that the division between Platonic and specifically Aristotelian runs through the *Metaphysics* also, while before him this work was taken to be in general one of the latest works of Aristotle. In the Platonic period, according to Jaeger, Aristotle considered metaphysics to be the doctrine concerning the transcendent as such. In the later, independent Aristotelian conception metaphysics became a general doctrine of being, concerned with the various areas of being and accordingly not exclusively aimed at the transcendent. Aristotle subscribed to the Platonic view of metaphysics in *De Philosophia* and in *Metaphysics* Λ.[19]

Jaeger's treatment of various other main groupings of the works of Aristotle, although also criticised on a number of points, have in

---

[15] Fragment 9 (R). Cf. chapter Four B and D of this study.
[16] W. Jaeger, *Aristotle*, pp. 307, 331; cf. note 14 above.
[17] As argued by J. Pépin, *Théologie cosmique*, p. 198.
[18] A. Mansion, 'La genèse', p. 323, attacks the vagueness of any conclusion built on this.
[19] Cf. W. Jaeger, *Aristotle*, pp. 219-221. Chapter Six B, section 2 will briefly consider the chronology of the *Metaphysics* and J. Owens' refutation of Jaeger's theory to the effect that the idea of metaphysics has gone through an evolution in Aristotle.

general been very stimulating and productive. But since this study is limited to *De Caelo* and those writings immediately surrounding it, I take the liberty not to summarize Jaeger's further results, and turn instead to a number of studies especially devoted to *De Caelo*.

B. H. VON ARNIM ON THE THEOLOGY OF ARISTOTLE (1931)

The new approach to the study of the works of Aristotle inaugurated by Werner Jaeger completely dominated the decades following.[20] Every new investigator had to state his position relative to Jaeger's theories clearly and motivate deviations from them solidly. Precisely because Jaeger aimed at a comprehensive view of the whole of Aristotle's work, his influence remained great even after many parts of his book had been refuted.

Of particular importance for the present study is the attack, undertaken comparatively soon, against Jaeger's thesis that the theory of the unmoved mover is already evident in *De Philosophia*, and that *Metaphysics* Λ (except for chap. 8) dates from the same period, i.e. shortly after Plato's death. A. Mansion has aimed some very good arguments against this thesis.[21] He points to the great distance that had come between Aristotle and his teacher in book Λ, and shows that *Physics* VIII is already presupposed in it.[22] According to him, the doctrine of the transcendent mover there expounded should be considered later than *De Philosophia* and *De Caelo* because in these works 'les moteurs des astres sont encore conçus comme des âmes'.[23] Mansion's attack was continued by H. Von Arnim,[24] although the latter makes no mention of the article by Mansion.[25]

---

[20] As mentioned earlier, this chapter does not aim at a comprehensive review of all studies published; I merely wish to sketch the main lines of the problems concerning *De Caelo*. Accordingly, I do not at this point discuss P. Gohlke's article, 'Die Entstehungsgeschichte der naturwissenschaftlichen Schriften des Aristoteles', published almost simultaneously with Jaeger's book. (A brief summary of it is given by A. Mansion, 'La genèse', pp. 428 ff.) An expanded sequel to it is P. Gohlke, *Die Entstehung der Aristotelischen Prinzipienlehre*. There will be occasion to consider his views in following chapters.

[21] A. Mansion, 'La genèse'.

[22] *Ibid*, pp. 327, 338.

[23] *Ibid*., p. 340.

[24] H. Von Arnim, *Die Entstehung der Gotteslehre des Aristoteles*.

[25] In this treatise no modern author is cited other than Jaeger and Von Arnim himself.

Von Arnim is mainly concerned to show that the teaching of the unmoved mover is the culmination of a long development and that within the *Corpus Aristotelicum* we find evidence of the early stage of Aristotle's thought in *De Caelo*.[26] In his opinion the doctrine of the fifth element, which we meet in *De Caelo*, renders such an unmoved mover superfluous. Von Arnim even goes so far as to call the two doctrines incompatible[27]: Aristotle would never have introduced the ether-hypothesis if he already subscribed to the dogma of 'Kein Bewegtes ohne Beweger'.[28]

According to Von Arnim the ether-theory of *De Caelo* does have to be distinguished sharply from the exposition in *De Philosophia*. In the dialogue the heavenly element is still pictured as 'ein mit seelischen Funktionen begabter Gott'[29], and according to fragment 21b (R) the motion of the stars is still 'voluntary'.[30] On this point Aristotle changes his mind soon after *De Philosophia* (also according to Von Arnim, written after 347): in *De Caelo* he no longer considers the ether to be psychically qualified but rather as a 'Körper der sich von Natur im Kreise bewegt, obgleich er [Aristotle] doch um seinetwillen den Himmel und die Weltkugel beseelt nannte'.[31] Nevertheless, a theory of an unmoved mover is still excluded here. The two passages in *De Caelo* where Von Arnim does note this theory[32] do not give him great difficulty: an Aristotle-scholar can always solve problems by branding relevant passages as 'späterer Zusatz'.

Von Arnim does not limit himself to distinguishing the three phases mentioned, but in passing constructs a chronology for the most important of Aristotle's works.[33] Especially here he evidences

---

[26] *Op. cit.*, pp. 8-9.   [27] *Op. cit.*, pp. 10, 13.

[28] *Op. cit.*, p. 35. cf. *Physics* VII, c.1, 241b34.

[29] *Op. cit.*, p. 5.   [30] *Op. cit.*, p. 7.

[31] *Op. cit.*, p. 17. Von Arnim thinks of *De Caelo* II, c.2, 285a29 and c.12, 292a18-b2. He pays no attention to the fact that *De Caelo* I, c.2-3 give the impression of being a first announcement of the doctrine of the fifth element. This fact induced Jaeger, *Aristotle*, p. 300, to consider an earlier draft of these chapters to have been written even before *De Philosophia*.

[32] *De Caelo* II, c.6, 288a27-b7; IV, c.3, 311a9.

[33] According to him the sequence is: *De Philosophia*; *Physics* I-VI; *De Caelo*; *De Generatione et Corruptione*; *Meteorologica*; *De Anima*; *Physics* VII-VIII; *Metaphysics* Λ (supposedly written shortly after *Physics* VIII, but before the death of Speusippus; c.8 is later according to Von Arnim also); *Metaphysics* K and N; *De Partibus Animalium* and *De Generatione Animalium*; *Eudemian Ethics*.

little sensitivity for the complexity of the process by which the various parts of the *Corpus* came into being. In *De Caelo* too he does not nearly see all the problems enumerated by for instance G. A. Seeck and L. Elders, and describes the work as a 'für die Veröffentlichung bestimmten und daher mit stilistischer Sorgfallt ausgearbeiteten Schrift'.[34]

One can gratefully note that Von Arnim was the first to posit explicitly that Aristotle did not always connect his doctrine of motion with a theory of an unmoved mover; but this certainly does not mean that with this all problems concerning *De Caelo* and the dialogues are solved. I forego detailed criticism here since chapters IV and V will deal with most of these matters.

C.   W. K. C. GUTHRIE ON THE DEVELOPMENT OF
ARISTOTLE'S THOUGHT (1933)

A further development in *De Caelo* interpretation was an article by W. K. C. Guthrie.[35] The author has subsequently elaborated on and revised the theory in his introduction to the Loeb edition of *De Caelo*.[36] Following the example of Jaeger, Guthrie also seeks to discover a developmental continuity in the views of Aristotle, but he orients himself far less to biographical and literary information, and far more to an analysis of a central philosophical theme of the *Corpus*, the theory of motion. He arrives at an extremely important conclusion: 'The progress of Aristotle's theory of motion was a simple development *and never a contradiction of what had gone before*'.[37] (italics mine).

In this development Guthrie distinguishes the phases actually already indicated by Von Arnim: 1. The phase of *De Philosophia*. The doctrine of the fifth element is already present, but, according to fragment 21b (R),[38] the ether appears still to be thought of as a divinity with a *nous*, and not as a body with natural motion. Guthrie does add however: 'for the possibility of this ... experimental form of the belief we have no further evidence than is provided by this one

[34] *Gotteslehre*, p. 8.
[35] W. K. C. Guthrie, 'The Development of Aristotle's Theology'.
[36] *Aristotle, On the Heavens.*
[37] *Op. cit.*, p. xvi.
[38] Cicero, *De Natura Deorum* II, 16, 44.

passage.'[39] 2. The next period in Aristotle's reflection on motion can, according to Guthrie, be traced in *De Caelo*, especially in books I and III. The telling fact here is that motion is no longer characterized as *voluntarius* but as φύσει. There is no thought here at all of an ether-soul which is, according to Guthrie, even polemicized against in *De Caelo* II, c.1, 284a18.[40] Originally he qualified this conception as 'pure materialism'.[41] Later, however, he considered a different interpretation of the passage 284a18 ff. possible, and the term 'materialism' 'too positive in expression'.[42] He did maintain his view that this phase ought to be distinguished from the preceding one and the third, insofar as no 'incorporeal first principle'[43] was posited here by Aristotle. 3. Not until the end of his thinking about *kinesis* did Aristotle unfold his theory of the primordial unmoved mover, which did not set aside the entire previous doctrine of motion, but formed 'the coping-stone on the previous construction'.[44] Many subsequent writers have expressed agreement with this view of three phases.[45]

Concerning *De Caelo* Guthrie, in contradistinction to Von Arnim, holds that 'the *De Caelo* is not a finished product, trimmed and tidied for the press. It was never planned for publication, but is a manuscript intended to serve Aristotle and his pupils as a basis for teaching and research.'[46] But as a whole it may be placed in Aristotle's second period: the passages I, c.9, 279a30; II, c.1, 284a18; III, c.2, 300b18; II, c.3, 286a9 (and IV, c.2, 309b12) exclude, in his opinion, an unmoved mover.[47] Books I and III do not even mention this highest principle at all[48]. That is why, Guthrie thinks, the *loci* II,c.6, 288a27

[39] 'Aristotle's Theology', p. 166.
[40] *Ibid.*, p. 169. [41] *Ibid.*, p. 169.
[42] *On the Heavens*, pp. xxxi (note a); xxxiv-xxxv.
[43] 'Aristotle's Theology', p. 98. In *On the Heavens*, p. xxxiv, Guthrie draws back on this point also to the extent that he considers it possible that Aristotle only for a time experienced difficulty with the 'intellectual reconciliation of his beliefs in the life and divinity of the heavenly bodies and his rational explanation of their movement', that is to say, Aristotle probably never relinquished the doctrine of an immaterial soul, but was merely unable to fit it into his system of the natural motions in a consistent way.
[44] 'Aristotle's Theology', p. 169; *On the Heavens*, p. xix.
[45] Cf. W. D. Ross, *Aristotle's Physics*, pp. 98 ff.; 'The Development of Aristotle's thought', p. 13 ff.; F. Solmsen, *Aristotle's System of the Physical World*, p. 241, p. 100 (note 23), and his review of I. Düring, *Aristoteles*, in *Gnomon* 37 (1967), p. 671.
[46] *On the Heavens*, p. xvi. [47] *Ibid.*, pp. xvi-xxiii.
[48] *Ibid.*, p. xxiii.

and IV, c.3, 311a9 must be later additions, since there the late theory is supposedly 'unambiguously referred to'. To these two passages he finally adds one more: I, c.8, 277b9.[49]

D. SOME EDITIONS AND TRANSLATIONS OF *DE CAELO*

On account of the investigations by Jaeger, Von Arnim and Guthrie interest in *De Caelo* received a new impulse. Simultaneously, other scholars aided increased familiarity with the text and content of the work. One could mention here: the English translation by J. L. Stocks (1930),[50] the edition of the Greek text by D. J. Allan (1936)[51], a French translation prepared by J. Tricot (1949),[52] a translation into German by O. Gigon (1950),[53] and, rather recently, a revised text with Italian translation by O. Longo (1962).[54]

The translation by J. L. Stocks is enriched with a large number of important notes which to a considerable extent have been used gratefully by later editors. But since his manuscript was finished already in 1922 he was unable to take the results of W. Jaeger into account.

The edition by D. J. Allan is the text used in this study, and quotations will always presuppose his text.

J. Tricot has not been impressed by Jaeger's genetic method. In his introduction he only mentions that the merit of Jaeger's study consists in the fact that he has put great stress on the 'tendance réalistique' of Aristotle's philosophical activity, which came to expression especially in the special-scientific investigations of the second Athenian period. Tricot still holds to an 'unité qui règne dans ses [Aristotle's]

---

[49] *Ibid.*, pp. xxiii-xxv. Guthrie considers it possible that II, c.6, 288b22-30 points to an external transcendent mover as well.

[50] *The Works of Aristotle*, translated into English under the Editorship of W. D. Ross, Vol. II: *De Caelo*, by J. L. Stocks.

[51] *Aristoteles De Caelo*, recognovit brevique adnot. instruxit D. J. Allan.

[52] *Aristote, Traité du Ciel, suivi du Traité pseudo-aristotélicien Du Monde*, trad. et notes par J. Tricot.

[53] *Aristoteles, Vom Himmel, Von der Seele, Von der Dichtkunst*, eingeleitet und neu übertragen von O. Gigon.

[54] *Aristotele, De Caelo.* In addition to the editions cited could be mentioned *Aristoteles, Die Lehrschriften*, herausgegeben, übertragen und in ihrer Entstehung erlautert von Dr. Paul Gohlke; Band VI, *Ueber den Himmel; Von Werden und Vergehen; Aristotele, De Caelo*, traduzione di M. Fausta Cini Guerri.

14

ouvrages consacrés à la science de la Nature'[55] and accordingly makes eager use of the commentaries authored by Neo-Platonists and Thomas Aquinas, who approached Aristotle similarly. According to Tricot, De Caelo is 'un des ouvrages les mieux ordonnés et les plus systématiques de tout le corpus.'[56] It seems to me that a 'unitary view' of the philosophical work of Aristotle may impair interpretation; nevertheless, the notes which Tricot added to his translation are often very helpful.

O. Gigon applies a rigorously analytic method to the work with which we are concerned.[57] The most important result of it is that no unity remains in the text at all. Having thus shown the disorder of De Caelo, Gigon does seek to re-order it, but he can only succeed by introducing a post-Aristotelian editor.[58] Among other things Gigon notes that I, c.4, seems odd: there is again talk of the circularly moving element after I, c.2 appeared to have treated it adequately[59], and he considers book IV to be 'a separate treatise' with only the most superficial of ties with the other books.[60] Although one could characterize Gigon's approach (though not his solutions) as progressive, with respect to a possible development in the thought of Aristotle one could call him quite conservative: 'The philosophical development of Aristotle has a relatively narrow scope.'[61] He once again considers the theory of an unmoved mover to be posited as early as De Philosophia and the fact that De Caelo treats this first principle so succinctly is to be explained by the circumstance that the theory was known from the dialogue![62]

The contribution of O. Longo is primarily in the area of textual criticism – an area which must remain outside the scope of this study.[63] In his edition of the text, however, he announces a systematic analysis

---

[55] *Traité du Ciel*, p.v.   [56] *Ibid.*, p. vi.
[57] Cf. also 'Aristoteles-Studien I'. His method is followed by G. A. Seeck, *Ueber die Elemente in der Kosmologie des Aristoteles*, p. 6. His conclusion with respect to the views of earlier authors regarding Aristotle's theory of the elements is: 'man hat sich hier zu sehr an groszzügige Beurteilung gewohnt' (p. 155). A rather negative evaluation of Gigon's method and results is found in *Aristote Du Ciel*, texte établi et traduit par P. Moraux, p. xi (note 1); p. xiii (note 3), and p. xxxvi (note 3). This writer holds that the work of Gigon contains 'hyper-criticism'.
[58] *Vom Himmel*, p. 44. 'Aristoteles-Studien I', p. 136.
[59] *Vom Himmel*, p. 17.   [60] *Ibid.*, p. 38.
[61] *Ibid.*, p. 44.   [62] *Ibid.*, p. 45.
[63] Cf. P. Moraux, *Aristote Du Ciel*, pp. clxxi, clxxxi.

15

of *De Caelo*[64], and offers a preview in his *Introduzione*. He views *De Caelo* in its oldest form as the original nucleus of the entire Aristotelian physics[65] and takes it to be written shortly after *De Philosophia*.[66] Next, he distinguishes three independent units within the work, books I and II, book III, and book IV.[67] In the main he follows Von Arnim and Guthrie as to the conception adhered to in the work, but expands their analyses by showing II, c.12 to be yet another later addition because here too, as in *Metaphysics* Λ, use is made of the astronomic system worked out by Callippus, which dates from approx. 330 B.C.[68] Finally, in I, c.9, 279a18 ff. and II, c.12, 292a22-b25 he discovers a theory which he takes to be inconsistent with the self-sufficiency of the *proton soma*. Longo thinks that a decision as to the consequences of such inconsistencies for the chronology is not possible until more insight is gained into the development of Aristotle's thinking in all its facets.

E. THE WORK OF PAUL MORAUX

In a 200-page introduction to the Budé edition of *De Caelo* Paul Moraux, Director of the Berlin Aristotle archives, has given us the result of years of intensive study of all the problems concerning this work.[69] His analysis of the work and of the questions which confront the exegete is excellent; but he relinquishes the attempt to resolve all these problems in a grand synthesis. It seems to him that contradictions in the work of Aristotle may have been occasioned by Aristotle approaching the same issues in different ways, or may be charged to Aristotle's aim to convince his opponents at all costs, at times even at the cost of consistency.[70] In fact, it seems as if Moraux rejects all the work accomplished by adherents of the genetic method.[71] An advantage, however, is that Moraux can consider it possible that the arrangement and order of *De Caelo*, as in the case of the other works, is largely accomplished by Aristotle himself. Hence Moraux

---

[64] O. Longo, *Struttura e composizione del 'De Caelo' di Aristotele.*
[65] O. Longo, *Aristotele, De Caelo*, p. xxxi, (note 3); but see also P. Moraux, *Aristote Du Ciel*, p. lxii, (note 1).   [66] *Aristotele, De Caelo*, p. xxxviii.
[67] *Ibid.*, p. xxxii.   [68] *Ibid*, pp. xx-xxiii.
[69] P. Moraux, *Aristote Du Ciel*. Cf. also various articles (see Bibliography).
[70] *Op. cit.*, pp. cxxv-cxxvi; xliii.
[71] *Ibid*, p. xxxviii (note 4); Moraux rejects (xlii ff.) the attempts made to find a development in Aristotle's psychology and theory of motion. They lack sufficient basis. Furthermore: 'l'hypothèse génétique risque de masquer la vraie difficulté au lieu de la résoudre', p. xliii.

is far less ready to call upon bungling or inexpert editors[72] as for instance O. Gigon, G. A. Seeck or L. Elders are. Moraux also considers books I and II, III, and IV to be main groups within *De Caelo*, while he does not think that book III is complete, and discovers its continuation in *De Gen. et Corr.* II. On the whole, Moraux takes books I and II to be written earlier than III and IV, but revised and expanded when joined with these. At that time the ether-theory was added as well.[73] In his detailed study of the content of Aristotle's work Moraux devotes an extensive part to the fifth element, including its history before and after. He acknowledges the originality of Aristotle's exposition which, contrary to Plato's mathematizing approach in the *Timaeus* and by other members of the Academy, explicates reality strictly in terms of physical principles.[74] But he follows S. Mariotti[75] in accepting an essential distinction between the astral *soma* of *De Caelo* and the *quinta natura* of the *De Philosophia* fragments. In his analysis of these fragments he sharply opposes all those who held that the early Aristotle is to be credited with a theory of a corporeal soul.[76]

As far as Moraux's investigation of the various parts of *De Caelo* is concerned: part I, c.8, 277b12-26 he considers to be a 'bloc erratique';

---

[72] *Ibid*, pp. ix-x.

[73] *Ibid*, p. xxxviii (note 4), where F. Solmsen, *Aristotle's System*, is quoted. Nevertheless, book III is based on the teaching of natural motion (cf. chapter Four, B below), as explained in I, c.2. It is not easy to see how this theory could have been developed without the doctrine of the five elements.

[74] *Ibid*, p. 1; cf. 'Quinta Essentia', 1196, and F. Solmsen, *Aristotle's System*, pp. 287 ff.

[75] S. Mariotti, 'La "Quinta Essentia" nell' Aristotele perduto e nell' Academia'. His hypothesis is accepted by H. J. Easterling, 'Quinta Natura' also, but is rejected by J. Pépin, *Théologie Cosmique*, p. 243 (note 3).

[76] P. Moraux, *Aristote Du Ciel*, p. liii (note 2) mentions attempts in this direction by H. Von Arnim, *Entstehung der Gotteslehre*, J. Moreau *L'Ame du Monde*; E. Bignone, *L'Aristotele perduto* and others. Moraux refers to a 'sorte de matérialisme', as Guthrie did: 'Aristotle's Theology'. Cf. chapter One, C (note 41). Von Arnim had spoken of a 'hylozoistische, pneumatische Theologie nach Art der Stoa', *Entstehung der Gotteslehre*, p. 28. It may be useful to point out that in any case a sharp distinction should be made between on the one hand the hypothetical view of Aristotle and that of the Stoa, and on the other hand the view of the Atomists. The difference between these two schools has already been pointed out by M. Pohlenz, *Die Stoa*, pp. 66-67. In the Atomists' view we find a reduction of all aspects of reality to the physical. The Stoa does not clearly distinguish the physical and biotic aspects of reality.

I, c.9 is composed of three pieces of different origin and date (of which the last, like II, c.1, derives from *De Philosophia*); I, c.12 also holds together quite loosely; II, c.2 clearly contains later materials, but does not seem to allow for a solution of the problems to which it gives rise; II, c.7 and 9 are mutually contradictory, etc. Moraux then, finds nothing of that compositional unity that Von Arnim and Tricot still considered evident.

Moraux's exceptionally valuable Introduction and the vast amount of learning brought to it have been of great service and will undoubtedly continue to aid investigators. Moraux has a keen sense for the weak points of many of the theories of his predecessors. All the same, his own work gives rise to yet other problems and so many issues remain unresolved that the case cannot be considered closed. The analysis has left so little of a unity of composition and philosophical conception intact that Aristotle is hardly recognizable as a thinker and author on a level suggested by the philosophical discoveries and writings with which he is credited. It seems to me that a search must be instituted towards a new synthesis in which continuous lines of development within Aristotle's works will become apparent once again.

F. A COMMENTARY ON *DE CAELO* BY L. ELDERS (1966)

The last book in this series of studies devoted to *De Caelo* I ought to mention is an attempt by L. Elders to administer to the need for a running commentary on the treatise.[77] One cannot really say, however, that this book fulfills the need. It does not only fall short as compilation of contemporary materials, but in addition Elder's interpretation of the text and his selections from the results of modern investigators suffer from a one-sided approach on the basis of a theory of an esoteric philosophy by Plato. Elders has given an exposition of this theory in a previous study, concerning the tenth book of the *Metaphysics*.[78] It was inspired by writers such as K. Gaiser, H. J. Kraemer and J. Stenzel. According to this view Plato, near the end of his life, placed the principles of the One and the Indefinite Dyad central;

---

[77] L. Elders, *Aristotle's Cosmology; a Commentary on the De Caelo.*
[78] L. Elders, *Aristotle's Theory of the One; a Commentary on book X of the Metaphysics.*

they must be taken as the two highest among ten interpenetrating 'levels of reality' or 'levels of being'. While some of the evidence supporting the theory can be derived from Plato's *De Bono*, I cannot but think that Elders credits Plato with many things that did not arise until later exegetes, such as Speusippus. But I prefer to leave these problems, as far as they concern Plato, out of consideration.

By reason of the fact that Elders accepts a completely Platonic phase in the development of Aristotle's thought, however, he seeks to unearth traces of such a system in the work of Aristotle, offering a compilation of facts of greatly varied scope and significance in order to bolster this position.[79] Elders believes it to be justified to hold that Aristotle 'admitted the reduction of being ... to the One and Plurality' in the *Eudemus*, *De Philosophia*, the *Protrepticus*, *De Contrariis*, *De Bono*, in large parts of *De Caelo*, in *Metaphysics* Γ, c.2 and I, c.3, and in Physics VII.[80] He considered his findings of 1961 affirmed in his study of *De Caelo*: 'in the *De Caelo* we have to do with a Platonic stage in Aristotle's cosmology'[81], although he does want to distinguish between various conceptions within the work: a. 'a first theory admits supra-mundane principles, ensouled heavens and the reduction of mathematical figures to principles'[82]; b. 'a second theory

---

[79] L. Elders, *Theory of the One*, pp. 13-22. According to Elders Aristotle must, on the one hand, have taught the reduction-theory, because he adhered to the doctrine of Ideas (*Eudemus*, fr. 5 W = fr. 5 R); on the other hand, the fact that in *De Philosophia* Aristotle rejects the theory of Ideas does not at all imply, according to Elders, that he also relinquished the reduction-theory. pp. 13, 16. The interpretation of *De Caelo* I, c.1, 268b1 ff., proposed on page 17, would have been one of the best proofs for Elders' view if only it were sound (but see ch. Four A of this study). The identification (p. 22) of 'Physis and Aletheia' with 'the realm of Ideas', (*Protrepticus* fr. 13 R), taken from Jaeger, has already been discussed in section A of the present chapter.

[80] *Theory of the One*, p. 24. The arguments regarding *De Philosophia* Elders presents in *Aristotle's Cosmology*, p. 28. In an article, 'The Topics and the Platonic Theory of Principles of Being', he attempts with but little success, to fit the *Topics* into the framework of his interpretation as well.

[81] *Aristotle's Cosmology*, p. 30.

[82] This is supposedly indicated by 268b1, mentioned earlier, and by I, c.2. The reduction of all *schemata* to simple ones in I, c.2, however, remains intra-modal. There is no hint of a metabasis to another category. In the same way Aristotle reduces all *somata* to non-complex *somata* in I, c.2, 268b27. Over against Elders' claim that in *De Caelo* 'mathematisation of reality' (disregarding the vagueness of this phrase) 'has taken place' (p. 14; cf. pp. 15, 44), one could

makes the heavenly bodies revolve in virtue of their own nature, and no reality higher than the first heaven is mentioned'; and finally, c. 'the theory of the First Mover', which must be viewed as later still.[83]

As far as the composition of the treatise *De Caelo* is concerned, Elders holds that the independent parts I and II, III, and IV have been put together by post-Aristotelian editors.[84] They have, of course, left their bothersome tracks, and hence Elders thinks that a rather large amount, up to 2.5% of the total text, should be eliminated to purify the true Aristotelian text.[85] Nevertheless: 'on the whole the text of *De Caelo* is remarkably good'![86] After all, one should not expect too much!

Elders appends an overview of the relative chronology of the various capita of *De Caelo*, divided into five groups.[87] This appendix makes

point to *De Caelo* III, c.1, in which Plato's theory of the triangles is under heavy attack. But Elders escapes again by positing that this chapter, together with c.7 and 8, were written after book I & II (pp. 44, note 2, 68). However, even c.1 of book I, which he cites, does not say of *to Hen* that it is *teleion*, but this is said of the *soma*. I recognize Elders' right to accept the existence of various conceptions within *De Caelo*, but when this is done it seems hardly possible to posit generalizations as for instance: 'The *De Caelo* does not distinguish clearly between mathematics and physics' (p. 44); 'in the *De Caelo* mathematisation of reality has taken place' (p. 14); 'the epistemology of the *De Caelo* therefore seems Platonic in character' (p. 44); 'the cosmology of the *De Caelo*' (p. 45); 'the idea of cosmology as contained in the *De Caelo*' (p. 46, 30), etc.

[83] *Aristotle's Cosmology*, p. 33.

[84] *Op. cit.*, p. 60. 'No strict uniformity of method presided over the redaction of the whole book'; p. 136: 'It would seem that the editors had at their disposition (*sic*) a collection of sheets and short notes which they brought together according to certain criteria' (!). In Elders' opinion the redactors posited were extremely incompetent folk: 'Lectures dealing with the same subject were brought together regardless of the purpose for which they had originally been written'. p. 231; 'We need ... not attach much significance to the arrangement of the individual chapters', p. 191.

[85] *Op. cit.*, pp. 63-64.

[86] *Loc. cit.*

[87] The first two phases mentioned on p. 33 Elders further divides into two sub-periods. An interesting datum in Elders' scheme (p. 68) is that he does not simply credit Aristotle's last phase with a number of interpolations, as Von Arnim and Guthrie did, but that to the last main phase, characterized by the heading 'A First Mover Affirmed', belong I, c.7, 12; II, c.6, 7; III, c.1, 2, 6, 7-8; IV, c.1, 2, 3, 4, 5, 6(?). Elders places in the same phase also *Analytica Priora*, I, c.46; *Physics* VIII, c.8; *Metaphysics* XI, c.4, and *De Generatione et Corruptione*.

clear that he no longer espies any kind of unity in *De Caelo*.[88] The genetic method, inaugurated by Werner Jaeger and meant to remove the later glosses from Aristotle's earliest conception in order to be left with a better portrait of the young thinker, turns out, in spite of itself, to have damaged its object of study to the extent that hardly any contours remain.[89]

[88] The scheme on p. 68 seems to militate against Elders' argument on p. 33. There I, c.1, 268a30 (placed in group IIa on p. 68) is used to prove that I, c.9 also accepts a Platonic cosmology (on p. 68, however, this chapter is classed under Ia). Similarly, on p. 33 the first main group (Ia and Ib) is characterized by 'the reduction of mathematical figures to principles', which reduction Elders noted in I, c.2. But on p. 68 these chapters are classed with the first sub-group of the second main phase. This brief critique will have to suffice. In the sequel Elders' views will be considered again. I agree with the evaluation of J. Long-rigg in *Class. Review*, 1968, pp. 166-168, who writes: 'Elders' work cannot be regarded by any means as definitive.' See also H. J. Easterling's review in *Mnemosyne* (IVa S. 22), 1969, pp. 199-202.

[89] *Synopsis* of the passages in *De Caelo* which, according to some authors, are not written simultaneously with the original version of the work.

H. VON ARNIM,	pp. (8), 19-20:	II, c.6, 288a27-b7
Entstehung der Gotteslehre	p. 21	IV, c.3, 311a9 seq.
W. K. C. GUTHRIE,	p. xxiii:	II, c.6, 288a27-b7
On the Heavens	p. xxiv:	IV, c.3, 311a9
	p. xxv:	I, c.8, 277b9-12
	p. xxiii:	II, c.6, 288b22-30 (?)
O. LONGO,	pp. xxi, xxiii:	II, c.12
De Caelo	p. xxvii:	I, c.9, 279a18 seq.*
		II, c.6, 288a27-288b6 *
	p. xxviii:	II, c.12, 292a22-292b25 *

* Longo considers these passages to militate against the hypothesis of a moving prime mover. A judgment as to the chronological implications he holds to be possible only within the framework of a comprehensive view of the whole of Aristotle's philosophical activity (p. xxix).

P. MORAUX,	p. xxii:	I, c.3, 269b21 seq.
Aristote Du Ciel		I, c.8, 277b23
	pp. xxii, xxvi:	II, c.3, (286a22-31)
	p. xxiii:	III, c.8, 307b19-24
	p. xxxviii nt. 4:	I, c.2-3
	p. lxxiii:	I, c.9, 277b27-278b8
	p. lxxv:	279a19-b3
	p. lxxxii nt. 1:	I, c.12, 282a14-21
	p. lxxxv:	I, c.12, 283a10-b22
	p. lxxxvi:	II, c.1
	p. xcvi:	II, c.2
	p. ciii nt. 1:	II, c.7

L. ELDERS,   p. 63:   I, c.9, 27(9)a30-b3
Aristotle's Cosmology   I, c.10, 280a28-32
                                p. 64:   I, c.7, 274a20-24
                                                II, c.6, 289a8-10
                                                III, c.1, 298a24 seq.
                                                I, c.4, 271a26-7
                                                I, c.7, 274b25-9
                                                I, c.11, 280b12-14
                                                    c.12, 283a8-10
                                                II, c.3, 286a11
                                                        286a25
                                                    c.4, 287a34
                                                    c.5, 288a7
                                                    c.6, 288a14-17
                                                    c.7, 289a22-23
                                                I, c.8, 277a31-3
                                                    c.11, 280b29-31
                                                         280b33-34
                                                         281a7
                                                II, c.2, 285a7
                                                        285a21-22
                                                    c.4, 287a20
                                                    c.13, 294a22-3
                                                    c.14, 296a16-17
                                                III, c.1, 299a18-19
                                                IV, c.3, 311a9-12
                                                    c.5, 312a31-32
                                                         312b17-18
                                                I, c.3, 269b21-23
                                                    c.8, 277b23-24
                                                II, c.2, 284b13-18
                                                    c.3, 286a21-22
                                                         286a30-31
                                                III, c.1, 299a9-11
                                p. 68:   chapters written in the period
                                                characterized by Elders as 'A
                                                First Mover Affirmed': I, c.7,
                                                12; II, c.6, 7; III, c.1, 2, 6, 7-8;
                                                IV, c.1, 2, 3, 4 *, 5, 6 (?).

* 'Certain chapters seem to have been compounded of earlier and later sections.
E.g. I, c.7, 8; II, c.13; IV, c.4.'

CHAPTER TWO

A RENEWED STUDY OF *DE CAELO:*
THE COMPOSITION

The first chapter has shown that no consensus regarding the inter-pretation of *De Caelo* has been reached; it seems as if the renewal begun with Jaeger cannot be brought to a conclusion, at least not in the case of this particular work. The only obvious trend one could point to in the monographs devoted to *De Caelo* since 1923 is the gradual proliferation of the number of passages held to be later additions, and the dissolution of the text into parts that hardly allow for re-integration. But a new interpretation of the separated parts will not easily be convincing: every passage dealt with must needs be treated in its context, and such treatment will almost always be open to attacks based on other views on the work as a whole.

Nevertheless, I intend yet another investigation of the work, with the aim of designing a new interpretative framework. It seems to me that within this framework it will be possible to assign a coherent and significant place to not only Cicero's statement as to the part played by a *quinta natura* in the psychology and theology of *De Philosophia*, but also to Von Arnim's late date for the doctrine of the Unmoved Mover, J. Moreau's treatment of the World-Soul with respect to *De Philosophia*, P. Gohlke's view on the difference between book I and II of the *Physics* as one between a substrate- philosophy and an *eidos*-philosophy, and W. Wieland's defense of the independence of the original Aristotelian physics. Initially, I prefer to postpone detailed discussion with other authors on each of the problem-areas to later chapters, since the view proposed will only derive its persuasive power, if any, from a more probable explanation of the texts within the frame of a philosophical development on the part of Aristotle.

A. THE TWO PROLOGUES OF *DE CAELO* III

Point of departure is the first part of the third book. I realize that this choice may seem arbitrary. P. Moraux[1] notes in section 298a24-b8

---

[1] P. Moraux, *Aristote Du Ciel*, pp. xiii-xv; 'Recherches', p. 181.

an incision in a27, and takes 298a24-27 to conclude books I and II, while 298a27ff. is a return to the stage set at the beginning of book I. G. A. Seeck[2], following F. Solmsen[3], finds a break after 298b5: 'die zweite Ueberleitung [b6-8] ist klar und in sich völlig befriedigend'. 'Der erste Satz dagegen [298a24-7], der versucht, die Verbindung zu dem astronomischen Fragen gewidmeten Buch II herzustellen, um einen Gedankengang Buch I-II-III zu konstruieren, ist ein ziemlich seltsames Produkt, dasz die angestrebte Funktion nicht erfüllen kann.'

It happens that one of the most interesting findings by Werner Jaeger, *viz.* the chronological difference between *Metaphysics* M, c.1-c.9, 1086a18 and M, c.9, 1086a21ff. & N, is based upon, among other things, the outstanding differences between the prologues preceding the two sections (1076a8-32 and 1086a21-32). The introduction to the portion which Jaeger considers to be written much later is more extensive and presupposes a greater part of the *Corpus Aristotelicum* than does the one in *Metaphysics* M, c.9.[4] It may be profitable to see whether something similar may not be the case in *De Caelo* III, c.1. By way of a preliminary I note that according to Seeck the extensive introduction (a24-b5) is secondary and aims to establish a connection of book III with books II and IV. The recapitulation in the first lines, however, is very unclear and the fact that the essay concerning the earth (II, c.13-14) and the part about the finiteness of the universe (I, c.5-8) are not mentioned, is a shortcoming.[5] On the other hand, the second introduction[6] refers to the first capita of book I.[7] I, c.2 clearly indicates a 'first element', and in c.2-3 a large number of properties of that *soma* are enumerated, the most important of which, i.e., its being ungenerated and indestructible (c.3,270a13), are referred to again because precisely at

---

[2] G. A. Seeck, *Ueber die Elemente*, pp. 74-75.

[3] F. Solmsen, *Aristotle's System*, pp. 293 ff.

[4] Cf. W. Jaeger, *Aristotle*, pp. 176-193, 205-208, and W. D. Ross, *Aristotle's Metaphysics* II, pp. 406-407. A similar phenomenon occurs in *De Longitudine Vitae*, c.1, 464b19-30 and b30-465a2. Concerning this see H. J. Drossaart Lulofs, *Aristotelis De Insomniis* I, p. xl, and W. D. Ross, *Aristotle, Parva Naturalia*, p. 52.

[5] Cf. O. Gigon, *Vom Himmel*, p. 31; O. Longo, *De Caelo*, p. xxxiii; P. Moraux, *Aristote Du Ciel*, p. xiii; furthermore, section a27-b5 appears to be an expansion of I, c.1; cf. P. Moraux, 'Recherches', p. 181.

[6] III, c. 1, 298b6-8: Περὶ μὲν οὖν τοῦ πρώτου τῶν στοιχείων εἴρηται, καὶ ποῖόν τι τὴν φύσιν, καὶ ὅτι ἄφθαρτον καὶ ἀγένητον· λοιπὸν δὲ περὶ τοῖν δυοῖν εἰπεῖν,

[7] G. A. Seeck, *Ueber die Elemente*, p. 76.

this point is the great difference with the elements to be dealt with in book III. Those remaining parts of the cosmos together make up the realm of becoming and passing-away.

Although it may be admitted that other parts of books I and II mention a 'first element', and that the concepts 'ungenerated' and 'incorruptible' are exhaustively treated in I, c.10-12, the second prologue of book III seems a correct and complete summary of I, c.1-3, at the same time giving a rather poor impression with respect to books I and II.[8] Hence I will continue on the hypothesis that a special relation obtains between I, c.1-3 and III[9], not present in the rest of *De Caelo*.

B. *DE CAELO* I, c.1-3 AND III IN THEIR RELATION TO THE REMAINDER OF THE TREATISE

Obviously, the first thing to investigate is the relation of I, c.1-3 to its context. The close of chapter 3 (270b26-31) has repeatedly drawn attention: P. Moraux calls it 'un bloc erratique' still showing that a treatment of the earthly elements was originally planned as sequel.[10] O. Longo[11] and G. A. Seeck[12] also note a lack of continuity with the preceding and with that which follows. Longo suggests that this be viewed as a later addition.[13] O. Gigon[14], on the other hand, remarks that in c.4, 270b32 – 'ziemlich überraschend' – the element which moves circularly is mentioned once again. The aim of that section is indeed merely to gird the thesis that the circular motion is without countermovement (c.2, 269a9-18 and c.3, 270a10-20) with more and better arguments.[15] The very fact that these arguments

---

[8] But cf. P. Moraux, *Aristote Du Ciel*, p. xiii on 'la fonction plus particulière de cette transition.' In 'Recherches', p. 171, however, he also considered the transition of book II to III to be very artificial.

[9] For the sake of brevity I will in the sequel refer to book III without making repeated mention of the fact that the first prologue, 298a24-b6, and the concluding lines, c.8, 307b19-24, should be excluded.

[10] 'Bemerkungen', p. 157.

[11] *De Caelo*, p. 303.

[12] *Ueber die Elemente*, p. 145.

[13] L. Elders, *Aristotle's Cosmology*, p. 97, suggests the solution that the section did belong with the 'original logos', but the 'editors' sought to improve upon Aristotle by relocating the piece. Elders has the habit of replacing single problems by a plurality of them.

[14] *Vom Himmel*, p. 17.

[15] Cf. P. Moraux, *Aristote Du Ciel*, p. xxxviii.

have not been fitted organically into the reasoning of c.2-3 leads one to suspect that they are later clarifications. Still, this suspicion offers insufficient foothold to arrive at a judgment concerning this fourth chapter relative to I,c.1-3. In principle one would have to leave room for the possibility that the second prologue of book III refers to I, c.1-4. But it seems that III, c.1, 298b6-8 fits much better with I, c.3, 270b28-31 than it does to c.4, 271a33.

It is generally recognized, on the other hand, that book IV contains no intrinsic connection with book III, and that the transition formed by III, c.8, 307b19-24 is quite artificial.[16] According to most interpreters *De Generatione et Corruptione* II would much sooner serve as sequel to *De Caelo* III than would the exposition about the light and the heavy now found in *De Caelo* IV.[17]

It may be worthwhile, therefore, to investigate the content of *De Caelo* I, c.1-3 & III[18] more closely, in order to verify the hypothesis to the effect that we are here dealing with two closely related parts. In advance I wish to point out that, in my opinion, the separation of I, c.1-3 & III need not be based exclusively on the arguments given above, derived from the composition of *De Caelo*, but that peculiarities of content require this separation as well.

---

[16] O. Gigon, *Vom Himmel*, pp. 37-38; P. Gohlke, *Prinzipienlehre*, pp. 71-79. Gohlke believes book IV of the *De Caelo* to have been written after *Physics* VIII, see 'Entstehungsgeschichte', p. 288; L. Elders, *Aristotle's Cosmology*, p. 329; O. Longo, *De Caelo*, p. xxxv; P. Moraux, *Aristote Du Ciel*, pp. xxi-xxiii, 'Recherches', p. 171; P. Steinmetz, 'Ansatzpunkte', p. 229 (note 18); G. A. Seeck, *Ueber die Elemente*, p. 74.

[17] P. Moraux, *Aristote Du Ciel*, pp. xxvi, xx; O. Longo, *De Caelo*, p. xxxviii.

[18] I, c.4, then, is not further discussed.

CHAPTER THREE

THE REFERENCES IN *DE CAELO* I, c.1-3 & III

1. INTRODUCTORY METHODOLOGICAL NOTES

If there is reason to think that it may be possible to indicate within the *Corpus Aristotelicum* not only a chronological order of the various writings, but also a correlate series of phases of thought, it is of great importance that one know which topics Aristotle had already treated, and consequently presumed his readers to be familiar with, before *De Caelo* I, c.1-3 & III. Commentators too often explicate even the early works in terms of the entire *Corpus* without restriction. The possibility mentioned, however, ought to urge us to allow the philological principle requiring that an author be explained in terms of his own work, to be valid only for those portions which we know with certainty, or have reason to believe, that they were written prior to the sections to be elucidated. To be sure, the restriction will reduce the length of commentaries considerably, but this can hardly be a decisive objection. One could perhaps object to the apparent circularity this entails: the interpretation of every text seems to be determined by a *Vorverständnis* of the context to the extent that every conclusion is in danger of entanglement in a *petitio principii*. Chronological determination of the parts of the *Corpus* is to be based upon a philosophical interpretation of the text. But this philosophical interpretation will be quite different depending on whether the section in question is considered to be early or more recent. If one would nevertheless observe the restriction it would mean that precisely for those parts concerning which there is the least certainty, no appeal to other Aristotle-texts may be made. Still, if a better foundation for the investigation must be considered unattainable, a restriction of this kind will be preferable to the age-old method of tracing '*the* philosophy of Aristotle' which led to a profusion of fancy. Awareness of the entire range of problems may perhaps cause one to allow for a greater number of possible explanations. Often the method used to date has obstructed avenues to possibly better insight into Aristotle's evolution.

2. AIDS TOWARDS CHRONOLOGICAL DETERMINATION

Basically, there are two kinds of data by which the chronological order of the various parts of the *Corpus* may be determined.

a. First, there are those which may be found on the basis of knowledge of Aristotle's development; specific insights may thus be marked as either still unconceived or already superseded. As noted above, Von Arnim, Guthrie and others hold that Aristotle hit upon the theory of the Unmoved Mover in the later years; hence, the passages in *De Caelo* which presuppose the theory are taken to be later additions, since the work as a whole is generally dated early. If accurate insight into the development of the thought of Aristotle were possible, this would yield the most reliable indications for the chronology by far. However, to reach this stage one must needs make use of quite different aids that are much less trustworthy – a circumstance which detracts from the value of the developmental theory based on it.

b. For these auxiliary aids one has recourse to philological techniques, i.e., study of the differences of style (such as between dialogues and lecture-notes), of the recurrences of certain words, of the ἅπαξ λεγόμενα, of the frequency of terms and expressions, of the geographical names occurring in the text (such as investigated by D'Arcy Thompson in the case of the *Historia Animalium*). Since the beginning of the twentieth century these have yielded good results. But the potential is limited and the results will always have to be checked in the context of a philosophical interpretation.

3. THE INTERNAL REFERENCES

Aristotle himself seems to have given very clear indications regarding the order of the various works: for compositional and didactic reasons he frequently refers to written or projected studies. But these internal references suffer from the same drawback as does the *Corpus* as a whole: they become chronologically valuable only if and when it is determined at which time they were incorporated into the text. Obviously, the references may well be the result of later revisions of an earlier text, either by Aristotle or by an editor. W. D. Ross' remark to the effect that 'cross-references only make it more easy to detect sequences which would be fairly certain even without the existence of the references' (*Physics*, p. 11), seems methodologically quite correct.[1] I believe, however, that many writers tend to neglect these references, and that for this reason references to later parts of the *Corpus*, for instance to *Physics* VIII, *Metaphysics* Λ, *De Progressu Anim.* etc., in *De Caelo* I, c.4-II, c.14, are too readily underestimated. At times, in II, c.2 for instance, it is not al all easy to show which part ought to be extrapolated as having been added later, because the whole context is closely interwoven with the reference.[2] Most commentators nevertheless believe that they may view such later references as independent, and continue uncritically to assign an early date to the whole of *De Caelo* I-IV.

At any rate, references do occur in *De Caelo* I, c.1-3 & III, and are part of the extant text. Hence they deserve as much attention as the rest. I will, accordingly, review them and take into account the remarks made by the various commentators.

a. I, c.3, 270a14-18

The section dealing with the 'first *soma*' contains a reference-note in c.3[3] Although one could point to the theory here proposed also in the *Metaphysics*[4], Guthrie is convinced that 'Aristotle's reference is to the *Physics* (I, c.7-9)', and all other commentators agree with him. It does indeed seem impossible that either Aristotle or an editor would,

---

[1] On the value of the references within the *Corpus* see also, E. Zeller, *Philosophie der Griechen* II,2, Leipzig 1921[4], p. 156; W. Jaeger, *Aristotle*, p. 294: 'What this method gives us is at best only the order that Aristotle at the close of his literary activity believed to be demanded by the nature of the subject-matter or by pedagogical considerations' – but see also pp. 295-296. A. Mansion, 'La Genèse', p. 424: 'Le système de références ... date évidemment ... de la dernière revision faite par Aristote des ouvrages en question.' This statement seems to preclude apriori the possibility that Aristotle may have made use of such references even in his very earliest works and that they were perhaps never removed. See also F. Nuyens, *Ontwikkelingsmomenten*, pp. 98-99; O. Gigon, *Vom Himmel*, p. 45 '... auf [die verweisende Bemerkungen] wird man sich besser nicht verlassen'. I. Düring, *Aristoteles*, pp. 34, 44 and note 268.

[2] Cf. P. Gohlke, *Prinzipienlehre*, p. 80, who points out that the whole of IV, c.3 presupposes the theory of the unmoved prime mover, while W. K. C. Guthrie, for instance, only abstracts 311a9-12. Cf. W. D. Ross, *Aristotle's Metaphysics*, pp. xiii-xiv.

[3] C3, 270a14-18 διὰ τὸ γίγνεσθαι μὲν ἅπαν τὸ γιγνόμενον ἐξ ἐναντίου τε καὶ ὑποκειμένου τινός, καὶ φθείρεσθαι ὡσαύτως ὑποκειμένου τέ τινος καὶ ὑπ' ἐναντίου καὶ εἰς ἐναντίον, καθάπερ ἐν τοῖς πρώτοις εἴρηται λόγοις.

[4] Guthrie mentions *Metaphysics* Λ, 1069b2-9; O. Longo, *Metaphysics* M, 1087a36; L. Elders, *Metaphysics* M, 1098a36 (but probably meant to refer to the place to which Longo points).

in one of the physical works refer to 'previous considerations' and mean the *Metaphysics*. Since, further, *Physics* I, c.7-9 agrees entirely with the brief representation in this text I will accept that Aristotle had already developed his theory concerning the three principles of all being (τὸ ὑποκείμενον, τὸ εἶδος and ἡ στέρησις) when he wrote *De Caelo* I, c.1-3.[5]

b. III, c.1, 299a9-11 and c.4, 303a23

In the third book more places demand attention.[6] To start with, c.1[7] and c.4[8]. With respect to the first-mentioned there is a consensus. Here is meant *Physics* VI, c.1-2.[9] The same holds for the c.4 reference, except that O. Longo mentions *Physics* III, c.4, IV, c.6-11, and VI, c.10. Evidently Longo has only looked for sections in the *Corpus* that could be referred to by the title 'concerning time and motion'; but the text also informs us that the work referred to deals with the contradictions in which those who maintain the existence of indivisible bodies involve themselves. The problem of divisibility and continuity is indeed presented in *Physics* VI, c.1-2. Consequently, it would be more correct to consider the reference to be directed to it.[10]

c. III, c.2, 301b32

Matters are more complicated in the case of III, c.2, 301b31-33.[11] Guthrie, Moraux and Tricot (hesitantly) point to *Physics* IV, c.6-9, Longo to IV, c.8. But G. A. Seeck notes, on pp. 77-79 of his book, that προειρημένων and εἰρημένων are always used by Aristotle for references within the same work. And on the basis of his view that an investigation of the reality of genesis, such as announced in III, c.1,298b9-12 is required he takes the passage to be a reference

---

[5] L. Elders' remark, *Aristotle's Cosmology*, p. 92, to the effect that this theory presupposes 'the theory of matter and form', appears unsound. H. E. Runner, *Development Illustrated*, pp. 104-107, distinguishes these two sharply – correctly so, I believe – and thinks that in the original design of *Physics* I the full-fledged hylomorphism was not present. See also P. Gohlke, *Prinzipienlehre*, pp. 28-31.

[6] Naturally, the references in the first prologue (298a24-27) are not included here.

[7] C.1, 299a9-11 περὶ δὲ τούτων ἐπέσκεπται πρότερον ἐν τοῖς περὶ κινήσεως λόγοις, ὅτι οὐκ ἔστιν ἀδιαίρετα μήκη.

[8] C4, 303a23 περὶ ὧν εἴρηται πρότερον ἐν τοῖς περὶ χρόνου καὶ κινήσεως.

[9] L. Elders believes this reference to stem from an 'editor or reader'. The passages mentioned in note 10 argue against this.

[10] *De Caelo* III, c.5, 304a22 and c.6, 305a4 proceed from the same treatment of the continually divisible. In I, c.1, 268a6 Aristotle builds on this as well.

[11] C.2, 301b31-33 ὅτι δ'οὔτε πάντων ἐστὶ γένεσις οὔθ' ἁπλῶς οὐθενός, δῆλον ἐκ τῶν προειρημένων.

to that exposition (which was apparently deleted later) and, 301b33-302a9 to be a secondary addition. Seeck's hypothesis regarding a lost 'Untersuchung zur Genesis' seems to me superfluous: to answer those who exclude becoming and passing-away Aristotle, in c.1, 298b14-24, refers to 'another study', just as he did in *Physics* I, c.2, 184b25-185a13.[12] There he said very clearly that ὁ φυσικός postulates the reality of motion (to which all genesis is reducible: c.7, 190b5-10). Entirely in harmony with that passage Aristotle also in *De Caelo* III, c.1, 298b18 rejects the Eleatic problematics (i.e. their theory of the non-reality of genesis), since these problems do not belong to the science of physics but to a study of the presuppositions of that science. Aristotle is sure that there is genesis. In c.3-8 it only remains to make clear in what sense one must speak of genesis.

In spite of this criticism directed at Seeck the question remains whether the reference in 301b32 is not in fact an internal reference to part of *De Caelo* itself. For, the text-argument is not that 'the preceding has made it clear' that there is no void, but a) that not everything is subject to genesis, and b) that it is not as if nothing at all becomes or passes-away. a) may readily be derived from the statements of I, c.3, 270a12-22. They explain that the primary *soma* is beyond the realm of genesis and *phthora*. b) is implied in III, c.1, 298b14-24.[13] If the reference is interpreted in this way, 301b33 ff. must be considered a further development of the theory that *creatio ex nihilo* is impossible, with the aid of an argument not yet advanced in *Physics* I.[14]

d. III, c.6, 305a21

In line with the above, it seems possible to view c.6, 305a21[15] as a reference to a part of *De Caelo* itself as well. In this case to c.2, 301b32 ff.[16]

---

[12] Here again it is not at all certain that the *Metaphysics* is referred to (Tricot, *Traité du Ciel*). As appears from Sextus Empiricus, *Math.* 10 (*Phys.* 2) 45, these problems were also dealt with in a lost writing, probably *De Philosophia*. Cf. fr. 9 (R).

[13] Cf. Simplicius, *In De Caelo* 598,3 ff. (Heib.), who does not point to any connection with *Physics* IV.

[14] Plato, *Timaeus* 58a, 80c had also rejected the possibility of a continuous vacuum. Cf. F. M. Cornford *Plato's Cosmology* p. 57. Accordingly, Aristotle is here able to appeal to a doctrine of the school.

[15] 305a21 εἰ δ'ἀσώματον, ἀνάγκη κενὸν εἶναι ἀφωρισμένον· τοῦτο δ'ὅτι ἀδύνατον, δέδεικται πρότερον.

[16] Cf. Tricot, *Traité du Ciel*. Most editors refer to *Physics* IV, c.6-9 exclusively.

e. III, c.5, 304b19

In addition to the passages mentioned above (c.1, 298b6-8 and c.2, 301b31-33) III, c.5, 304b19 also tightens the bond between I, c.1-3 and III, by referring to I, c.2.

f. III, c.1, 300a1; c.2, 300b17; c.8, 306b19 refer to Plato's *Timaeus*.

In accordance with the restriction mentioned under section 1 of this chapter I will, to explicate the text, rely only on Plato's dialogues up to and including the *Timaeus*[17] and Aristotle's *Physics* I and VI, c.1-2. The current view to the effect that *De Caelo* presupposed far more of the *Physics*[18] is based especially on numerous references to parts of the *Physics* in *De Caelo* I, c.4-II, c.14. But if it can be shown that I, c.4-II, c.14 is a later section, the chronological indications elicited from it will, of course, become irrelevant, at least as far as *De Caelo* I, c.1-3 & III is concerned. It certainly seems more likely, I should think, that Aristotle first conceived the main outlines of a cosmology, and that he would only subsequently concentrate on certain details (as for example in *Physics* III and IV).

[17] For, the possibility exists that *Laws* X is later than *De Caelo* I, c.1-3 & III. It also contains important cosmological remarks and I. Düring, for instance, believes it to contain references to the philosophy of the early Aristotle (*Aristoteles*, p. 187).

[18] H. Von Arnim, *Entstehung der Gotteslehre*, p. 8, mentions *Physics* I-VI; cf. F. Solmsen, *Aristotle's System*, p. 302 (note 47). But without the theory of *De Caelo* I, c.2 and III, c.2, *Physics* V, c.6, 230a18-b26, for instance, is inconceivable. In *Physics* III and IV also, the doctrine of the five elements is assumed to be known, and it even seems as if Aristotle has already come much closer to the theory of *Meteorologica* I, in which fire as distinct area within Aristotle's doctrine of layers has lost much of its significance by way of the ὑπέκκαυμα-theory, and has been made into a sub-form of ἀήρ; cf. IV, c.5, 212b20-22. (Unlike Ross, I deem it quite unlikely that in this passage 'Aether' would stand for fire).

CHAPTER FOUR

THE CONTENT OF *DE CAELO* I, c. 1-3 & III

The clue found so far, the hypothesis of chronological differences within the various parts of *De Caelo*, will obviously have to be verified. Possible differences in philosophical conception which appear in the various parts will have to be analyzed. I will therefore treat the views of *De Caelo* I, c.1-3 & III at some length, and attempt to show that this part constitutes a unity and ought to be assigned an early date. As to the remainder of *De Caelo*, only those sections in which Aristotle's conception can be shown to date from a later phase in his development will be dealt with. The greater part of the investigation, then, will concern I, c.1-3 & III.

A. ARISTOTLE'S STARTING-POINT (I, c.1)

As appears from the opening lines Aristotle will, in *De Caelo*, be dealing mainly with bodies and spatial magnitudes, with their qualities and motions.[1]

1. The *Soma* (Physical Body) as Central Theme

Aristotle begins his cosmology by pointing out the central position of the *soma* in reality, and devotes the first chapter to a description of it. It is important to understand Aristotle's point of view here, because these lines give expression to one of his fundamental convictions which will control the entire subsequent argument, but which is not

---

[1] I, c.1, 268a1-3. It is basically incorrect to understand this (as does O. Gigon, *Vom Himmel*, p. 14) as a delimitation over against 'das wesenhaft Unkörperliche'. Gigon would first have to demonstrate that Aristotle has introduced this distinction between corporeal and non-corporeal substances already. In *De Caelo* I, c.1-3 & III there is, I think, not a hint of it. But Gigon would be right if in the first prologue of book III (added later), in 298b5 for instance, he were to note a delimitation of the area of knowledge of nature, which is the result of the fact that the immaterial substances, accepted by Aristotle at a later date, remain outside of the field of investigation of physics.

itself subjected to critical examination. This basic principle is formulated in 268a22: 'The body is the only perfect spatial entity'.

2. The Basic Principle Posited, Not Demonstrated

It does indeed seem as if Aristotle offers an argument for this thesis in section 268a10-20, but that section has often, and not without reason, failed to impress the commentators. A proof in the strict sense is not given at all; rather, a dogmatic stance is being 'fortified' by every means at his disposal. He begins his argument with the thesis that everything which is continuous, and therefore infinitely divisible[2], may be distinguished into the one-dimensional, the two-dimensional, and the three-dimensional.[3] By means of a proposition derived from the Pythagoreans[4], a reference to a cultic practice, and an example from the common use of language[5], Aristotle works out something like an identification for 'three' and 'all', and in turn replaces this with 'perfect', 'complete'.

The quality of 'completeness' is thus proper to the body since it is three-dimensional, and the 'all' is complete because it is the totality of all bodies (b8); for the same reason neither the one-dimensional nor the two-dimensional have a right to this predicate.

3. No *Metabasis eis allo genos*

Once it is realized that in this first chapter Aristotle is concerned to maintain the priority of the physical[6] body, the conclusion may well

---

[2] 268a6 seems to contain a reference to *Physics* VI, c.1-2; cf. Tricot, *Traité du Ciel*. In chapter Three this section was shown to be presupposed in *De Caelo* I, c.1-3 & III.   [3] 268a7-9.

[4] 268a11: τὸ πᾶν καὶ τὰ πάντα τοῖς τρισὶν ὥρισται. It must be emphasized that this implies no 'Pythagoreism' on the part of Aristotle, anymore than in a26. By way of this old thesis the priority of the physical *soma* with respect to lines and planes is posited, so that Aristotle comes into conflict with 'Pythagoreistic' philosophers: Plato in the *Timaeus* and some other members of the Academy. Aristotle's position here is clear in a30-b5 and III, c.1, 299a16-300a14; c.8, 306b24-6. The Pythagorean teaching is explicitly rejected in III, c.1, 300a14-19.

[5] These two examples make clear that Aristotle introduces *endoxa* into the debate in order to forestall further critical questions with the help of their authority.

[6] At this point already I should remark that the term *physis* in *De Caelo* covers a far broader area than that which modern usage ascribes to 'the physical'. I return to this broader meaning in chapter Four, F.

be that 268a28-b5[7] requires an interpretation different from the one accepted until now. Almost every commentator from antiquity to modern times has understood the core of this text to be this: Aristotle rejects the possibility of the existence of a four-dimensional magnitude.[8] In 268a9 Aristotle had already noted that next to the line, the plane and the body no other divisible magnitude exists, but the danger that people might hold four-dimensional or multi-dimensional magnitudes to exist apparently was so great that Aristotle would once more warn against it. W. K. C. Guthrie translates (beginning at a30): 'This much, however, is clear, that there is no further change to a fourth species of magnitude like the changes from length to surface and from surface to body. Otherwise body would not be the complete magnitude that we have shown it to be, for any advance on it could only be made where it fell short; but that which is complete cannot fall short; it extends in every possible direction.'

Now, it does not seem very likely that Aristotle has rejected the possibility of magnitudes of more than three dimensions as emphatically as here suggested. No one appears to have defended such a theory until the nineteenth century. There is yet a second objection: when οὐκ ἔστιν εἰς ἄλλο γένος μετάβασις is translated with 'there is no further change to a fourth species of magnitude' the implication would be that Aristotle accepts a *metabasis* from line to surface and from surface to body! L. Elders[9] does indeed note the implication and concludes that 'there is no basis for Ross' remark that Aristotle never thought of points, lines and planes as forming a chain of entities.'[10] Elders sees a connection with the important text of Plato's *Laws*, X, 894a[11],

---

[7] ὅσα μὲν οὖν διαιρετὰ τῶν μεγεθῶν, καὶ συνεχῆ ταῦτα. εἰ δὲ καὶ τὰ συνεχῆ πάντα διαιρετά, οὔπω δῆλον ἐκ τῶν νῦν· ἀλλ' ἐκεῖνο μὲν δῆλον, ὡς οὐκ ἔστιν εἰς ἄλλο γένος μετάβασις, ὥσπερ ἐκ μήκους εἰς ἐπιφάνειαν, εἰς δὲ σῶμα ἐξ ἐπιφανείας· οὐ γὰρ ἂν ἔτι τὸ τοιοῦτον τέλειον εἴη μέγεθος· ἀνάγκη γὰρ γίγνεσθαι τὴν ἔκβασιν κατὰ τὴν ἔλλειψιν, οὐχ οἷόν τε δὲ τὸ τέλειον ἐλλείπειν· πάντῃ γάρ ἐστιν.

[8] Thus Simplicius, Tricot, Moraux and Stocks; cf. Elders, *Aristotle's Cosmology*, p. 79, and O. Longo, *De Caelo*, p. 298. O. Gigon, 'Aristoteles-Studien I', p. 120: 'eine fast pedantische Explikation dessen was in a9 schon gesagt war.'

[9] *Aristotle's Cosmology*, pp. 81 ff.

[10] *Op. cit.*, p. 82 (note 1), in which W. D. Ross, *Analytics* p. 14, is quoted, and p. 17.

[11] Plato, *Laws* X, 894a: γίγνεται δὴ πάντων γένεσις, ἡνίκ' ἂν τί πάθος ᾖ; δῆλον ὡς ὁπόταν ἀρχὴ λαβοῦσα αὔξην εἰς τὴν δευτέραν ἔλθῃ μετάβασιν καὶ ἀπὸ ταύτης εἰς τὴν πλησίον, καὶ μέχρι τριῶν ἐλθοῦσα αἴσθησιν σχῇ τοῖς αἰσθανομένοις.
Cf. Ph. Merlan, in A. H. Armstrong, *The Cambridge History of Later Greek and*

which, he believes, teaches a theory of derivation. It seems to me that this is so: Plato here explains the becoming of all concrete, visible things by deriving them from higher entities which are not considered to belong to the realm of sense-perception. Immediately preceding the sensorily perceptible must be the two-dimensional and one-dimensional mathematical entities (surface and line). With respect to the principle (ἀρχή) meant in 894a3 one can in the same scheme think of the mathematical point as 'origin of the line', or, perhaps, of an origin no longer mathematical but purely intelligible. The becoming (in phases) of things perceptible takes place by means of 'growth'.[12]

In whatever way one would wish to interpret further details, it is clear that in Plato's scheme the sensorily perceptible three-dimensional is fourth in line from the ἀρχή which is itself supra-physical and non-sensory. This, it seems to me, provides a conclusive argument against Elders' thesis that in De Caelo I, c.1 Aristotle holds the same derivation-theory[13], and that Aristotle is merely concerned to emphasize the impossibility of continuing towards the four-dimensional. It is not only inconceivable that Plato should have called the physical, perceptible bodies 'complete' without any restriction, but it is equally impossible that a derived entity should receive the predicate τέλειον. This predicate, according to pre-Socratic and Platonic thought, belongs exclusively to the origin, the totality or the whole.[14] The very fact that Aristotle grants the body the predicate 'complete' (in a23) proves that he also considers it to have the character of ἀρχή and that he views it to be an *irreducible* magnitude.

Early Medieval Philosophy, 1970², p. 19: 'Here, it seems, Plato indeed derives the sensible from the mathematical and does so, strangely enough, as a matter of course.'

[12] λαβοῦσα αὔξην

[13] L. Elders, *Aristotle's Cosmology*, p. 78, also explains the *archai* spoken of in 268a3 as 'the principles ... out of which the three dimensions evolve, viz. the One and Plurality', even though according to I, c.3, 270a14-17, *Physics* I (containing Aristotle's own *archai*-theory) had already been written; cf. also *De Caelo* III, c.7, 306a9-11! On p. 81 Elders is of the opinion that in 268a26 Aristotle agrees with Plato and Xenocrates in accepting indivisible lines as principles for lines, while the very fact that Aristotle holds the line to be characterized by the number one entails the rejection of Academic views and intends to stress the continuous divisibility of every line in one direction; 268a6-8, 27-8.

[14] *De Caelo*, I, c.2, 269a19: τὸ γὰρ τέλειον πρότερον τῇ φύσει τοῦ ἀτελοῦς is rooted in the same tradition.

That is why treatment of it is accorded the place of honour at the beginning of his argument! But this means that he is diametrically opposed to Plato's reasoning, and that the text, when compared to *Laws* X, 894a4, does not express agreement with but criticism of one of the most fundamental points of Plato's philosophy.

I would therefore suggest the following paraphrase for section 268a30 ff.: 'This much is clear: no *metabasis eis allo genos* is possible, such as (for instance) from line to plane and from plane to body; for the product of such a *metabasis* (τὸ τοιοῦτον) would no longer be a complete magnitude; for, the *ekbasis* necessarily goes hand in hand with a decrease of completeness (thus the body would be incomplete). But the complete (the body) cannot fall short. For it possesses extension in every possible direction.'

This means that I would explicate οὐκ ἔστιν εἰς ἄλλο γένος μετάβασις as being an attempt to understand the various aspects of reality in accordance with the nature proper to each of them, and to do justice to this nature by means of the principle of mutual irreducibility.[15] The critique of the doctrine of the 'indivisible lines' (in the work of that name) is based on this principle also. Again, this principle serves as the basis of Aristotle's argument about continuity and discontinuity in *Physics* VI, c.1-2[16], which is equally directed against Plato, and presupposed in *De Caelo* I, c.1. His refutation of Democritus' physicalistic atomism and of the mathematical atomism of Plato's *Timaeus* in *De Caelo* III, c.1, 299a11-300a14 rests upon this principle. The *Categories* defend the same insight against Plato's late reduction-theory.

The implications of this ontological principle for logic Aristotle has expounded in the *Posterior Analytics* I, c.7: 'In a proof one may not pass from one *genus* to another; for instance, prove a geometric proposition by arguments derived from arithmetic.'[17] 'Concerning those things of which the genus differs, such as in the case of geometry and arithmetic, a proof derived from the one discipline

---

[15] Cf. H. Dooyeweerd, *A New Critique of Theoretical Thought* I, pp. 101-106; II, pp. 36-54; D. H. Th. Vollenhoven, *De Noodzakelijkheid ener Christelijke Logica*, Amsterdam, 1932, p. 41.

[16] *Physics* VI, c.1, 231a24: ἀδύνατον ἐξ ἀδιαιρέτων εἶναί τι συνεχές, οἷον γραμμὴν ἐκ στιγμῶν. c.2, 232a24; 233b16-17.

[17] 75a38: οὐκ... ἔστιν ἐξ ἄλλου γένους μεταβάντα δεῖξαι, οἷον τὸ γεωμετρικὸν ἀριθμητικῇ. This insight is considered to be an important anti-Platonic trend by G. E. L. Owen, 'The Platonism of Aristotle', pp. 141-142.

(arithmetic) cannot be applied to the properties of the objects of the other (the extended entities of geometry) – unless extended entities and numbers are identifiable.'[18] 'A *metabasis* is allowed in a proof only when, either in an absolute sense or in some respect, the genus is in both cases the same.'[19]

The fact that Aristotle has used this principle against Plato and his other pupils is evident not only from the lines quoted above from *Laws* X and from the *Timaeus*-doctrine of the elements, but also from data Aristotle offers us on theories that are usually associated with Plato's lecture *De Bono*. I do not intend to go into the problems connected with this, but rather take as example a passage from the criticism of Plato and the Academy as found in *Metaphysics* A, c.9.[20] The reduction of all spatial magnitudes and of the discontinuous numbers to the *same* principles, i.e., the One and the Great and Small (cf. as early as *Physics* I, c.4 and 9) is rejected on the conclusion that the three-dimensional and the two-dimensional are not to be viewed as species of one and the same genus, just as in the case of the one-dimensional and the two-dimensional or lines and points. The *allo genos* of *Metaphysics* A, c.9, 992a14 interferes with *De Bono*'s theory which would, with the aid of a universal method of logical diaeresis reduce all being to an all-embracing genus, τὸ "Ον or τὸ "Εν (or τὸ 'Αγαθόν). Aristotle was keenly aware of the multiplicity of meaning of the concept of 'being'.

Apriori it seems probable that this fundamental discussion with

[18] 75b3: ὧν δὲ τὸ γένος ἕτερον, ὥσπερ ἀριθμητικῆς καὶ γεωμετρίας, οὐκ ἔστι τὴν ἀριθμητικὴν ἀπόδειξιν ἐφαρμόσαι ἐπὶ τὰ τοῖς μεγέθεσι συμβεβηκότα, εἰ μὴ τὰ μεγέθη ἀριθμοί εἰσι.

H. Tredennick, *Posterior Analytics* (Loeb) p. 61 (note d) correctly remarks in connection with the last of this part: 'for Aristotle they are not.' Aristotle has no doubt as to the irreducibility of continuous entities from discrete ones. He only indicates that for Platonists the preceding argument does not hold. NB. the use of ὥσπερ in the sense of 'for instance', also occurring in *De Caelo* I, c.1, 268b1; IV, c.2, 308b7; *Rhet.* II, c.21, 1394b19.

[19] 75b8: ὥστ' ἢ ἁπλῶς ἀνάγκη τὸ αὐτὸ εἶναι γένος ἢ πῇ, εἰ μέλλει ἡ ἀπόδειξις μεταβαίνειν.

[20] 992a10-19: βουλόμενοι δὲ τὰς οὐσίας ἀνάγειν εἰς τὰς ἀρχὰς μήκη μὲν τίθεμεν ἐκ βραχέος καὶ μακροῦ, ἔκ τινος μικροῦ καὶ μεγάλου, καὶ ἐπίπεδον ἐκ πλατέος καὶ στενοῦ, σῶμα δ' ἐκ βαθέος καὶ ταπεινοῦ. καίτοι πῶς ἕξει ἢ τὸ ἐπίπεδον γραμμὴν ἢ τὸ στερεὸν γραμμὴν καὶ ἐπίπεδον; ἄλλο γὰρ γένος τὸ πλατὺ καὶ στενὸν καὶ βαθὺ καὶ ταπεινόν· ὥσπερ οὖν οὐδ' ἀριθμὸς ὑπάρχει ἐν αὐτοῖς, ὅτι τὸ πολὺ καὶ ὀλίγον ἕτερον τούτων, δῆλον ὅτι οὐδ' ἄλλο οὐθὲν τῶν ἄνω ὑπάρξει τοῖς κάτω. ἀλλὰ μὴν οὐδὲ γένος τὸ πλατὺ τοῦ βαθέος· ἦν γὰρ ἂν ἐπίπεδόν τι τὸ σῶμα.

Plato has occupied the young Aristotle intensely; it is in fact demonstrable with the aid of numerous data concerning Aristotle's dialogues and early parts of the *Corpus* (*Physics* I for instance). My exposition of the *metabasis* meant in *De Caelo* I, c.1, therefore, is not easily refuted by referring to places such as *History of Animals* VIII, c.1, 588b4 and 11.[21] The investigation of which the *History* is the result was not started until Aristotle had left Athens in 347 BC, and hence the passages mentioned are probably to be dated well after *De Caelo* I, c.1. Furthermore, the biological problems there are hardly comparable to the ontological discussion where the relation is at stake between the arithmetical and mathematical to physically qualified entities.

My interpretation of the lines 268a30-b2 is, I trust, clear from the above: *Derivation of mutually irreducible entities from each other is not permissible.* The lines b2-5 which follow, and which serve to explicate a30-b2 further, still need some elucidation. Particularly my translation of b3, ἀνάγκη γὰρ γίγνεσθαι τὴν ἔκβασιν κατὰ τὴν ἔλλειψιν, 'for the *ekbasis* necessarily goes hand in hand with a decrease of completeness', is diametrically opposed to W. K. C. Guthrie's 'any advance on it could only be made where it fell short.' To clarify the view here taken I would, for the concept of *ekbasis*, refer to an important section of Plato's *Republic* II, where Plato speaks about the divinity and about how it is to be spoken and written of in the newly designed state. The point of departure is that the divinity is good.[22] Hence it is the cause of all good only, not of evil.[23] The question following is whether god is mutable or whether he never 'steps out of his own *idea*'.[24] The proof of god's immutability is given by means of a dilemma: if he departs from his own *idea*, he would either do so himself or be brought to it by something else.[25] 380e3-381b7 proceeds to show that change from without[26] must be considered impossible. When the second possibility is next investigated Socrates

[21] b4: ἐκ τῶν ἀψύχων εἰς τὰ ζῷα μεταβαίνει κατὰ μικρὸν ἡ φύσις and b11: ἡ μετάβασις ἐκ τῶν ἀψύχων εἰς τὰ ζῷα συνεχής ἐστιν. Worked into *Part. Anim.* IV, c.5, 681a12: ἡ γὰρ φύσις μεταβαίνει συνεχῶς ἀπὸ τῶν ἀψύχων εἰς τὰ ζῷα

[22] 379b1.

[23] 379b15.

[24] 380d1: ἆρα γόητα τὸν θεὸν οἴει εἶναι καὶ οἷον ἐξ ἐπιβουλῆς φαντάζεσθαι ἄλλοτε ἐν ἄλλαις ἰδέαις... ἢ ἁπλοῦν τε εἶναι καὶ πάντων ἥκιστα τῆς ἑαυτοῦ ἰδέας ἐκβαίνειν;

[25] 380d8: οὐκ ἀνάγκη, εἴπερ τι ἐξίσταιτο τῆς αὑτοῦ ἰδέας, ἢ αὐτὸ ὑφ' ἑαυτοῦ μεθίστασθαι ἢ ὑπ' ἄλλου;

[26] 381a4: ἔξωθεν

asks whether this would be a change for the better or for the worse. The answer: 'Necessarily for the worse, if he were to change at all. For of god we are not likely to maintain that he is deficient in beauty or perfection.'[27] Here then are all the elements required for a correct understanding of *De Caelo* I, c.1, 268b2-5. If the divinity would step out of his own *idea*, which is to be qualified as complete and not inadequate in any respect, then the form adopted by him could no longer be called complete. The *ekbasis* out of his completeness would necessarily be for the worse, that is, it would go hand in hand with a decrease of perfection. (In his biological works Aristotle has tried to prove this thesis of the perfection of the truly real – in Plato's *Republic* the perfection of god – by constantly searching for purpose in the realm of biology. Theophrastus is rather sceptical about it and remarks that one would have to offer a better argument as to why more order (τάξις) is not possible and why every change would really imply a change for the worse.[28])

The above was not meant to argue that the section in *De Caelo* I, c.1 is directed against the philosophy of Plato in *Republic* II, but to show that the form of argumentation agrees. In this connection it is interesting to note that, as Simplicius, *In De Caelo* 288, 28-289, 15 (Heib) informs us, Aristotle has transposed the entire argument as to the immutability of god found in *Republic* II to his dialogue *On Philosophy* to apply to the divinity of his own conception. Aristotle has defended the *immutabilitas Dei* with the same argument, *viz.* that change as improvement is excluded because god is not ἐνδεής; every change therefore must be one for the worse.[29] On the basis of this datum the association with *Republic* II need not seem farfetched. But, I repeat, Aristotle's criticism is not directed against Plato's views in *Republic* II. In that work Plato has not yet attempted to close the gap between the perceptible and the intelligible worlds by thinking of the sensorily perceptible as derivation from supra-physical,

---

[27] 381b10: Πότερον οὖν ἐπὶ τὸ βέλτιόν τε καὶ κάλλιον μεταβάλλει ἑαυτὸν ἢ ἐπὶ τὸ χεῖρον καὶ τὸ αἴσχιον ἑαυτοῦ; 'Ανάγκη, ἔφη, ἐπὶ τὸ χεῖρον, εἴπερ ἀλλοιοῦται· οὐ γάρ που ἐνδεᾶ γε φήσομεν τὸν θεὸν κάλλους ἢ ἀρετῆς εἶναι.

[28] Theophrastus, *Metaphysica*, c.4, 7b7: διὰ τί τὸ πλέον ἀδύνατον ἢ εἰς τὸ χεῖρον ἡ μετάβασις;

[29] ἀλλ' οὐδὲ ἑαυτὸ μεταβάλλει ὡς καλλίονός τινος ἐφιέμενον· οὐδὲ γὰρ ἐνδεές ἐστι τῶν αὑτοῦ καλῶν οὐδενός· οὐ μέντοι οὐδὲ πρὸς τὸ χεῖρον, ὅτε μηδὲ ἄνθρωπος ἑκὼν ἑαυτὸν χείρω ποιεῖ, μήτε δὲ ἔχει τι φαῦλον μηδέν. ὅπερ ἂν ἐκ τῆς εἰς τὸ χεῖρον μεταβολῆς προσέλαβε.
= *De Philosophia* fr. 16 (R).

40

i.e. mathematical and intelligible *principia*. That tendency does not become manifest until later (*Timaeus* and *Laws* X) and seems to have been dominant in the lecture *De Bono*.

The criticism of *De Bono*, very compactly present in a30-b5 can be made explicit in line with my interpretation by means of a more extensive paraphrase.

The body is the only complete continuous entity. Consequently, a series of derivations in the sense of Plato's later philosophy is impossible. For in such a derivation-series the body would not appear until the fourth place, after the origin, the line, and the surface. But in that case the body would not be complete. For in the Platonic series of derivations the Ἕν is at the highest point of the ontological scale (According to a *testimonium* of Aristoxenus, *Harm. Elem.* II, p. 30 Meib., it may be identified with τὸ 'Αγαθόν[30]. In other places it is as Being opposed to non-Being.) It is perfect and does not fall short in any way. Now, on the Platonic view the body can only be thought to originate from the One if an *ekbasis* of the One from out of itself be accepted. But such an *ekbasis* can only occur for the worse (ἐπὶ τὸ χεῖρον) and to the measure that this process of *ekbasis* continues and the distance to the origin increases, the lack of perfection increases also. (One could speak of an alienation of the One from itself). Consequently, the line is less complete than its origin, the plane less complete than the line, and the physical body less complete than the mathematical plane.[31] (After all, extension means divisibility and thus lack of unity.) But this is in disagreement with the thesis found in *De Caelo* I, c.1, 268a23, to the effect that the body is the only complete entity. Thus the late-Platonic doctrine of the derivation of physical reality should be rejected.

The meaning attached in this paraphrase to the One of Plato's doctrine of principles may be clarified some more in connection with c.9 of *Physics* I, a book which must have preceded *De Caelo* I, c.1-3[32];

---

[30] Cf. also *Eth. Eud.* I, c.8, 1218a25. Perhaps texts such as this chapter may allow us to deduce that over against the genesis of all perceptible things from the Ἕν, stood the ἔφεσις, ὄρεξις of all things to the Ἕν or 'Αγαθόν.

Thus over against ἡ ἀπὸ τῶν ἀρχῶν ὁδός (*Eth. Nic.* I, c.4, 1095a34) stands the ἀνάγειν εἰς τὰς ἀρχάς (*Metaph.* A, c.9, 992a10), parallel with the two pillars of the Platonic dialectic, i.e. the διαίρεσις and the συναγωγή (*Phaedrus*, 266b).

[31] This may be compared with *Metaphysics* Z, c.2, 1028b16: δοκεῖ δὲ τισι τὰ τοῦ σώματος πέρατα, οἷον ἐπιφάνεια καὶ γραμμὴ καὶ στιγμὴ καὶ μονάς, εἶναι οὐσίαι, καὶ μᾶλλον ἢ τὸ σῶμα καὶ τὸ στερεόν.

[32] Cf. *De Caelo* I, c.3, 270a17.

I am inclined to think that it was originally very closely bound up with *De Caelo* I, c.1-3 & III. Comparing his own newly developed teaching of the three principles with the Platonic doctrine, in which the ῾Εν and τὸ μέγα καὶ μικρόν are mutually opposed as positive and negative poles, Aristotle posits that, in their system, Platonists must accept an ὀρέγεσθαι (ἐφίεσθαι) of the one principle to the opposed principle. 'But it is not possible for the *eidos* (Aristotle identifies this with the One in c.4, 187a18!) to have an ὄρεξις to itself, since it has no imperfection[33], nor can the negative principle strive towards the *eidos*, for that would mean self-annihilation.' This criticism in *Physics* I, c.9 also evidently directs itself, be it from a different point of view, against the late-Platonic doctrine of principles, in which the One, the perfect and the really real, is understood as Origin of all reality. It is likely that *De Caelo* I, c.1, in its original context and in the time of its composition, when the discussion concerning the principles was central, was readily understood by its hearers or readers. *Physics* I, c.9 equally presupposes a great deal of knowledge of the debates in the Academy. But the present location of the *De Caelo* I, c.1-3 among the physical works may be the reason why this chapter has not appeared to discuss such fundamental philosophical issues as it in fact does.

I do not consider the fact that this interpretation of the *ekbasis* and the theory of the One on which it is based parallels central themes of Plotinus' thought to be a serious objection, but rather an advantage. I should consider this an argument in favour of the acceptance of a continuous connection on an important point between the later Plato and Neo-Platonism. Plotinus, *Enneads* I, 8 (no. 51 Harder) c.7,17 may serve as example.[34]

---

[33] C.9, 192a20: καίτοι οὔτε αὐτὸ αὑτοῦ οἷόν τε ἐφίεσθαι τὸ εἶδος διὰ τὸ μὴ εἶναι ἐνδεές, οὔτε τὸ ἐναντίον. (φθαρτικὰ γὰρ ἀλλήλων τὰ ἐναντία)

[34] ἐπεὶ γὰρ οὐ μόνον τὸ ἀγαθόν, ἀνάγκη τῇ ἐκβάσει τῇ παρ' αὐτοῦ (Volkmann/ Harder; αὐτό ms. en Henry-Schwyzer, 1964), ἤ, εἰ οὕτω τις ἐθέλοι λέγειν, τῇ ἀεὶ ὑποβάσει καὶ ἀποστάσει, τὸ ἔσχατον, καὶ μεθ' ὃ οὐκ ἦν ἔτι γενέσθαι ὁτιοῦν, τοῦτο εἶναι τὸ κακόν.

Cf. Ph. Merlan, *From Platonism to neo-Platonism*, p. 2: '... the system of Plato as set forth by him [Aristotle], exhibits unmistakable similarities to a neo-platonic system'; p. 191: 'As presented by Aristotle, and as confirmed by what we know about Speusippus and Xenocrates the derivation of physicals from non-physicals was a principle accepted by Plato and his disciples. It is this principle which is the clearest anticipation of some tenets which we are wont to term neoplatonic.'

To complete my treatment of this difficult passage from the first chapter of *De Caelo* I refer to the translation by P. Moraux: 'il n'est pas possible de passer du corps à un autre genre de grandeur, comme on le fait pour aller de la ligne à la surface, puis de la surface au corps, car s'il permettait cette opération le corps cesserait d'être une grandeur parfaite. De toute nécessité, en effet, le passage d'un genre à un genre supérieur ne peut avoir lieu que parce que quelque chose fait défaut au genre d'ou l'on part.' In his Introduction[35] he adds the following elucidation: 'quand Aristote parle du passage de la ligne à la surface et de celle-ci au corps, il entend *simplement classer* les genres d'étendues et ne veut pas dire que la surface soit engendré à partir de lignes et le corps à partir de surfaces. Au premier chapitre du livre Γ, il combat en effet la théorie de Platon qui, dans le *Timée*, constituait au moyen de triangles les molécules des corps'[36] (italics mine), and: 'La μετάβασις εἰς ἄλλο γένος dont il est question ici n'a rien de commun avec le procédé de raisonnement qu'Aristote interdit dans les *Anal. Post.*, A,7.'[37] It seems to me however that the emphasis noticeable in ἐκεῖνο μὲν δῆλον of a30 is more readily understood if the passage is directed against a theory held by some members of the Academy, rather than that the subsequent section fought against windmills or were a purely 'academic' argument.[38] A more telling objection to this translation seems τὸ τοιοῦτον in b2, where one would expect τοῦτο (if it were to refer exclusively to τὸ σῶμα). The Greek text would have gained in clarity if in a30 it read ὡς οὐκέτι εἰς ἄλλο γένος ἔστι μετάβασις. Further, why does it not say εἰς ἄλλο μέγεθος or εἰς ἄλλο εἶδος τοῦ συνεχοῦς? Precisely because of the fact that Aristotle, after having expounded his own theory, often immediately

---

[35] P. xxxiii, (note 2).

[36] L. Elders circumvents this powerful argument by positing that III, c.1 (on the basis of parallels with *Physics* V and *De Anima* noted by him) 'does not seem to be early' (*Aristotle's Cosmology*, p. 279). I, c.1, on the other hand, is 'likely to be early' according to p. 82.

[37] Is this remark aimed at P. Gohlke's translation? Cf. *Lehrschriften* 6, p. 20: 'Aber das ist klar, dass es keinen Uebergang gibt von einer Grössengattung zur andern, z.B. von der Länge zur Fläche oder von der Fläche zum Körper, weil so etwas dann nicht mehr vollkommene Grösse sein könnte; der Uebergang müsste ja Ausfüllen einer Lücke sein, und das Vollkommene kann eine solche Lücke nicht haben, weil es allseitig erfüllt.'

[38] In this way I would view Ptolemaeus' book περὶ διαστάσεως, in which this author, according to Simplicius, *in Ar. De Caelo* 9,21 (Heib.) καλῶς ἀπέδειξεν ὅτι οὐκ εἰσὶ πλείονες τῶν τριῶν διαστάσεις.

uses it as the critical touchstone for the opinions of his predecessors (for instance *Physics* I, c.9), and because a30-b5 gains a much profounder philosophical meaning in the defended interpretation, I considered it permissible to explicate this interpretation at length. In this way all arguments for and against can be weighed, before one could conclude that Moraux' view, which is certainly to be preferred over that of W. K. C. Guthrie and that of L. Elders, is to be accepted.

4. Does *Protrepticus* B33 Provide a Counter-argument?

To counter the above exposition of 268a30 ff. one could argue that a fragment of Aristotle's *Protrepticus*[39] seems to show that its author accepted a derivation of lower areas of being from higher ones. P. Wilpert has demonstrated that the argument used there constituted one of the pillars on which *De Bono* was built.[40] With its aid Plato tried to order the whole of reality in terms of a hierarchic system with the One at its summit. The great difficulty with this approach by Plato is the equalization of a logical priority and an ontological one: it causes the physical to be placed lower in the scale than the mathematical and the numbers, which implied a disqualification. It is certainly correct to say that Aristotle, in *Protrepticus* fragment B33 (Düring) was still strongly influenced by the Academic way of thinking. It is less certain, however, whether one ought to, in line with Wilpert,[41] conclude that its author still thinks 'ganz platonisch', at least, when this is meant to say that Aristotle also subscribes to derivation of a lower genus from a higher. In his commentary on the *Protrepticus* (p. 200), I. Düring points to two related places[42] in works which certainly

---

[39] Fr. B 33 (Düring); 5b (R.): αἴτιά τε μᾶλλον τὰ πρότερα τῶν ὑστέρων· ἐκείνων γὰρ ἀναιρουμένων ἀναιρεῖται τὰ τὴν οὐσίαν ἐξ ἐκείνων ἔχοντα, μήκη μὲν ἀριθμῶν, ἐπίπεδα δὲ μηκῶν, στερεὰ δὲ ἐπιπέδων, στοιχείων δὲ αἱ ὀνομαζόμεναι συλλαβαί. Cf. also Ch. Lefèvre, 'Du Platonisme' on the problems regarding the text of this section (pp. 226-227, note 39).

[40] *Zwei Frühschriften*, pp. 148 ff. Aristotle, *Metaphysics* Δ, c. 11, 1019a3 credits Plato with this method.

[41] *Loc. cit.* p. 151. This Platonizing interpretation is already found in W. Jaeger, *Aristotle*, pp. 94-95; also F. Solmsen, *Logik und Rhetorik*, p. 83.

[42] *Topics* VI, c.4, 141b5-8; *Anal. Post.* I, c.4, 73a34-36. W. D. Ross, *Analytics*, p. 14, had already taken the same view with respect to the passage of the *Protrepticus* and had exhaustively refuted Solmsen's interpretation. Cf. also W. G. Rabinowitz, *Aristotle's Protrepticus*, pp. 85 ff. In note 132 this writer mentions the various passages in which, according to him, Aristotle refutes the derivation-

do not subscribe to a Platonic derivation-theory. In these cases the issue is clearly an epistemological priority in the sense that to understand the concept of a line, the concept of a point must be known, since 'line' must be defined as 'the connection of two points'. Aristotle can accept Plato's epistemological starting-point, but does not connect it with the ontological implication that his teacher thought necessary. According to Aristotle, as for Plato, scientific investigation should penetrate to the non-composed, primary elements. But this did not lead Aristotle to neglect the proper character of the physical as compared to the arithmetical and the geometric, or to use the *principia* of number as the *principia* for bodies, as his teacher did. According to Aristotle every genus ought to be studied in terms of its own *principia*.[43]

5. The Physical is Irreducible

Over against the Platonic derivation of the physical out of its mathematical and arithmetical substrate Aristotle vindicates the perfection of the body and with that its irreducibility and primacy. That this position is not inconceivable in the period of Aristotle's stay in the Academy may appear from Plato's *Sophist* 240b1, where the Eleatic stranger attacks the rough-hewn, earthy philosophers from the race of giants, and summarizes their philosophy with these words: ταὐτὸν σῶμα καὶ οὐσίαν ὁριζόμενοι. In Aristotle the body has once again attained the character of ἀρχή as it did for the early Ionian philosophers of nature. The rejection of Plato's derivations does not imply that for Aristotle the various genera distinguishable in reality enjoy equal rank. In his doctrine of the categories, already presupposed in *Physics* I, the genus of the οὐσία is clearly central. Quantity and quality can only be predicated of something else; but the *ousia* on the contrary is completely independent. (*Physics* I, c.6, 189a14; c.7, 190a34-b3). Just as Plato's later system centered on τὸ Ἔν (Ὄν), for Aristotle's first independent conception the centre was the *ousia*. And during this early period, in which hylomorphism is not yet de-

---

theory: *Metaphysics*, A, c.9, 992b13-18; B, c.5, 1001b26-1002b11; Z, c.2, 1028b16-27; K, c.2, 1060b6-19; M, c.2, 1076b11-39; 1077a24-36; c.6, 1080a12-b36; c.9, 1085a7-b34; N, c.3, 1090b5-32.

[43] Cf. *De Caelo* III, c.7, 307a7-17. J. Stenzel's remark, *Zahl und Gestalt*, p. 140, concerning Aristotle's habit 'nicht mehr Ableitbares ruhig in seiner Gegebenheit hinzunehmen' also holds for his early writings.

veloped, *ousia* is still conceived of as a physically qualified bearer of properties. In agreement with this Aristotle, in *De Caelo* I, c.1, calls the body the only 'perfect' spatial magnitude. Instead of a logistic approach to reality this chapter evinces physicalism.[44]

The function of section 268a30 ff. in the argument, then, is in my interpretation that after Aristotle has given his own positive point of departure, the fundamental difference with regard to contemporary school-conceptions is indicated. Aristotle proves to subscribe to a view of the 'really real' quite different from that of Plato. Every accusation to the effect that Aristotle is guilty of a questionable lack of lucidity fails the moment it is realized that Aristotle's audience consisted of people who were sufficiently informed by these 'hints': they were quite familiar with Plato's theories, and perhaps even with those of Speusippus and Xenocrates.

B. THE DOCTRINE OF MOTION (I, c.2,268b11-26)

Once Aristotle has thus deliniated his field of investigation in the first chapter he continues by saying that he would postpone awhile the treatment of the problem as to whether the mass of the whole is limited or unlimited.[45] He fixes his attention on the primary parts

---

[44] Aristotle's evaluation of the *soma* has changed profoundly when, in *Metaphysics* Z, c.16, he suddenly claims that earth, fire and air cannot really be understood as *ousiai*, but only as *dunameis*, i.e. as material for the biotically qualified.

[45] C.2, 268b11-13; all commentators agree that the ὕστερον of line 12 refers to I, c.5-7, where an extensive treatment of this issue is given. In 268b13 Aristotle enters upon a discussion of the κατ' εἶδος αὐτοῦ (sc. τοῦ παντός) μόρια, that is to say, the first *soma* (in I, c.2-3) and the four remaining components of the All (together in book III). Compositionally speaking, it is not clear why treatment of the finitude of the All is not presented here, but that it is given after only one of the five elements that are to be studied has been discussed. This problem exists, however, only if I, c.5-7 belong to the same phase of composition as does I, c.1-3. If this be questioned a number of alternatives suggest themselves. One might view this, as Moraux, Longo and Elders do with respect to c.3, 269b21-23 and book IV, as an attempt to connect a newer text with an older one in the case of 268b11-13 as well. It seems possible, however, that Aristotle, in view of his eagerness to arrive at an exposition of his own theory on the first element, foregoes discussion of the *apeiron*-issue. He does grant Plato, who had begun his cosmology by discussing the ὅλον, that embraces τὰ ἐν μέρους εἴδει πεφύκοτα (*Timaeus*, 30c-33b2), and who had described this ὅλον as τέλεον ἐκ τελέων, that a treatment of the whole ought to precede

46

of the universe, the 'elements'. To deal with them he posits a new point of departure:

1. Aristotle's New View of Motion

'All physical bodies and magnitudes are able to move themselves locally by themselves: for we posit that nature is their principle of motion.'[46] Aristotle here candidly opposes his standpoint to that of Plato. In the *Phaedrus* 245c-246a the latter had argued that only a self-moved thing could guarantee the continuity of motion in the cosmos, and that the body, understood by Plato as 'put into motion by another'[47] depends for its impulse on an (a-somatic) self-moving psyche. (cf. *Laws* X, 893b ff.) Apparently, Aristotle considered the argument of the *Phaedrus* convincing to the extent that for him too, motion must ultimately be reduced to something that is self-moved.[48] With respect to this point, therefore, *De Caelo* I, c.2[49] is much closer to Plato than for instance *Physics* VII and VIII are; there the rule is that everything which moves is moved by something else. Self-movement is then degraded to a secondary level *after* the unmoved first mover. Here, in *De Caelo*, Aristotle refuses to accept a non-physical principle for this auto-motion: the impetus does not come from outside the body, but all bodies possess, according to him, a principle of motion of their own which he calls 'physis'. In this central issue then, for Aristotle 'physis' takes over the part played by 'psyche' in Plato. I. Düring[50] is not unjustified in saying that 'Aristotle's

discussion of the parts. But for Aristotle such a study is not interesting since on this score he agrees with Plato on all important points (cf. *Timaeus*, 32c, 35c). Aristotle's primary goal in all of his early writings is to clarify his differences with Plato and with the Academy. Later, as established leader of a philosophical school, he is especially concerned to offer a complete, systematic treatment of all important philosophical problems.

[46] I, c.2, 268a14-16 πάντα γὰρ τὰ φυσικὰ σώματα καὶ μεγέθη καθ' αὑτὰ κινητὰ λέγομεν εἶναι κατὰ τόπον· τὴν γὰρ φύσιν κινήσεως ἀρχὴν εἶναί φαμεν αὐτοῖς.

[47] 245c6: ὑπ' ἄλλου κινούμενον, either from without or from within, 245e5-6; cf. *Laws* X, 894b8.

[48] Cf. W. K. C. Guthrie, 'Aristotle's Theology', p. 162.

[49] The same view is found in *De Caelo* III, c.2, 300a20; 301b17 and c.5, 304b13-22 (with a reference to I, c.2).

[50] I. Düring, 'Nature and Reality', p. 42; cf. F. Solmsen, *Aristotle's System*, pp. 99, 102. This change may be understood as an annulment of the breach in the 'hylozoistic' *arche* of the Ionic philosophers of Nature, caused by Plato's sharp opposition between *psyche* and *soma*. Cf. J. B. Skemp, *Theory of Motion*, p. 35.

physis is endowed with most of the attributes with which Plato endows his intelligent soul.'

2. No A-somatic *Psyche*

It is not easily conceivable what sort of function Aristotle would assign within this system of self-moving bodies to a world-soul or to astral souls. One could far more readily accept that Aristotle, by introducing the theory of *De Caelo* I, c.2, sought to offer a replacement for that Platonic speculation in order to bring all cosmic phenomena together in terms of physical bodies and their motions.[51] The passages in *De Caelo* II, c.2, 285a29 and c.12, 292a18-21 and 292b1-2, which nevertheless speak of the first heaven (the sphere of the fixed stars) and of the stars being endowed with soul must not close the eyes to the conclusions forced upon us by *De Caelo* I, c.2,3. They must rather be understood as an argument for dating *De Caelo* I, c.4-II, c.14 later. For II, c.2, 284b32-34 and 285a27-30 clearly indicate that there ψυχή is understood as ἀρχὴ κινήσεως, as Aristotle has worked out in *De Anima* (cf. chapter V, G of this study).

3. The Same Doctrine of Motion in *De Philosophia*

It is of great importance that Aristotle very probably also subscribed to the theory of *De Caelo* I, c.1-3 & III in the dialogue *De Philosophia*, in which he calls the Eleatics ἀφύσικοι, 'because the *physis* is the principle of motion, which they excluded by saying that motion is impossible.'[52]

---

[51] Cf. O. Gigon, *Vom Himmel*, p. 15; According to Gigon the doctrine of natural motion is 'ein Stück in dem Versuch des Aristoteles, die sichtbare Welt, die bei Parmenides, Demokrit und Platon der Bereich des Widersprüchlichen und unfassbar Veränderlichen war, in eine Ordnung und damit in das Sein und in die philosophische Erkennbarkeit zu bringen', cf. 'Aristoteles-Studien I', p. 119.

[52] *De Philosophia* fr. 9 (R). The terms στασιώτας τῆς φύσεως καὶ ἀφυσίκους indicate that Sextus' quotation does not stem from *Physics* I, c.2, 184b16 ff. and *De Caelo* III, c.1, 298b14-24, but that the work from which these words were taken is indeed closely related to these two. The treatment of the concepts '*physis*' and '*kinesis*' in *De Philosophia* does not allow us to agree, it seems to me, with W. Jaeger, *Aristotle*, p. 151, who finds in this dialogue the 'lower conception of nature' which fits with Plato's doctrine of the soul as 'chief principle of becoming'. In the dialogue also, *physis* is not a part of reality, but rather embraces the whole of it.

Here again it is not very easily seen how the Platonic psychology could be made to agree with this Aristotelian view. Now, the very fact that fragment 21b (R) of *De Philosophia* still seemed to contain a Platonic psychology, provided Von Arnim and Guthrie with the most important reason for considering this dialogue to have been written before *De Caelo*. But if one accept such a distinction one is confronted with the problem that in *De Philosophia* the 'first element' is indeed introduced, but not yet connected with the doctrine of natural motion.[53] This view must be rejected. Just as the treatment of the four elements of Book III cannot be viewed as a complete cosmology apart from I, c.1-3, so also the *proton soma* cannot be thought of as if it were independent of the doctrine of natural motion. In any case the conclusion is that acceptance of such a distinction between *De Philosophia* and *De Caelo*, merely on the basis of fragment 21b, seems to rest on a rather weak foundation. The chronological relationship between *De Philosophia* and *De Caelo* I, c.1-3 & III, therefore, needs to be investigated once again.

C. THE METHOD OF DIVISION IN *DE CAELO* I, c.1-3 & III

Aristotle continues his argument in I, c.2, 268b17 by dividing the local motion posited into two simple motions: the circular and the linear. The latter can be subdivided still further: a movement away from the cosmic center and one towards it (268b17-24; c.3, 270b29-31).

1. The Basic Division

The basic division of the work as a whole runs parallel to this main distinction: in I, c.2, 268b26-c.3, 270b31 the circularly moving body is treated, book III is concerned with the bodies that move linearly.[54] In the former Aristotle adds no further differentiation; he only

---

[53] For instance, F. Solmsen, *Aristotle's System*, p. 287 (note 1); cf. pp. 450-451.
[54] In later studies Aristotle maintains this sequence. In the section on the impossibility of an infinite universe the *proton soma* is treated first I, c.5, 271b26-273a6, and next the *somata* which move upward or downward, I, c.6. This arrangement is similar to that of Plato's cosmology, in which the orbits of the world-soul are described, *Timaeus* 34b-47e, followed by a description of the four *somata* which are correlated with rectilinear (53c8) figures. The division is so 'natural', that Aristotle unquestioningly retained it in later revisions: hence, explanations and remarks to expand the theory of the astral bodies and the heavenly sphere are placed after I, c.3, and a renewed treatment of the most important characteristics of the sublunar world is located after book III.

49

attempts, after having 'proven' the existence of such a circularly moving body (268b26-269a18), to track down a number of determinations by *negation* of the properties that play a part in the realm of the other four bodies (cf. chapter IV D of this study).

2. Diaeresis

The other pole, the realm of linear motion, is treated after the transition in I, c.3,270b26-31 & III, c.1,298b6-8 in the rest of book III. 'If there is to be becoming and passing-away, it will have to occur in the realm of the four *corpora*'. Thus Aristotle begins his treatment, and he continues by analyzing whether there is genesis or not.[55] In III, c.2 follows a positive exposition of Aristotle's own view on motion and relevant matters. The opposition of motion to rest, and within both the subdivision of 'natural' and 'unnatural' play an important part. Aristotle's view of genesis is put forward in the next chapters of book III as the result of repeated diaeresis of the problem, where one pole is continually pared off and put aside like an onion-peel, while analysis is carried on into the remaining possibility. Following the course of the argument closely one is confronted with a unity of method in III, c.1-8 which renders it highly unlikely that within this section one would have to distinguish differently dated parts.[56]

Aristotle had discussed the method of diaeresis as '*the* method required' in *Physics* I: within the primarily (sensorily) given which, as long as it is not analyzed gives the impression of chaos, the elements and principles must be made evident with the aid of diaeresis.[57]

---

[55] III, c.1, 298b12 poses the problem discussed in the remainder of the first chapter. For the interrelations of the relevant issues recognized by Aristotle see the schematic summary at the end of the present section.

[56] According to L. Elders, *Aristotle's Cosmology*, p. 68, however, c.3 and 4 are from phase IIa; c.5 from phase IIb, and c.1, 2, 6, 7-8 from phase III.

[57] *Phys.* I, c.1, 184a21 ἔστι δ' ἡμῖν τὸ πρῶτον δῆλα καὶ σαφῆ τὰ συγκεχυμένα μᾶλλον· ὕστερον δ' ἐκ τούτων γίγνεται γνώριμα τὰ στοιχεῖα καὶ αἱ ἀρχαὶ διαιροῦσι ταῦτα.

H. E. Runner's paraphrase of the last line, 'these elements the principles divide' (*Development Illustrated*, p. 87) suggests that he has overlooked the fact that διαιροῦσι is a participle; Cf. *Physics* VIII, c.4, 255a20; I, c.7, 190b3. In *Physics* I, c.2, 184b15-22 Aristotle presents a clear example of such a diaeresis. Lines b22-25 appear to be a methodical indication for *De Caelo* III. For the relation between *De Caelo* III, c.3, and *Physics* I, c.1 cf. G. A. Seeck, *Ueber die Elemente*, p. 82.

In agreement with the intentions expressed by Aristotle in *Physics* I, c.1, *De Caelo* III, c.3, 302a15-18 describes the 'element' as an entity εἰς ὃ τἆλλα σώματα διαιρεῖται, but itself ἀδιαίρετον εἰς ἕτερα τῷ εἴδει. No great risk is involved when this is seen in connection with the method propagated by Plato in *Phaedrus* 270c3 ff. According to Socrates one should for every object of scientific inquiry investigate whether the entity is simple or whether it appears to us under different εἴδη. In the first instance one should consider the function (*dynamis*) of the object and its ability to influence other objects or to undergo action from without. In the second case the various εἴδη should be *counted* and then each εἶδος individually should be accorded the same treatment.[58] The eidos may be counted; this seems to be connected with its being distinguishable. Apparently, for Plato knowledge of a complex object consisted of knowing the number of εἴδη and their functions.[59] For only in this way a definition could be given of a specific object, since the definition must necessarily include the genus to which the object belongs and that property which renders it numerically and eidetically distinguishable with respect to the other εἴδη within the genus. It seems to me, despite the distance that, in *Physics* I and in *De Caelo* I, c.1-3 & III, had come between Plato and his pupil, that Aristotle's scientific method was still closer to the Academic approach than to the syllogistic method[60] which he himself developed later, and which was closely connected with his later eidos-conception.

3. The Role of the Number Three

Plato's great interest in the diaeretic method designed by him is perhaps occasioned by the fact that with it he had found a new way of solving the problem of the relation between unity and diversity (Parmenides). With this method one could recognize a diversity of two or more εἴδη within one genus. Continued reflection finally brought Plato to the acceptance of two principles, τὸ ῞Εν and ἡ ἀόριστος δυάς, which are closely connected with the method.[61] In the philosophical

---

[58] 270d5: ἐὰν δὲ πλείω εἴδη ἔχῃ, ταῦτα ἀριθμησάμενον ... ἰδεῖν ...
[59] Cf. *Timaeus* 53b8: ταῦτα πρῶτον διεσχηματίσατο εἴδεσί τε καὶ ἀριθμοῖς and *Laws* X, 894a8: ὡς ἐν εἴδεσιν λαβεῖν μετ' ἀριθμοῦ.
[60] Investigation of the number of *eide* plays a part in Aristotle's study of the principles and elements as well, in *Physics* I, c.4-6 and *De Caelo* III, c.4-5.
[61] The Dyad is called διαιρετική by Alexander Aphrod., *in Metaphysica* 57, 3-7 (= Aristotle, *De Bono*, fr. 2a R).

works of Plato's old age especially the first of these principles was attributed profound, even religious meaning. Aristotle rejected these principles. But for quite some time he made eager use of the diaeretic method. Perhaps his decided preference for the number three (the number of the All – I, c.1, 268a9-20) may also be associated with the diaeretic scheme. Triads are repeatedly used in his inquiries: in I, c.1 he holds that only the body can be complete because it possesses three dimensions; in c.2, 268b24-26 he believes that his doctrine of motion fits very well because here too he arrives at three natural motions corresponding to three specifically different *somata*; and in *Physics* I Aristotle had shown that physical phenomena can be explained only with the aid of three principles which relate to each other as do a genus and its two species.[62] These three doctrines not only cohere because they date from the same period, but also because all three clearly indicate the rejection of Plato's views, and constitute important nuclei of Aristotle's early independent philosophy.[63]

Schematic *Aperçu* of the argument in *De Caelo* I, c. 1-3 & III.

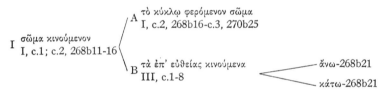

---

[62] *Physics*, I, c.7-9; 191a1; 192a9.

[63] Should the possibility not be considered that between the doctrine of the three principles (*Physics* I) and of the three elements (*De Caelo* I, c.1-3 & III) originally belonged a theory concerning the three causes? (*Physics* I, c.1, 184a13-14 points to a division in the study of the *physis* into a chapter on the *archai*, one on the *aitia*, and one on the *stoicheia*!). Does Plato's *Laws* X, 888e not indicate that about 350 BC. a philosophy was current which accepted φύσις, τέχνη and τύχη as causes of the coming-into-being and passing-away of all things, and could it be that in Aristotle's *Protrepticus* fr. 11 (R) one finds the traces of this? If so, *Physics* II, in which the doctrine of the *four* causes is introduced rather abruptly could be the result of a later incisive revision of the original 'De Causis'. Cf. chapters Five J and Six B of this study.

II (=IB). Περὶ τοῖν δυοῖν – = Περὶ γενέσεως καὶ φθορᾶς.

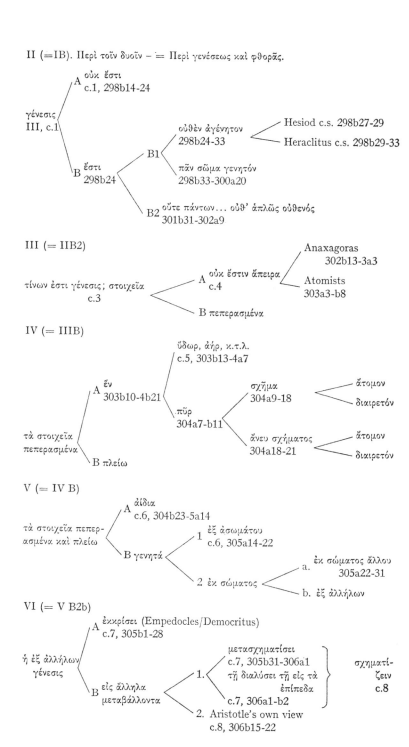

γένεσις
III, c.1

A οὐκ ἔστι
c.1, 298b14-24

B ἔστι
298b24

B1

οὐθὲν ἀγένητον
298b24-33

Hesiod c.s. 298b27-29
Heraclitus c.s. 298b29-33

πᾶν σῶμα γενητόν
298b33-300a20

B2 οὔτε πάντων... οὐθ' ἁπλῶς οὐθενός
301b31-302a9

III (= IIB2)

τίνων ἐστι γένεσις; στοιχεῖα
c.3

A οὐκ ἔστιν ἄπειρα
c.4

Anaxagoras
302b13-3a3

Atomists
303a3-b8

B πεπερασμένα

IV (= IIIB)

τὰ στοιχεῖα
πεπερασμένα

A ἕν
303b10-4b21

B πλείω

ὕδωρ, ἀήρ, κ.τ.λ.
c.5, 303b13-4a7

πῦρ
304a7-b11

σχῆμα
304a9-18

ἄτομον
διαιρετόν

ἄνευ σχήματος
304a18-21

ἄτομον
διαιρετόν

V (= IV B)

τὰ στοιχεῖα πεπερ-
ασμένα καὶ πλείω

A ἀΐδια
c.6, 304b23-5a14

B γενητά

1 ἐξ ἀσωμάτου
c.6, 305a14-22

2 ἐκ σώματος

a. ἐκ σώματος ἄλλου
305a22-31
b. ἐξ ἀλλήλων

VI (= V B2b)

ἡ ἐξ ἀλλήλων
γένεσις

A ἐκκρίσει (Empedocles/Democritus)
c.7, 305b1-28

B εἰς ἄλληλα
μεταβάλλοντα

1.

μετασχηματίσει
c.7, 305b31-306a1
τῇ διαλύσει τῇ εἰς τὰ
ἐπίπεδα
c.7, 306a1-b2

σχηματί-
ζειν
c.8

2. Aristotle's own view
c.8, 306b15-22

53

1. Introduction

In parts A and B of this chapter two important points of divergence appeared between Aristotle and his teacher, i.e., the question as to where the origin of the perceptible ought to be sought, and the question: what is the origin of all motion. It will become clear that also in the case of the first element which Aristotle is about to explicate in the first part of his treatment of the elements there is a decided change of standpoint with respect to Plato. It is true that traces of this theory are to be found in other Aristotelian works[64], but no proof for the existence of a special fifth body and a systematic treatment of its properties is found anywhere except in *De Caelo* I, c.2, 268b26 ff. This section is generally supposed to be of an earlier date than are the other works handed down in the *Corpus* that also refer to this doctrine.[65]

Two testimonia inform us that in the case of the fifth element Aristotle offers a theory completely his own.[66] The texts in Plato and other authors that might perhaps point to a fifth element display differences with the theory found in Aristotle on essential points.[67] In the *Timaeus* ether is a variant of air and is not ordered into the series as if it were an independent entity (58d).[68] The fifth polygon is not ascribed to an element in this dialogue but rather to the All (55c). In the *Laws* Plato speaks exclusively of the same four bodies which in the *Timaeus* he had construed from triangles (X, 889b). *Epinomis* 981c ff. and 984b cannot detract from the originality of Aristotle's theory of the *proton soma*, in view of the different arrange-

---

[64] The dialogue *De Philosophia* (fr. 21a), fr. 26; 27 (R) may be mentioned explicitly. In addition: *Meteor.* I, c.1, 338b21; c.3, 340a20; 341a3; *De Gener. Anim.* II, c.3, 736b31; 737a1; *De Caelo* II, c.4, 287a3; c.12, 291b32; *De Anima* II, c.6, 418b9, 13.

[65] With respect to *De Philosophia* matters are somewhat different; cf. chapters Four E and Six D of this study.

[66] Cicero, *Tuscul.* I, 26, 65: 'Quinta natura, ab Aristotele inducta primum' (*De Philosophia*, fr. 27d R); Ps. Clemens, *Recogn.* 8, 15: 'Aristoteles etiam quintum introducit elementum' (*De Philosophia* fr. 27e R).

[67] As to the 'prior history' cf. P. Moraux, 'Quinta Essentia', col. 1171-1196; *Aristote Du Ciel*, pp. xlvii-l which concludes: 'l'originalité d'Aristote en la matière ne fait aucun doute.' F. Solmsen, *Aristotle's System*, pp. 287 ff.

[68] Cf. G. S. Claghorn, *Aristotle's Criticism*, p. 22.

ment of the elements and their secondary position relative to the soul. Furthermore, it may be questioned whether this dialogue was indeed written prior to the publication of Aristotle's new discovery, as J. Pépin believes.[69]

It is necessary, therefore, to analyze all data available in order to be able to pose the question as to what motives led Aristotle to introduce this theory. Here again, close attention will first be given to the text itself.

2. The Proof for the Existence of the First Element

All local motions may, according to Aristotle, be reduced to two non-complex ones (circular and linear); since each of these movements must correspond to a simple *soma*, the existence of a naturally circularly moving, simple body is necessary (c.2, 268b26-269a7). The weakness of the argument used here may be left out of consideration; it has been pointed out by various writers.[70] More important is to see how Aristotle describes this element.

3. Characteristics of the First Element

Aristotle goes to great lengths to ascertain that the important difference between the four 'earthly'[71] bodies and the element postulated by him be delineated clearly. Its circular motion must be first among all possible motions (269a18). Its substance must be more divine than that of all other elements (269a30). It is separated from the elements that surround us and comparatively higher in value the further it is removed from us.[72] In c.3 Aristotle adds still more de-

---

[69] *Théologie Cosmique*, p. 221. W. Jaeger, *Aristotle*, p. 144 (note 2), however, held that the ethertheory of Aristotle was absorbed into the Platonic doctrine of the elements by the author of the *Epinomis*. This is also the view of E. Berti, *La Filosofia del primo Aristotele*, p. 408. Cf. A. H. Chroust, 'Probable Date', p. 290.

[70] Cf. P. Moraux, 'Quinta Essentia' col. 1196-97. Especially the principle of ἓν ἑνὶ ἐναντίον, used by Aristotle in 269a10, 14, immediately gives rise to problems. In his attack on the Aristotelian world-view Gallileo was sure to point to this. Did Aristotle himself recognize weakness here and attempt to strengthen his position in I, c.4?

[71] C.3, 269b14: τὰ σώματα τὰ δεῦρο; b16 τὰ ἐνταῦθα.

[72] C.2, 269b15 κεχωρισμένον, τοσούτῳ τιμιωτέραν ἔχον τὴν φύσιν ὅσῳπερ ἀφέστηκε τῶν ἐνταῦθα πλεῖον.

terminations: the element possesses neither heaviness or lightness; it is ungenerated and indestructible, not subject to growth or change; finally, according to Aristotle, it does not age and does not undergo influence from without.[73] The terms speak for themselves. The author effects, as it were a *chorismos* between the ungenerated, immutable world of the eternal and the realm of becoming and passing-away,[74] just as Plato placed the being that always is over against that which is always in becoming.[75] The difference between the two conceptions is nevertheless great indeed: Plato opposes the intelligible world to the visible world, including all bodies. For Aristotle the νοητά have completely lost the place of honour accorded to them by Plato.[76] Consideration is given only to bodies.

4. The Intention Behind the Introduction of the First Element

The properties of the first element, recounted above, remind one on the one hand of Plato's world of Ideas, on the other hand they recall his teaching concerning the soul. The problem forces itself upon us: what moved Aristotle to build his own philosophy around a newly introduced physical body? What difficulty did he seek to overcome?

W. Jaeger's view, i.e. that the calculations of the relative volume of the various elements forced Aristotle to this,[77] leaves too many obvious features of this body unexplained and the lines to which Jaeger refers for support look more like an afterthought than a strong inducement towards the development of the new theory. It seems to me that this innovation must be seen as a reaction to a number of points in Plato's philosophy with which Aristotle could not agree. In the *Timaeus* and, very extensively, in the *Laws* Plato proves the priority of the soul relative to the body. The soul, the origin of all motion, must precede everything that is able to move.

---

[73] C.3, 269b30 ἀδύνατον ἔχειν βάρος ἢ κουφότητα
270a13 ἀγένητον, ἄφθαρτον, ἀναυξές, ἀναλλοίωτον.
270b2 ἀγήρατον, ἀπαθές.
[74] I, c.3, 270a20-22 and III, c.1, 298b8-11. Cf. O. Gigon, 'Aristoteles-Studien I', p. 132: '... der Begriff κεχωρισμένον, hinter dem unverkennbar die platonische Lehre vom Chorismos auftaucht.'
[75] *Timaeus* 27d; cf. *Philebus* 53c-55a.
[76] Cf. Chapter Four G, par. 1 of this study.
[77] *Aristotle*, p. 154, with reference to *Meteor.* I, c.3, 339b2 ff.; 340a1.

Plato's argument actually comes down to this, that *motion precedes the body which moves*, and hence motion may be abstracted from the body. Aristotle emphatically rejected this. His thinking is centered on the body, the *ousia*, of which motion is a property. To him, motion apart from a moving physical body is unthinkable. It is not accidental that in *De Caelo* the body (I, c.1) is dealt with before motion (I, c.2). This fact by itself already points to an approach different from that of Plato. For Aristotle, the young Academic, the treatment of the composition of the world-soul in the *Timaeus* was unacceptable. In its famous section on the soul 34c-36d which, according to Plato, is related to the intelligible and sharply opposed to all things somatic, Plato, spoke of 'mixing', 'splitting', 'uniting', 'inner and outer'. This impressed Aristotle as being too mythical to be worthy of a real 'physiologist'. Motion cannot occur without a bearer of it. Hence, according to Aristotle, the problem of the relation between body and soul can be solved only when this is not seen as an influence of an asomatic entity upon a body, but as a relation between bodies, though of different character. In this regard one could once more point to the fact that in the *Sophist*, 246a ff., Plato answers at length, be it in general terms, the criticism of those who deny any reality to non-bodies. Aristotle has rejected the foundation of visible reality in a world beyond, such as Plato had proposed in his doctrine of the Ideas. He has also rejected the attempt to make motion independent, apart from concrete, visible things, thus not accepting Plato's theory on the soul.

None of this however, excludes the fact that the first element displays characteristics which remind one of Plato's worldsoul,[78] and his teaching of the background. The note is clearly sounded in the various predicates of the *proton soma*. The lofty, religious meaning which the astral world came to have for Aristotle is also often brought into connection with the loss of the world of Ideas in his cosmological conception.[79] Atticus has already, in order to explain the character-

---

[78] F. Solmsen, *Aristotle's System*, p. 289: 'this body aspires logically to the same status as Plato's soul' is in fact too weak. In *De Philosophia* fr. 27 the fifth element is nothing less than the substance of the soul. Cf. also Ph. Merlan, in Armstrong, *Cambridge History*, p. 41; I. Düring, 'Heritage', p. 94; A. J. Festugière, *La Révélation* II, pp. 252-257!

[79] Cf. W. Jaeger, *Aristotle*, pp. 141, 164; C. J. de Vogel, *Greek Philosophy* II, p. 31; J. Moreau, *L'Ame du Monde*, pp. 82, 125; E. Berti, *La Filosofia del primo Aristotele*, p. 350; M. Untersteiner, *Aristotele Della Filosofia*, p. xiii. For the

istics of the first element, considered a combination of the properties Plato ascribed to the intelligible and the realm of the stars.[80] In agreement with him, I hold that an historical explication of Aristotle's introduction of this new theory is possible only when seen against the background of Plato's doctrine of the Ideas and of the soul; no explanation on the basis of Aristotle's own later reinterpretation of this early phase of his thought can be convincing.

5. Two Kinds of *Ousia*

Once Aristotle has proven the existence of a special heavenly element and now attempts to indicate a number of its characteristics, he does so, I noted, by way of *negation* of the properties of 'earthly' elements. But these other elements and their properties have not yet been analyzed to any great length. Treatment of them does not begin until book III.[81] From the opposition of the first element to all the others

sake of completeness it should be mentioned that J. Pépin, *Théologie Cosmique*, pp. 498-499, continues to believe 'qu'aucun argument n'est vraiment décisif pour établir que l'auteur du *De Philosophia* aurait rejeté la théorie platonicienne des Idées.'

[80] Fr. 5, 49-58 ed. Baudry, p. 20 = Eusebius, *Praep. Evang.* XV, 7, 6 ed. Mras, II, p. 365, 5-12. Cf. W. Theiler, 'Aristoteleszeugnis', pp. 127-131; J. Pépin, *Théologie Cosmique*, p. 246.

[81] Hence, before Aristotle can speak of the fact that the first element cannot be characterized as either light or heavy, he must anticipate his later exposition in 269b20: δεῖ δὲ ὑποθέσθαι τί λέγομεν τὸ βαρὺ καὶ τὸ κοῦφον, νῦν μὲν ἱκανῶς ὡς πρὸς τὴν παροῦσαν χρείαν, ἀκριβέστερον δὲ πάλιν, ὅταν ἐπισκοπῶμεν περὶ τῆς οὐσίας αὐτῶν. Book IV seems to be the announced sequel and hence P. Moraux, *Aristote Du Ciel*, p. 155 (note) and p. xxii; O. Longo *De Caelo*, p. 300, and L. Elders, *Aristotle's Cosmology*, p. 90, consider the passage to have been added later. The use of the term οὐσία, however, if interpreted as the 'essence' of the light and the heavy, is remarkable. The word *ousia* is primarily used by Aristotle to stand for 'the concrete things', anything referred to by a substantive. To be sure, in the *Metaphysics* a certain differentiation in usage comes to the fore: when the concrete thing is viewed as a σύνθετον, the term *ousia* may be applied to this combination of form and matter, but also to the *substantia formalis* and the *substantia materialis* separately, cf. Bonitz, *Index*, p. 545a18. The meaning of *substantia formalis* has become so expanded that it can finally be identified with the ὁρισμός, the λόγος and τὸ τί ἐστιν. But the examples given by Bonitz apply only to substantives and, as far as I could see, not to qualities. Yet, 'light' and 'heavy' are consistently viewed as πάθη by Aristotle. In view of these considerations I would approach this passage from a different point of view: in the text of b20 the lemma in the Simplicius-commen-

58

it is clear that the realm of becoming is conceived of as constituting a whole. Aristotle can do so since in III, c.8, 306b15-22 he points to *hyle* as the common basis of the realm of the four elements. But there is no connection between the *protè ousia* and the substance in the area of becoming; on the contrary, the *chorismos* between them is heavily underscored.[82]

In *Timaeus* 35a and 27d Plato had struggled to find a link between the indivisible and ungenerated realm of being, and the divisible and becoming, and in *Philebus* 27b8 he had looked for the relation between the real *ousia* and the γεγενημένη οὐσία. Aristotle sought to escape this dialectic by rejecting the teaching of an intelligible world. But the tension has not disappeared in his own conception in which he drew the 'really real' into the area of the *Physis*; it is still fully present in his doctrine of the fifth element.[83] Although use of the term *soma* for all five elements indiscriminately might suggest a relationship or common characteristic, the conclusion must be that the language here is not univocal but equivocal. The fundamental opposition between the two realms cannot be overcome by it.

tary reads: τὸ βαρὺ καὶ κοῦφον. Just as expressions such as τὸ πολὺ καὶ ὀλίγον or τὸ πλατὺ καὶ στενόν or τὸ βαθὺ καὶ ταπεινόν, which were used in the late-Platonic philosophy to refer to one specific realm characterized by two contrasts (for instance, *Metaphysics* A, c.9, 992a10-15), τὸ βαρὺ καὶ κοῦφον could refer to the area of genesis as a whole. And would it not be possible that ἡ οὐσία αὐτῶν, in contrast to ἡ πρώτη οὐσία (c.3, 270b11), stood for the *ousia* which is characterized by the light-heavy contrast? (for *ousia* in this sense cf. *Physics* I, c.2, 185a20-b5; c.7, 190a31-b5; c.9, 192a6, and P. Gohlke, *Prinzipienlehre*, pp. 27-28). Could the passage not imply that that which will be said of the realm of the four elements in book III is presupposed? The qualities light and heavy play an important part in the discussions of book III, for instance in c.2, 301a22-b3; cf. also 299b31-300a20 and c.6, 305a24-6. Further, I, c.3, 269b26, for example (ἀνάγκη δὴ πᾶν τὸ φερόμενον ἢ κάτω ἢ ἄνω ἢ κουφότητ' ἔχειν ἢ βάρος ἢ ἄμφω), receives a basis in III, c.2, 301a22-301b17.

[82] *De Mundo* c.2 concurs exactly. Ether as οὐρανοῦ καὶ ἄστρων οὐσία (392a6), which is ἄτρεπτον, ἀπαθῆ and ἀνετεροίωτον, is sharply distinguished from ἡ δι'ὅλων παθητή τε καὶ τρεπτή, καὶ φθαρτή τε καὶ ἐπίκηρος (sc. φύσις), a32-35. Later, when Aristotle no longer identifies the ether with the highest deity, this element moves much closer to the others; cf. for example, *Meteor.* I, c.2, 339a22 συνεχής; c.3, 340b13 προσεχές; 340b4-14; cf. F. Solmsen, *Aristotle's System*, pp. 397, 407 .

[83] W. Jaeger, *Aristotle*, p. 153, was already aware of the tension in the doctrine of the first *soma* in *De Caelo*, I, c.2-3; cf. G. A. Seeck, *Ueber die Elemente*, p. 128.

6. First or Fifth Element?

A brief remark must be made with respect to the appellation πρώτη, πρῶτον, used by Aristotle in I, c.2, 269a18; c.3, 270b11; III, c.1, 298b6. From chapters I, c.2-3 it is evident that Aristotle here gives a value-judgment.[84] This does not exclude the possibility, however, that he may perhaps have approached this *soma* from an historical point of view in another work, and noted that it was 'discovered' subsequent to the four elements of Empedocles.[85]

7. The First Element Moves by Virtue of Its Own Nature

I should like to pay attention to something which does not seem to have been treated anywhere: according to c.2, 269a7 the first element moves 'by virtue of its *own* nature'. The same formulation is used in c.3, 270a8, also in connection with the *proton soma*. With regard to other bodies this phrase is not used. In book III we read of these elements that they 'by nature' possess 'gravity' and 'levity'.[86] I would ask here whether perhaps Aristotle has tried, in this subtle way, to differentiate within 'natural motion' between a natural motion in virtue of its *own* nature *and* a natural motion on account of impulse (κατὰ ῥοπήν)?[87]

---

[84] Accordingly, Gigon's translation: 'das ursprüngliche Element' should be rejected.

[85] Cf. *De Philosophia* fr. 27a, b, c, d, e (R). Especially in connection with the extensive review of the history of philosophy Aristotle gives in book I of the dialogue, it is conceivable that he called the element he himself introduced 'the fifth', if he was able to refer back to the exposition of *De Caelo* I, c.2-3 (cf. chapter Four, E, par. 3 of the present study). It will be difficult to ascertain this. At any rate, it is incorrect to conclude to a contradiction when one time πρῶτον, and at another *'quintum'* is used, as H. J. Easterling, 'Quinta Natura', p. 80, does; πρῶτον is evaluative; there is no 'renumbering' at all. Furthermore, I would be inclined to believe that when first introducing the astral element Aristotle speaks of πρῶτον σῶμα (i.e. in *De Caelo*, I, c.1-3), and only later of πέμπτη φύσις (i.e. in the *De Philosophia*). Cf. J. Pépin, *Théologie Cosmique*, p. 223.

[86] ῥοπὴ βάρους ἢ κουφότητος III, c.2, 301a22-26; cf. c.7, 305a25. The term ῥοπή is not used for the first element.

[87] Schematically arranged:

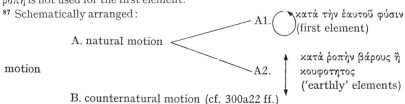

60

Even if one is not inclined to think so it is still legitimate to ask that some attention be paid to this peculiarity in the text. Virtually all commentators however, understand natural motion to be a fixed, determined motion, and, making respectful mention of the natural-scientific possibilities implied in such a system,[88] they qualify it as a disappointing materialism,[89] meager in comparison with the Platonizing phase in the early years and the teleological phase of Aristotle's later thought. But is has already been suggested that the concept '*physis*' in *De Caelo* may not at all justify such a view. The sections I, c.1, 268a13, 19; III, c.8, 306a15; I, c.3, 270a20 much rather point to a far broader significance of the word which has nothing to do with materialism or determinism. (cf. chapter IV F of this study.) The profound respect for the astral world evidenced by Aristotle in his treatment of the fifth element, which is in complete agreement with the note sounded in fragments 12, 13, and 18 (R) of *De Philosophia* and the *Epinomis* (from approximately the same time), excludes a deterministic interpretation. Once it is noted that in *De Caelo* I, c.1-3 & III the relation of the first element to the other bodies corresponds with Plato's main distinction in the *Timaeus* where the realm of the *nous* is dealt with prior to that of *anangké* (cf. *Timaeus* 47e3 ff.), and where circular motion is explicitly called characteristic for *nous* and *phronesis* (34a), no possibility remains but to consider the realm of determinateness to be limited to the area of genesis and not to think of the astral world as being included in it.[90]

[88] Cf. F. Solmsen, *Aristotle's System*, p. 291: 'Physics itself now includes a divine element, and God himself is subject to physical laws and an object of physical studies'; G. A. Seeck, *Ueber die Elemente*, p. 127.

[89] Thus, among others W. K. C. Guthrie, 'Aristotle's Theology', p. 169. In his *On the Heavens* he deletes this term since it is too strong, and he represents the views of *De Caelo* I, c.2 & 3 as a temporary transitional phase, in which Aristotle has not yet thought through all the implications.

[90] In that case motion 'according to its own nature' could not be understood as orbital motion determined by natural laws, but rather as a regular path accomplished in freedom. The stars, if fragment 27a of *De Philosophia* may be considered dependable (cf. chapter Six D, par. 4 of the present study), consist of the same substance as does the human mind. Hence they will naturally have to be understood to be of the highest intelligence. Concerning the relation of the greatest regularity and the highest intelligence cf. Plato's *Epinomis* 982a4-d4.

8. The Interpretation of *De Philosophia* fragment 21b (R)

Whoever would maintain this thesis will have to take a stand with regard to the well-known and troublesome datum in Cicero's *De Natura Deorum*, 2.16.44: in a section which until recently was unanimously thought to derive from the dialogue *De Philosophia* (fr. 21b, R) the natural motion of the four elements is opposed to the *voluntarius motus* of the stars. It led W. Jaeger, H. Von Arnim, and W. K. C. Guthrie to transpose the limited, deterministically conceived physis-concept of that fragment to *De Caelo*. Now, it is clear that in the latter work the astral world also belongs to the area of *physis*; hence, these authors were forced to hold that Aristotle, while writing *De Caelo*, had drastically revised his astronomic opinions: the astral motion must be explicated in *De Caelo* as 'lawful', 'determined'. This problem has caused fragment 21b to become the subject of extensive discussion.[91]

Although with due regard for the Ciceronian text, I hold that this one passage may not be used as the basis for the acceptance of an inconceivable discontinuity in Aristotle's development and of an extraordinary contradiction in the data concerning *De Philosophia*. One will have to look for an error in the tradition from Aristotle to Cicero and, if possible, an explanation will have to be given for the cause of this error. My own attempt I offer with due humility: Is it not conceivable that at some point or another in the tradition leading to Cicero, the motion which Aristotle qualified as 'natural motion κατὰ ῥοπήν' was no longer understood as a species of (more inclusive) 'natural motion', but as *the* natural motion? Instead of the more extensive scheme given by Aristotle (cf. note 87), inattention or a stoicizing transposition could have caused a simplified scheme:

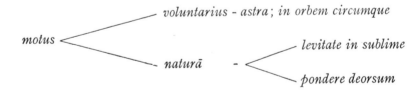

Within this simplified scheme it is actually nonsensical to prove the impossibility of '*ut contra naturam astra moveantur*'; in *De Caelo* I,

[91] Cf. M. Untersteiner, *Della Filosofia*, pp. 228-235; J. Pépin, *Théologie Cosmique*, pp. 192 ff.

c.2, 269b6 and c.3, 270a11 such a consideration does make sense. A proof to the effect that stars cannot move 'contra voluntatem' would fit Cicero's approach.

In part B of this chapter I noted that fragment 9 (R) of *De Philosophia* is not in accordance with an interpretation that delimits the physis-concept there such that the first body would remain excluded. The argument against the Eleatics would largely loose its force and the debate against their logicism would have had a different focus. Accordingly, a deterministic view of the *physis* for this phase of Aristotle's thought should be rejected and replaced by a *teleological* one. It seems to me that this is the conception encountered in the fragments of the *Protrepticus*, in the other fragments of *De Philosophia* and in *De Caelo* I, c.1-3 & III. *Protrepticus* fragment 11 (R) (= B11-21 Düring) proclaims the teleological character of Nature very clearly and *physis* is placed even above *techne*. The *techne* is able to copy and complete Nature, but it can never supersede Nature. The most highly developed creatures, such as man, cannot have come into being by chance, nor are they the result of technical production: they must be viewed as the product of a divine, creative Nature, with the character of a demiurge.[92]

It also seems that this is the teleological view of Nature Plato opposes in *Laws* X, 888e4-889e2, in spite of the fact that he connects *physis* with *tyche* and *anangke* (889c6; b2; a5). The conception objected to is held to posit that only those *technai* may be considered 'serious' which 'join their own craft with (that of) Nature', i.e. medicine, agriculture and the care of the body.[93] And is not Aristotle, with his teaching of Nature as *artis magistra*, the very person to debate Plato's theory of the world of Ideas? According to Aristotle *Physis* was not made by a demiurge after an example of far higher order, but Nature itself displays, to every patient student, the models for cultural and ethical acts. It is inconceivable that the philosopher(s) meant in these passages of the *Laws* would recommend to a physician to place his own abilities in service of nature if they took nature to

---

[92] Cf. *De Philosophia* fr. 8b: τὴν δημιουργὸν αὐτῶν φύσιν. *Ibid.* fr. 12b, 13c (R).
[93] 889d5 ὁπόσαι τῇ φύσει ἐκοίνωσαν τὴν αὐτῶν δύναμιν, οἷον αὖ ἰατρικὴ καὶ γεωργικὴ καὶ γυμναστική. The evaluative scale of the various *technai* here attacked agrees with Aristotle's *Protrepticus* fr. 8b (R). According to that text τὰ περὶ τὴν τροφὴν καὶ τὸ ζῆν are primary. Τὰς πρὸς ἡδονὴν τέχνας are next in line, and only after that, still farther distantiated from first necessities, geometry. rhetoric and other παιδείας are listed.

63

be an irrational incomprehensible power. That is why I cannot agree with the interpretation of, for instance, F. Solmsen, *Aristotle's System*, p. 15, who understands this section to contain a fairly correct picture of the view of the Atomists. Plato's conception of the principle of motion and becoming in the *Laws* is opposed to that of the 'hylozoists' such as Diogenes of Apollonia and the early Aristotle, just as much as it is opposed to the view held by Democritus c.s. The conception of *Physis* objected to is like the one developed by the writers of the *Corpus Hippocraticum*. This doctrine is attacked by Plato on the basis of a view in which *Physis* is reduced to the material, the chaotic, the somatic, and in which it is secondary with respect to the order-creating psyche.[94]

The conclusion must therefore be that Cicero's testimonium has been influenced by a physis-conception such as held by Plato and as has been usual in consistent materialism.[95] E. Berti correctly stresses the fact that Jaeger's interpretation of fragment 21b implies 'un concetto di natura come assenza di rationalità e di ordine, ben diverso da quello che risultà dallo stesso Περὶ Φιλοσοφίας'. For him also it is therefore incorrect to construe a difference between the views of *De Philosophia* and *De Caelo*.[96] In this phase 'natural motion' does not *exclude*, but *includes* voluntary motion for Aristotle! Hence I do not think there are convincing arguments against the acceptance of agreement between *De Philosophia* and *De Caelo* I, c.1-3 & III.[97] In the introduction of the first element Aristotle's argument is emphatically aimed at denying that circular motion clashes with the nature of that first element. This, it seems to me, is the burden of both fragment 21b of *De Philosophia* and of *De Caelo* I, c.2, 269b6-10. The thesis that this motion is 'natural', intrinsic to the body, brings with it that Aristotle, already in this period, must have objected strenuously to his predecessors' theories of motion, especially Plato's.[98]

---

[94] F. Solmsen, *Aristotle's Cosmology*, p. 97.

[95] It hardly requires mention that for Plato nature only constituted a (lower) part of reality; for Epicurus c.s. it is the totality of all being.

[96] *La Filosofia del primo Aristotele*, pp. 368-370. Berti, however, falls into another error: he subordinates the motion of the stars in both writings to an unmoved prime mover.

[97] Similarly M. Untersteiner, *Peri Philosophias*, p. 148; but unlike J. Pépin, *Théologie Cosmique*, p. 223 with note 2.

[98] For Empedocles cf. III, c.2, 300b1-6 and II, c.1, 284a24-26, discussed again in II, c.13, 294b3 ff. For Plato cf. chapter Four B of this study.

He interpreted their views in this sense, that they accepted a *soma* with the propensity to fall, but whose fall was held back by the forceful action (actually going against the nature of that *soma*) of a world-soul or some such entity. (cf. *De Caelo*, II, c.1, 284a15,27.) Aristotle thought this conception sufficiently discredited by his substitution of *physis* for the *psyche* as principle of motion. Later, when Aristotle nevertheless feels bound to accept a *psyche* as condition for the auto-motion of the heavenly sphere and of the planets (dependent on the Unmoved Mover)[99] an interesting reconsideration occurs. In *De Caelo* II, c.1, 284a27 he argues that the continued existence of the first heaven cannot possibly be the result of forceful action by a world-soul. W. D. Ross[100] correctly saw that this may not be identified with the doctrine of motion in I, c.2, in the sense that the *psyche* is denied every role. Emphasis is here on 'forceful', which does not exclude that the *ouranos* may be called 'ensouled'.[101] P. Moraux completely agrees with Ross.[102] My hypothesis, i.e. that I, c.4-II, c.14 have together been composed after I, c.1-3 & III agrees with this interpretation of II, c.1 by Ross and Moraux, who prefer association with the remainder of book II to a rather forced link with I, c.2.[103]

9. The Home of the Gods

Near the end of the description of the primary substance there is a treatment concerning the abode of the gods, as pictured in popular belief (c.3, 270b5-11). The fact that Greeks and Barbarians, to the extent that they accept the existence of gods, believe the stars to be their home is an additional argument for Aristotle in favour of the divine character of the heavenly element he accepts. But Aristotle must have been acquainted with persons who did not take heaven to be the most important object of religious worship, but rather the

---

[99] Cf. Chapter Five G below.
[100] *Physics*, p. 98.
[101] II, c.2, 285a29; cf. 284b33; and II, c.12, 298a18-21, b1-2. W. K. C. Guthrie, *On the Heavens*, p. xxxi.
[102] *Aristote Du Ciel*, pp. lxxxviii-lxxxix. F. Nuyens, *Ontwikkelingsmomenten*, p. 109, and L. Elders, *Aristotle's Cosmology*, pp. 180, 182, however, hold that II, c.1 contains a rejection of any function on the part of an asomatic *psyche*.
[103] II, c.1 displays a relationship with *De Philosophia* noted by many investigators. On the basis of the exposition above I conclude that there has been a slight shift away from the view-point of the dialogue in II c.1.

center of the universe. In the description of the journey of the gods through the heavens in Plato's *Phaedrus* the remark that Hestia remained behind, alone in the 'home of the gods',[104] plays on the Pythagorean doctrine which called the center of the universe Διὸς φυλακή.[105] The final sentence of the *Critias*[106] may indicate that the lines in the *Phaedrus* must be understood to be less 'playful' than De Vries does,[107] and that there may well be an element of disagreement on the part of Aristotle in the view as to the abode of the gods he defends.[108] I am inclined to see here an anti-Platonic and anti-Pythagorean tendence, and once again evidence of independence in Aristotle's view of the cosmos.

E. THE REALM OF BECOMING AND PASSING-AWAY (BOOK III)

1. The Sublunar Bodies

In I, c.2, 268b21-26, c.3, 270b30 and III, c.1, 298b8 the realm of genesis is dominated by the division into a body moving upwards and one moving downwards.[109] In Aristotle's scheme the two poles further split into fire and air moving upwards and water and earth moving downwards (269a17-18). It is remarkable that Aristotle offers no argument to support this further distinction. Evidently, with Plato he accepts the four elements posited by Empedocles as 'roots' of all that is,[110] but the mathematical argument given

---

[104] 247a1; cf. G. J. de Vries, *Commentary*, p. 131, for literature on the identification of Hestia and the earth (cq. the central fire in the 'Philolaic' system).

[105] Aristotle, *De Caelo*, II, c.13, 293b1-4. According to the Pythagoreans under attack the centre is τὸ κυριώτατον τοῦ παντός. cf. Simplicius, *in De Caelo*, 512, 12-14 Ζανὸς πύργον and Διὸς θρόνον (= Aristotle, *De Pythag.* fr. 14a R).

[106] 121b-c Ζεὺς ... συνήγειρεν θεοὺς πάντας εἰς τὴν τιμιωτάτην αὐτῶν οἴκησιν, ἢ δὴ κατὰ μέσον παντὸς τοῦ κόσμου βεβηκυῖα καθορᾷ πάντα ὅσα γενέσεως μετείληφεν.

[107] *Loc. cit.*, see note 104 above.

[108] *De Mundo*, 391b9-16, which renders Aristotle's position very explicit, indeed names τὸ μέσον as ἑστία and μήτηρ, but τὸ ὑπερθεν αὐτῆς, the heavens θεῶν οἰκητήριον. Cf. in addition *De Caelo* I, c.9, 278b14.

[109] 'Moving away from the centre' and 'moving towards the centre', 270b31.

[110] In *Physics* I, c.4, 188a17, in a context similar to *De Caelo* III, c.5, Aristotle judges Empedocles' solution to be better than that of others. In spite of this, P. Moraux, *Aristote Du Ciel*, p. xix, considers *De Caelo* III to be incomplete because a specification of the number of elements is not given. But it may be questioned whether this provides a basis to conclude that Aristotle did intend

by his teacher[111] does not fit into his own scheme. Just as Plato had done, Aristotle relates becoming and passing-away to these four elements, but there is an important difference: for Plato these constituted the totality of the somatic (including the astral bodies),[112] while Aristotle accepted yet another *soma* beyond these.

2. A Critical Attitude Towards the Eleatic Philosophers

In a brief treatment of the problem of becoming in general Aristotle confronts himself with the Eleatic views (III, c.1, 298b14-24), but, as in *Physics* I, c.2, for a counter-argument to their a-physical standpoint he refers to a separate study, which is to deal with the presuppositions for any investigation of nature.[113] These cannot be dealt with in *De Caelo* III since it is itself part of an inquiry into *physis* (I, c.1, 268a1). It would be wrong to think that the reference is to *Physics* I: that book also concerns itself, as part of the science of *physis*, only with foundational concepts and basic structures that obtain *within* the physical. It so happens that this work too announces a forthcoming discussion (with Parmenides c.s.) in the very same way.[114]

to give a specification (in *De Gen. et Corr.* for instance, which in that case would have to be simultaneous with *De Caelo* III). While on other issues Aristotle investigated Plato's conception critically, he could have taken this part for granted and only later have tried to present a further explanation for this view.
It seems to me that *De Gen et Corr.* is more readily understandable if seen as a later study of largely the same topics as in *De Caelo* I, c.1-3 & III, in which Aristotle seeks to solve problems in his former conception and attempts to approach other issues from his new standpoint occasioned by his biological investigations. The differences I will point out in the sequel between *De Caelo* I, c.1-3 & III and I, c.4,-II, c.14 & IV mostly exist between *De Caelo* I, c.1-3 & III and *De Gen. et Corr.* as well.

[111] *Timaeus* 31b4 ff. Plato ascribes a certain priority to fire and earth, which seems to influence Aristotle; cf. c.2, 269a26; a35; b5; III, c.3, 302a22, a29; cf. J. Burnet, *Early Greek Philosophy*, par. 147.
[112] *Timaeus* 28b; Aristotle, *De Caelo* III, c.1, 298b34.
[113] 298b19: τὸ γὰρ εἶναι ἄττα τῶν ὄντων ἀγένητα καὶ ὅλως ἀκίνητα μᾶλλόν ἐστιν ἑτέρας καὶ προτέρας ἢ τῆς φυσικῆς σκέψεως. In addition to the ὂν ἀκίνητον of the Eleatics (*Physics* I, c.2, 184b26) the νοητά of Plato's conception could, of course, have been treated in the 'other' study (as was probably the case in the *De Philosophia*). The lines b21-24 point to this. It is decidedly incorrect to read into b19 that Aristotle himself posits the existence of ἀγένητα καὶ ὅλως ἀκίνητα.
[114] *Physics*, I, c.2, 184b25.

3. The Chronological Relation of Book III to *De Philosophia*

Both passages occasion a difficulty for those who hold that *De Philosophia* was written prior to *De Caelo*. Why is it that Aristotle did not, as in *De Caelo* I, c.9, refer to that dialogue, in which he dealt extensively with the Eleatic view and in that connection discussed Plato's doctrine of Ideas (fr. 9, 10, 11 R)? After all, Aristotle is not at all reluctant to supply references throughout book III!

Two additional points indirectly related to this may witness *e silentio* with respect to the chronology of *De Philosophia*. As appears from fragment 6a and 6c Aristotle, in the first book of *De Philosophia*, has devoted a lengthy review to the principia adhered to by his predecessors, and opposed these with his own theory of *eidos* and *steresis* found in *Physics* I, c.7-9.[115] There is further, as shown earlier, reason to believe that in the dialogue Aristotle debated the Eleatics with the *physis*-theory of *De Caelo* I, c.2. If *De Philosophia* did in fact precede *Physics* I and *De Caelo* I, c.1-3 & III, these central theories surely should have figured quite prominently in the dialogue otherwise their meaning would have remained completely in the dark. In that case would a reference in *Physics* I and in *De Caelo* I, c.1-3 & III to that recently written dialogue not be very natural, when Aristotle so readily refers to the dialogue in *De Caelo* I, c.9?

The current placement of *De Philosophia* before *De Caelo* I and *Physics* I leaves us with these two remarkable facts: two passages in *De Caelo* III and *Physics* I refer to a later study which, as to content, could well be the dialogue *De Philosophia*; and, on the other hand, if the dialogue had been written earlier, these books should refer to *De Philosophia* since it treats important doctrines such as the principia of all genesis and the origin of motion. These difficulties are caused by the fact that, following Jaeger, most scholars held that fragment 21b of *De Philosophia* forced one to conclude that the dialogue contains an astro-kinetic conception more Platonic than the one in *De Caelo* I. In section D.8 of this chapter I have already mentioned this fragment and argued that this single testimonium is not sufficient to determine that *De Philosophia* is earlier than *De Caelo*. The matter that concerns us at this point once more gives reason to doubt the correctness of the current placement of *De Philosophia* within the relative chronology,

---

[115] Cf. J. Pépin, *Théologie Cosmique*, p. 468; E. Berti, *La Filosofia del primo Aristotele*, p. 331.

and the question comes to mind: is it not possible that Aristotle has indeed given the studies promised in *Physics* I, c.2, 184b25 and in *De Caelo* III, c.1, 298b20 (and probably also in 299a1[116]) in *De Philosophia*, which, then, was written subsequently?

4. A Further Criticism of Plato

While Aristotle now leaves the 'metaphorical',[117] a-physical language of Parmenides out of further consideration, he seriously discusses the pseudo-physical theories of Plato who, he thinks, has failed to recognize the intrinsic nature of the physical as compared to the mathematical (III, c.1, 299a6). A theory considering all things to to be made up of planes, as is the case in the *Timaeus*, must, if it is to be consistent, teach that a line is composed of points.[118] But in *Physics* VI, c.1-2 Aristotle had already explicated that this runs counter to the structure of the continuous. III, c.1 could accordingly be considered to complement I, c.1 (cf. part A of this chapter).

5. Motion in the Realm of the Four Elements

In c.2 Aristotle once again speaks of the 'natural motion' postulated in I, c.2, and about the factors 'light' and 'heavy' briefly mentioned in I, c.3.[119] The order of treatment of these topics is parallel to that of c.2-3 in book I. It is incomprehensible that L. Elders, *op.cit.*, pp. 281, 282, holds that Aristotle's exposition here 'involves a certain degradation of motion'. To Aristotle motion is pre-eminent, and his doctrine of natural motion inherent in all bodies he defends with all available means, including arguments derived from the negation of motion, the state of rest. (c.2, 300a27-b8). Only a superficial reader

[116] This contains an oblique reference to a consideration of Hesiod, Heraclitus and thinkers in their tradition. It is most probable that they were also discussed in *De Philosophia* I, since there Aristotle was concerned with an account of the historical development of the concept σοφία. C. Prantl, *Aristoteles, Vier Bücher*, p. 322, indeed viewed this as a reference to the *De Philosophia*.

[117] III, c.1, 298b23 μετήνεγκαν.

[118] III, c.1, 299a6-11. A similar metabasis is made in either case. The τοῦ αὐτοῦ λόγου ἐστι could indicate that Aristotle himself draws the consequences of the *Timaeus*-argument, thus arriving at a thesis not (yet) posited by Plato. In a12, however, there is mention of τοῖς ποιοῦσι τὰς ἀτόμους γραμμάς in a general way.

[119] Purposely kept to the absolutely necessary in I, c.2 and 3 in order to bring out his theory of the fifth element; cf. O. Gigon, 'Aristoteles-Studien I', p. 123.

could see a resemblance between the prime unmoved mover of Aristotle's latest phase and the 'primary resting' and the 'primary moving' of c.2, 300b1, b13, 15, 21.[120] The 'primary resting' and the 'primary moving' have only logical status, just as in this period 'proton' is constantly used to denote that which cannot be further reduced to anything else.[121] The criticism directed at Empedocles, the Atomists, and Plato's *Timaeus* clearly shows that Aristotle means the very doctrine of motion found in I, c.2

A proof follows for the existence of elements characterized by the qualities light and heavy, correlated to a natural motion of their own. Here 'lightness' is not understood as that which is 'least heavy'. The immanent levitational force that Aristotle supposes to be present in fire and air is another instance where part of the Platonic cosmology is rejected. In *Timaeus* 62c, 63d, Plato had credited everything belonging to the category of *soma* with motion towards the center of the universe. Upward motion did not have independent status. It seems as if Aristotle's argument in 301b16, 30 embraces all bodies.[122] But this must not be taken to mean that the ether-theory is a later addition to book III. Circular motion is an essential part of the doctrine of natural motions: it is not easy to see how Aristotle could have developed a cosmology including only elements with a natural motion upward or downward. This section shows, rather, that Aristotle here accepts a separation between the world of the first element and that of genesis, sufficiently rigid to allow him to believe that, since the former has been dealt with, it can completely be left out of further consideration.

6. Genesis

Once it is clear that the realm of perishable things consists of bodies possessing a natural motion upward or downward, Aristotle can proceed with the exposition of his view on the problem of all

---

[120] Thus Elders, *Aristotle's Cosmology*, p. 282, in spite of H. Von Arnim's remarks, *Entstehung der Gotteslehre*, chapter V.

[121] Cf. c.3, 302a11; c.5, 304a17; 303b21, 22; *Physics* I, c.1; *Protrepticus* fr. 13 (R). Compare also the πρῶτον φίλον in Plato's *Lysis* 219c-d (A. W. Begemann, *Plato's Lysis*, dates this dialogue far later than is generally done, i.e. close to the *Parmenides*), the πρῶτα ὀνόματα of *Cratylus* 414c-d, 422b-d, the πρῶτα (σώματα) of *Theaetetus*, 201e, 205c, and *Laws* X.

[122] But see 301a22, ἔνια.

genesis – a problem which has fascinated the whole of Greek philosophy, especially since Parmenides. Aristotle believes that the preceding part (I, c.1-3 & III, c.1,2) has sufficiently shown that not everything is subject to genesis. Positively, there is the proof for the existence of an element that has not become, and negatively, he has rejected the conceptions of Hesiod and Heraclitus (referring to a later, definitive treatment) and of Plato.[123]

When considering motion Aristotle already indicated that he intended to get to the bottom of the matter: if one would study a phenomenon, he thinks, one should ask whether or not it may perhaps be derived from something else; if so, the inquiry immediately shifts to that more primary entity. One could possibly return to that which was derived later and consider it as related to its origin. In phenomena of motion, therefore, he looks for simple, non-composed motion; in every instance of being moved he seeks the prime motion; and, in the case of an inquiry into the genesis of visible things, he is concerned with the coming-to-be and passing-away of their primary components, τὰ πρῶτα ἐνυπάρχοντα, 302a12.

Aristotle mentions secondary forms of genesis,[124] based on the four primary constituents of the sublunar world: change of shape, for instance, and addition, reduction and composition. Here genesis remains limited to changes in the spatial or numerical aspects of the parts (quantity, mathematical form). But for him the real problem is: how ought one to think of a becoming and passing-away of the entities fire, air, water and earth?

7. The Components of the Physical World

The third chapter presents a definition of the concept 'primary component':[125] that which remains after consistent application of diaeresis to other, composed bodies, and which is itself no longer reducible to entities that differ eidetically. Immediately thereafter he points to the difference of his own theory compared to that of Anaxagoras, to whose views he paid a great deal of attention in his

---

[123] III, c.2, 301b31. As noted in chapter III, par. 3 above, 301b33 ff. is not directly connected with the προειρημένων of b32. That part of the text is intended to present additional arguments.
[124] In *Physics* I, c.7, 190b5 ff.: μετασχηματίσις, πρόσθεσις, ἀφαίρεσις, σύνθεσις.
[125] 302a15-18; cf. c.4, 302b17-19.

early period.[126] Next he determines the number of elements. This he does in the same way as he proceeded in *Physics* I, c.2, 184b15-25 and c.4, when he established the number of principia of all perishable things. Here too, his rejection of an infinite number of elements is greatly influenced by the principle of the economy of thought discovered by the mathematicians.[127]

In his critique of predecessors Aristotle constantly compares their position to his own with respect to the issue of the doctrine of motion and its implications.[128] Once the close relationship between book III and I, c.1-3 is recognized, this can only be viewed as an indication of Aristotle's careful method: it seems impossible that later additions could be found here, as for instance G. A. Seeck *op.cit.* p. 80, and L. Elders, *Aristotle's Cosmology*, p. 297, believe there to be.

With respect to the question as to whether the elements of all that becomes and passes-away are themselves subject to genesis or whether they are immutable, as the Atomists think, Aristotle adds another indirect argument in favour of the correctness of his theory of the fifth element: fire too, is subject to 'dialysis', since it is 'put out' or 'dies down.'[129] Hence it cannot possibly be eternal, which means that the eternal astral bodies cannot consist of fire, as Plato had taught (*Timaeus*, 40a-b; 41a-b).

In c.7, 306a1-306b2 and c.8, 306b22-9 Aristotle returns to Plato's reduction of the physical entities to mathematical ones. The criticism expressed in I, c.1, and III, c.1 is reiterated, but in different words: Plato has wrongly looked for the principia *outside* of the physical and thereby illicitly overstepped the boundaries (c.7, 306a7-11). To Aristotle the resultant antinomies have become so obvious that the tone of his argument becomes almost passionate: he is convinced that a true 'phycisist's' greatest concern is not a formal, logically consistent *system* but rather a consistent *explication* of the phenomena perceived (306a11-17; a29).

8. The Intent of Book III is not Exclusively Critical

Thus by far the greater part of book III is a refutation of the views

---

[126] Cf. *Physics* I, c.4, 187a22 ff., in which Anaxagoras in also placed over against Empedocles, and *Protrepticus*, fr. 10c; 11 (R). Also, *De Caelo* III, c.4.

[127] C.4, 302b20-30; 303a17-8; cf. *Physics* I, c.4, 188a17; 189b21-2; 191a6-7.

[128] C.3, 302b5-10; c.4, 303b4-9; c.5, 304b11-22.

[129] C.6, 304b27; 305a9-11; cf. *De Philosophia* fr. 19a and 16 (R).

of Plato and others. Even this fact may argue for early dating: philosophical insights are often first developed in relation to problems inherent in a teacher's system. But this does not mean that in book III Aristotle does not propose a view of his own concerning the genesis of the elements.[130] In c.8, 306b15-22 quantitative physics is rejected in favour of qualitative physics. The passage contains an appeal to Nature itself,[131] and a clear reference to the treatment of the ὑποκεί-μενον and of ὕλη as the 'πρῶτον ὑποκείμενον' in *Physics* I, c.7-9.

Since Aristotle wishes to explicate *physis* from within he holds it to be illegitimate to reduce beyond its components. But he is able to say something about the components considered together. All composite entities, he says, (306b20) exist by virtue of these four elements, which constitute their substrate. But the substrate out of which concrete things are formed cannot itself possess form. Plato was right when he proposed an ἀειδὲς καὶ ἄμορφον ὑποκείμενον as the basis for all things somatic. That is why the *stoicheia* together must be viewed as ὕλη without eidos and without (mathematical) form. Each of the four elements taken singly is the result of a specification of the common basis which, just as in *Physics* I, Aristotle calls *hypokeimenon*. The term διαφοραί in 306b22 may help recall the fact that in *Physics* I, c.7, 190a15-6; b24 Aristotle conceived of the substrate as genus specified by the eidos. In the same way here the four sublunary elements are related as species to one genus. And, while Aristotle has (in I, c.1) rejected every metabasis from one genus to another (for instance, from mathematical quantity to physical *soma*) he unhesitatingly accepts metabasis within one and the same genus: there is an exchange of *diaphorai*[132] such that one eidos may turn into another.

Structurally, this conception of a common basis for the elements of all things that are subject to becoming displays many similarities to the old Ionic theories of the one *arche* out of which the various distinct bodies arose. It cannot be denied that the *hypokeimenon* and therefore also the *proton hypokeimenon* (*hyle*) display this character

---

[130] Thus P. Moraux, 'Recherches', p. 186 and *Aristote Du Ciel*, pp. cxxxiii; cxl.
[131] Cf. I, c.1, 268a19 and *Protrepticus* fr. 13 (R).
[132] For instance, light, heavy; rarefied, dense; warm, cold. Book III is not at all exclusively preoccupied with the qualities warm, cold; dry, wet. Cold, warm is a pair of opposites like any other, c.8, 307b5-18; cf. G. A. Seeck, *Ueber die Elemente*, p. 86. On this point there is a characteristic difference compared to *De Gen. et Corr.*

of *arche*.[133] But Aristole has corrected these Ionic views considerably in that for him the universe cannot have a 'beginning' in any temporal sense. Because of his conviction that reality as a whole is indestructible, the word *arche* looses its meaning of 'beginning' and becomes equivalent to 'principle'.

It may be admitted that on the basis of the later Aristotle many astute questions can be asked as to the how and why of this metabasis of elements, but it seems more to the point to note that Aristotle here holds to an anti-atomistic conception of his own, sharply opposed to Plato's *Timaeus*. And even if, as in *Physics* I, he is still very much preoccupied with the views of the *Timaeus*, and therefore analysis is not pushed as far as in *De Generatione et Corruptione*,[134] this should not induce one to claim that *De Caelo* III is not complete without the latter work and that both writings must, therefore, stem from the same phase of composition. Only gradually, by way of his biological investigations in the period after 347BC, Aristotle gained the insight that knowledge of that whereof something consists does not constitute the only and highest knowledge, but necessarily requires supplementation.

9. A Connection Between III, c.8 and I, c.3, 270a32

III, c.8 indicates that to Aristotle the most genuine kind of genesis is the μεταβολή from one *eidos* to another, which he takes to be characteristic for the primary components of reality. All other kinds of genesis are less far-reaching. As example of such μεταβολή Aristotle repeatedly mentions the change from illness to health,[135] which implies a complete shift in the make-up of the patient. An interesting passage in I, c.3 yields additional information to the effect that Aristotle did not conceive of the elements as simply 'dead matter': on the contrary, they are the building material for the entire organic world, and themselves classified under the category of life. According

---

[133] Cf. *Physics*, I, c.6, 189a31-2 and c.9, 192a29-32; J. Burnet, *Early Greek Philosophy*, p. 12 (note 1).

[134] Cf. F. Solmsen, *Aristotle's System*, p. 321 and note 1. This author (on p. 379 note 1) correctly describes *De Gen. et Corr.* as being 'less Platonic in outlook than Book I of the *Physics*.' In my opinion, *De Caelo* I, c.1-3 & III belongs to the phase of *Physics* I in its least evolved form.

[135] *De Caelo* I, c.3, 270a29; *Categories* c.8, 8b37; 9a1.

to the passage,[136] the first, eternal element cannot be subject to change (ἀλλοίωσις), for it is not subject to growth or decay (cf. 270a22-25). 'For, we see that all physical bodies that change in *pathos*, also display growth and its opposite; for instance, the bodies of animals and the plants and their parts and equally the *somata* of the elements.' In III, c.8, 306b20-22 the elements are considered subject to *metabole kata pathos*. Here even growth and diminution is ascribed to them. And although one should probably think here of volume-changes on account of water turning into steam etc., the passage does imply that Aristotle believed the elements to belong on the level of the living. L. Elders[137] correctly notes: 'Elsewhere, e.g. in *De Gen. et Corr.* I, c.5, he reserves the terms increase and diminution for growth and decrease of organisms'.

Aristotle's views as to growth etc. have gone through profound changes in the course of his career as scientific investigator. But the present text makes quite clear that no '*anima nutritiva*' as principle of growth has as yet come into view, and that, therefore, Aristotle is still in an early stage of his development in I, c.3 and III, c.8.

F. THE PHYSIS-CONCEPT IN *DE CAELO* I, c.1-3 & III

The entire argument of the *De Caelo*-sections under investigation was probably part of a study 'Περὶ φύσεως'.[138] This prompts the question as to what Aristotle understood by 'Nature' in this phase of his thinking. It is true that the text presents no separate treatment concerning this central concept of Aristotle's system. Still, I believe that the passages in which the concept *Physis* occurs can yield some important conclusions.

In the first place *Physis* may have macro-cosmic meaning. When Aristotle speaks of the importance of the number three[139] and, among other things, adduces that three is the number of the All, he continues: 'hence also we make use of that number in the cultic worship of the gods, since we have derived it from Nature as *one of her laws*';[140] and a little later he repeats: 'thus we act upon the prompting of

---

[136] I, c.3, 270a25-35. Cf. *Categories* c.8, 8b25 ff. for the terms *pathos, hexis, diathesis*.
[137] *Aristotle's Cosmology*, p. 93. Compare *De Gen. et Corr.* I, c.5, 321a9 ff.
[138] I, c.1, 268a1.
[139] I, c.1, 268a9-23.
[140] I, c.1, 268a13: παρὰ τῆς φύσεως εἰληφότες ὥσπερ νόμους ἐκείνης.

Nature itself'.[141] In another place (where, as in I, c.1 supporting arguments are not given, because the most basic philosophical convictions are at stake), in III, c.8, when Aristotle chooses in favour of a qualitative physics in contrast to Plato's mathematical approach of the physical – to Aristotle this seemed a Procrustean method – he says: 'Nature itself seems to point us in this direction which agrees with the *logos*'.[142] *Physis* has a directive character in I, c.3, and displays some of the features of a demiurge: 'very properly *Physis* seems to have kept the element which was to be ungenerated and indestructible separated from the realm of the opposites'.[143] In I, c.2 *Physis* is further mentioned as the principle of motion for the five natural elements which together constitute the All.[144] In still another place Aristotle uses the word as synonym for 'reality in its entirety'.[145] All these passages taken together seem to justify the conclusion that in this early phase of Aristotle's thinking *Physis* stands for *the whole of reality*, somatically qualified, *and* at the same time for the rational normative principle of reality.

On the basis of all this, therefore, it will be difficult to maintain that Aristotle still holds to the intelligible world of Plato's conception. The law for reality is here no longer sought *outside* of that which is subject to it, but once again, as was done before Plato, *within* reality. This conclusion may be helpful with respect to Aristotle's lost writings, the *Protrepticus* for instance. For, if this conclusion is not difficult to accept in the case of *De Caelo* I, c.1-3 & III, it seems rather dangerous to think in terms of Plato's doctrine of Ideas in the case of fragment 13 (R) of the *Protrepticus* where, after all, a very similar *Physis*-concept is put forward.[146]

---

[141] I, c.1, 268a19: διὰ τὸ τὴν φύσιν αὐτὴν οὕτως ἐπάγειν ἀκολουθοῦμεν.

[142] III, c.8, 306b15: ἀλλ' ἔοικεν ἡ φύσις αὐτὴ τοῦτο σημαίνειν ἡμῖν, ὃ καὶ κατὰ λόγον ἐστίν.

[143] I, c.3, 270a20: ὀρθῶς ἔοικεν ἡ φύσις τὸ μέλλον ἔσεσθαι ἀγένητον καὶ ἄφθαρτον ἐξελέσθαι ἐκ τῶν ἐναντίων.

[144] I, c.2, 268b16; cf. III, c.2, 301b17; c.5, 304b13.

[145] III, c.1, 300a16; cf. translation by J. Tricot.

[146] Thus W. Jaeger, *Aristotle*, pp. 90 ff. On this point Jaeger has been repeatedly and extensively refuted by I. Düring (for example, in his study *Aristotle's Protrepticus*, pp. 212 ff.). Düring is in agreement with Diels (1888), who concluded 'that Aristotle here goes much further than in any other known writing of his in using Platonic language, but that the context in which these expressions occur forbids to interpret αὐτὰ τὰ ἀκριβῆ and other similar expres-

Physis does not only have the character of law and norm in a macrocosmic sense. Where the *physis* of the various entities of sensory perception is concerned there is a close connection with the idea of order and regularity (*taxis*) as well.[147] Everything has its own *taxis* within the order of *Physis* as a whole. Via this notion of an ordered world *Physis* is related to *kosmos* in the sense of beautifully composed reality.[148] The nature of a thing and of the entire universe is 'that which it usually is'[149] *and that which it ought to be!* Incongruities with it are evil and ought to be corrected by re-instatement of the old *physis*. To this extent it is meaningful to speak of deriving 'guidelines', ὅροι, from Nature itself.[150] It seems that this remarkable

---

sions as referring to transcendent forms in Plato's sense.' (transl. Düring). On p. 217 Düring offers various parallels to ἡ φύσις αὐτή and concludes: 'The word φύσις in B 47-50 [= fr. 13 R] is not synonymous with "idea", it is "the cosmic order".' (p. 218) Cf. also his article 'Nature and Reality', pp. 42-55. Düring's interpretation of fr. 13 and the connections with pre-Platonic thought pointed to are especially helpful in clarifying the position of the early Aristotle. Even C. J. de Vogel, who has always defended Jaeger's theory of a Platonic first phase in Aristotle, has moved away from his interpretation of fr. 13 of the *Protrepticus*; cf. her article 'Transcendent Ideas', p. 284: '... as to the αὐτὰ τὰ πρῶτα and αὐτά of fr. 13 I join Ingemar Düring with a grateful acknowledgment that on this point he led the way to a better understanding', and *ibid.*, note 85: 'Though I have some reservations to make about certain details of his argument, I do think that his interpretation of the αὐτὰ τὰ πρῶτα is essentially right. No doubt this implies an important correction of Jaeger's interpretation which, on this point at least, appears to have been accepted somewhat too easily.' For a similar discussion regarding the αὐτὰ τά ... in *De Philosophia* fr. 8 (R), cf. M. Untersteiner, 'Peri Philosophias' pp. 341-342 against P. Wilpert, 'Ueber die Philosophie', pp. 155-162.

[147] III, c.2, 301a4-11. Cf. I. Düring, 'Nature and Reality', p. 43. Unfortunately he does not point to the important shift that occurs with respect to the order of Nature as well, when Aristotle introduces his theory of the unmoved metaphysical mover. In his early phase this orderliness is an irreducible datum. Later it is explained in terms of the directedness of the entire material *physis* towards the immaterial highest being.

[148] III, c.2, 301a10. Compare *De Philosophia* fr. 12a,b (R).

[149] 301a7-9. J. Burnet, *Early Greek Philosophy*, pp. 363-364, relates the stem φυ - to that of 'to be' (fu-isse etc.), in rejection of W. A. Heidel's view, who refers to φύομαι. W. D. Ross, *Physics*, p. 505, and *Metaphysics*, I, p. 269, follows Burnet, as does D. Holwerda, *Commentatio*, pp. 104-109. Cf. chapter Six B, note 52 below.

[150] Thus the *Protrepticus*, fr. 13 (R); B 47-8 (D).

characteristic may be related to Aristotle's Asclepiadic background.[151] To the physician only the *physis* of his patient could function as guide but never an ideal construction as to 'health itself'. Precisely this aspect of Aristotle's *physis*-concept enabled him to restore to visible reality the rank of the 'really real'.[152]

There is an ambiguity in this approach to *Physis*: that which is subject to the law and object of scientific inquiry is identical to that from which the law proceeds.[153] The totality of the five elements together makes up *Physis*, but at the same time *Physis* can be called the principle of motion for these. Man, animal, plant, things and elements are subject to the 'laws' of *Physis*, but simultaneously there is nothing beyond the totality of these entities that could be referred to as *Physis*. In point of fact, however, this difficulty is inherent in all immanence-philosophy.

The universal character here ascribed to *Physis* is expressed also when the Presocratic philosophers, elsewhere referred to as φυσιόλογοι, are called 'men who philosophize concerning truth'[154] in III, c.1. Just as in *Physics* I, c.8[155] *Physis* is apparently identical with 'truth'. The φυσικός is philosopher *par excellence*. It is not until Aristotle accepts an origin outside and above the realm of *Physis* that the φυσικός is degraded to a man of (a special) science. But *Physis* is then also degraded to 'the material universe' which no longer comprehends reality in its entirety, but depends upon an immaterial, a-physical prime mover. The preceding has shown, I trust, that Aristotle has not yet reached this stage at this point. Especially the clear agreement of the *Protrepticus*, the *De Philosophia*, and *Physics* I[156] with *De Caelo* I, c.1-3 & III with respect to the concept of *Physis* justifies the belief that Aristotle has conceived and devel-

---

[151] Cf. I. Düring, 'Nature and Reality', p. 50: 'In the *Corpus Hippocratcum* φύσις is a. the normal status regarded as a constant; b. the active and creative force, δημιουργὸς φύσις, in every organism, in man and in the Cosmos; c. the essential reality behind or beyond the changing phenomena'.

[152] Cf. O. Gigon, *Vom Himmel*, p. 45.

[153] A. Mansion, *Introduction*, p. 158 (1946², p. 266) was aware of the difficulty involved. But he held that exactly because of this inner contradiction this conception could not possibly be ascribed to Aristotle.

[154] III, c.1, 298b13; cf. b29.

[155] 191a25; cf. c.5, 188b30; *Protrepticus* fr. 5a, b and 12b, 13 (R); B 47, 44, 32 (D); I. Düring, 'Nature and Reality', pp. 39, 49.

[156] Cf. Chapter Six below.

oped the work *De Natura* (of which *De Caelo* I, c.1-3 & III probably was a part) when there was as yet no thought of a *meta*physics.[157] After Aristotle had rejected the world of Ideas in which his teacher sought the law for visible reality, he apparently returned to the old Ionic tradition, which believed the totality of meaning discoverable in visible and tangible somatic reality,[158] even if Aristotle had learned to see this reality through Plato's eyes.

Excursus: Aristotle on 'First Philosophy'

In this connection I should like to touch upon another issue. In section D,5 of this chapter I concluded that according to Aristotle within *Physis* there is a distinction between a πρώτη οὐσία and another δεύτερα (?) οὐσία. It is possible that knowledge concerning *Physis* might accordingly be subdivided into a science regarding the above-mentioned first *ousia* and a science concerning the remaining realm, i.e. that of the four elements. But in that case the question is: which science now is the actual, the most essential form of knowledge-concerning-Nature (= Philosophy)? This question runs parallel to the problem as to which is the most essential, most authentic *ousia* within *Physis*. In view of the specification πρώτη, given to the substance of the astral

---

[157] A. Mansion, *Introduction*, p. 159 (1946², p. 268) has pointed to the tension between these two phases, but tried to erase it. Cf. P. Gohlke, *Aristoteles und sein Werk*, p. 81; 'Entstehungsgeschichte', p. 305, who displays more insight on this point.
W. Wieland, *Aristotelische Physik*, p. 61 has, with respect to *Physics* I, pointed to the fact that the design of the book is far more readily understood 'wenn man den Gedanken eines Metaphysikprimates aufgibt und von der Voraussetzung ausgeht, dass die Physik so wie sie in *Physik* A entwickelt wird, der aus sich verständliche Entwurf der allgemeinen theoretischen Philosophie ist, die höchstens der praktischen und der poietischen Wissenschaft gegenüber abgegrenzt werden musz.'
[158] Cf. A. Mansion, *Introduction*, p. 52: 'en tant qu'Aristote pouvait se regarder comme l'héritier des Ioniens primitifs, et surtout d'un Empédocle ou d'un Anaxagore, il y avait une continuité certaine entre leur spéculations cosmologiques et sa philosophie de la nature, pardessus Socrate et Platon, chez qui les préoccupations de cet ordre avaient fait presque totalement défaut. Les anciens écrits, que la tradition intitule περὶ φύσεως, avaient pour objet, au moins partiel [like the 'De Natura' of Aristotle] la somme des phénomènes du monde et leur enchainement' (cf. 1946², p. 90). See also I. Düring, 'Nature and Reality', p. 52; F. Solmsen, *Aristotle's System*, p. 98; E. Frank, 'Fundamental Opposition', p. 172.

bodies in *De Caelo* I, c.3, 270b11, the answer is not difficult. Compared to knowledge of the perishable world insight into this first substance is obviously to be viewed as the first and highest form of philosophy. This knowledge concerns divine, eternal, indestructible and immutable being.

While this question of status is still fairly readily answerable, a second question may arise which is far more difficult, *viz.* what is the relation of the science of the first *ousia* to knowledge of *Physis* as a whole, and which of these two deserves priority? If the order of the sciences is determined by way of their objects of study then knowledge of *Physis* as a whole should come first, since the first substance is to be viewed as merely part of *Physis*, and in a relation of genus to species the genus seems to be first in rank.

A second tendency evident in Aristotle's work from the beginning, however, is the hierarchical ordering of everything that is distinguished and variously evaluated. The anthropological remarks found in fragments of the *Protrepticus* offer clear examples of this. Body and soul are placed in an hierarchical relationship. The body is the instrument of the soul.[159] The soul 'rules',[160] and is 'better', because more ἀρχικός, than the body.[161] The highest function of the soul, the φρόνησις, is considered the goal and meaning of being-man and the perfect life is connected with it.[162] Aristotle even goes so far as to claim that actually man, either completely or to a great extent, may be identified with that function (that part) of the human soul.[163] The essence and meaning of man may be grasped in the doctrine concerning the *nous*.[164]

It is conceivable that in the doctrine of the macrocosmos Aristotle leaned towards a similar reduction, and that in this case too there was the tendency to seek the essence of Nature in its highest *eidos*, the first substance, the divine. The divine possesses the highest τιμή.[165] Concerning the divinity of Aristotle's early period it may also be

---

[159] Fr. 4 (R) = B8 (D); fr. 6 (R) = B59 (D).
[160] Fr. 6 (R) = B59 (D).
[161] Fr. 5b (R) = B34 (D); cf. B61 (D).
[162] Fr. 5b (R) = B38-40; B 53 (D); fr. 6 (R) = B 60-61 (D).
[163] Fr. 6 (R) = B 62 (D): καὶ γὰρ ἂν τοῦτο, οἶμαι, θείη τις, ὡς ἤτοι μόνον ἢ μάλιστα ἡμεῖς ἐσμεν τὸ μόριον τοῦτο.
[164] Cf. a similar reduction in Pseudo-Plato, *Alcibiades Maior*, (130c-d), 133c. C. A. Bos, *Interpretatie*, pp. 107-112, dates this work about 346 BC.
[165] *De Caelo* I, c.2, 269b16; *Metaphysics* K, c.7, 1064b4.

said, as will be seen in chapter Six,D, that he 'rules', and is more ἀρχικός than is the ὕλη which is his working-material. In addition, his perfect happiness may be considered to be the goal to which every man, even all perishable being, strives. This tendency might suggest that according to the early Aristotle 'first philosophy' was not primarily directed towards *Physis* as a whole but rather to the first *ousia*, that is to say, towards the divine element.[166]

One might remark here that I am attempting to solve problems that do not exist at all. After all, in *De Caelo* these problems are nowhere in evidence. Still, it is perhaps possible to defend the thesis that for Aristotle the issue was indeed important. In the *Metaphysics* it recurs repeatedly.[167] The basic pattern there remained the same even though various parts receive a different meaning. The concept of *Physis* as 'total reality' is replaced by the more abstract concept of 'being qua being'. The πρώτη οὐσία is no longer the fifth element of *De Caelo* I, c.2-3. The tendency, already present in *De Caelo* I, c.2-3, i.e. to separate the divine from everything else as sharply as possible (which there resulted in an internally contradictory theory of the fifth element which could hardly be called a σῶμα any longer) appears to have gained the upper hand. The divine has been deprived even more of any commensurability with the perceptible world: it is even denied somatic character. The only predicate which is still applicable to both the divine and material things is the completely abstract and contentless *to on*. Πρώτη οὐσία is now the highest species of the genus *to on*, i.e. transcendent and immovable (unmoved) being. Knowledge of *Physis*, on the other hand, is limited to the special science dealing with all things material (*Metaphysics* Γ, c.3, 1005a31-4).

It may be noted that the more abstract concept of *to on* evinces the same problems and tension found in the concept of *soma*. (cf. chapter IV, D,5). Here too the term *on*, held in common, suggests a relationship which in fact cannot pertain. Here, as there, the conclusion must be that Aristotle's philosophy runs stuck in equivocal use of terms. Secondly, it is of some importance to note that Aristotle now asks whether authentic philosophy ought to treat of the

---

[166] Which implies that the 'first philosophy' ought to treat *theology* (the doctrine concerning the divine element in a macrocosmic sense) and *psychology* (the divine in man). Association can hardly be avoided with the dialogue *De Philosophia* from the same period, the entire positive part of which, it seems, was devoted to a treatment of these two disciplines!

[167] *Metaphysics* Γ, c.1-3; E, c.1; K, c.7.

doctrine of 'being qua being' as *genus* embracing the objects of theology, physics and mathematics, or be concerned with the highest species of being. Aristotle chooses the latter and with the aid of a questionable artifice he subsumes the general science of being under theology.[168]

It seems to me that more insight is gained into the motivation for this hotly debated choice on the part of Aristotle when its relationship to an earlier conception is kept in mind. In the first period Aristotle already identified highest philosophy with the teaching concerning the being of god. The fact that theology may at the same time be the doctrine of universal principles rests on the circumstance that everything else owes its meaning and existence to divine activity. The major difference between this early and his later phase is this: while originally the first *ousia* was an immanent part of *Physis* as a whole, the opposition between this *ousia* and that which is subject to it has been increased to the point where finally it occupies a transcendent station above *Physis*.

Regarding Aristotle's concept ὂν ᾗ ὄν it may be said that it occurs exclusively in the (late) *Metaphysics* and has a purely logical function. For these two reasons it may certainly not be brought into connection with τὸ Ὄν which, as data concerning *De Bono* indicate, was strongly ontologically loaded in the late-Platonic philosophy.

G. THE THEORY OF KNOWLEDGE

It may seem a little strange that a section on the theory of knowledge should occur in an analysis of Aristotle's theory of the cosmos. But in classical Greek philosophy epistemology is still closely interwoven with cosmology, so that there is reason to ask whether perhaps the portion of *De Caelo* under consideration does contain epistemological material.

1. Rejection of the Platonic Doctrine of the Intelligible World

Aristotle rejects the doctrine of the intelligible world of which the visible world is supposedly a copy. This may be concluded from the tenor of the work as a whole[169], with its attention to concrete reality,

---

[168] *Metaphysics* E, c.1, 1026a29-32; K, c.7, 1064b11-14.
[169] I, c.3, 270b5; 12-15; c.2, 270a31; III, c.2, 301a6, 8; c.7, 306a17; c.6, 304b26.

its appeal to observed fact, and its stress on the *soma* as point of departure for physics within the framework of a rejection of any derivation of it from higher metaphysical principles.[170] Furthermore, in the one passage that speaks of τὸ νοητόν, Aristotle makes very clear that he ascribes no separate existence to it: a renewed refutation of Plato's theory to the effect that all physical bodies are constructed out of surfaces argues that subscribers to this theory 'come into conflict with the mathematical sciences, the most exact sciences there are! For these consider even τὸ νοητόν divisible, while Plato and his followers, to maintain their own hypothesis, must hold that not even everything sensorily perceptible is divisible' (III, c.7, 306a26-30; cf. c.1, 299a4-6). For Aristotle the noetic has a different meaning, as becomes clear from III, c.1, 299a11-8, where the relation of the mathematical and the physical is briefly mentioned. Mathematical entities such as surfaces, lines, etc. can only be studied by *abstracting* them from concrete things (cf. III, c.6, 305a25; c.8, 307a19). Visible reality, its great diversity of moving bodies with their variegated properties, remains point of departure.

2. Aristotle's Scientific Method

On account of this difference it is inevitable that, compared to Plato, Aristotle's scientific inquiry into reality will proceed along different lines. In *Physics* I Aristotle had announced his program: investigation of first principles, first causes, and first components. In *De Caelo* I, c.1, 268a3,5 (cf. III, c.7, 306a8-11) this intention is briefly noted once more. In III, c.3, 302a11 the reason for his search for the elements of the perishable part of the cosmos is formulated as follows: 'the way to knowledge runs via τὰ πρῶτα.' This remark may be

---

[170] I. c.1. I believe that a phase in which Aristotle supposedly adhered to the Platonic theory of Ideas is insufficiently supported by the extant texts. I. Düring's arguments against the acceptance of this phase seem conclusive: 1. Cicero is unaware of a Platonizing phase – I. Düring, *Biographical Tradition*, pp. 322, 325 (in spite of C. J. de Vogel's attempt, 'Transcendent Ideas', p. 271, to refute this argument). 2. Aristotle conceives of values and standards for theoretical knowledge as to be found within the realm of *physis* (I. Düring, *loc. cit.*, p. 332). 3. His distinction between οὐσία and τὸ συμβεβηκός is meant to replace Plato's doctrine of the Ideas (I. Düring, *Aristoteles*, pp. 81 ff.). Since many of Jaeger's views prove to be untenable it is no longer necessary to hold on to his hypothesis of a Platonic phase. This does not mean, however, that I agree with Düring's rejection of virtually any development at all.

clarified with the help of *Physics* I, c.4, 187b11: 'Not before we know of which and how many components it consists do we consider a complex entity known.'

The position here taken by Aristotle is remarkable. It typefies his physicalistic starting-point: the theory holds for the realm of the inorganic. For other areas of reality, however, this approach is not adequate. On the basis of the passages cited, however, I conclude that Aristotle was not yet sufficiently aware of this in the beginning period of his philosophic work. But in the course of the years his insight has deepened. His biological and logical investigations taught him that another aspect is at least equally important: knowledge concerning the type or kind to which something belongs. I think that *Metaphysics* B, c.3, 998a20-b14 offers significant evidence for this broadening of Aristotle's perspective. There he stresses the fruitfulness of analysis of components in phonetics, in mathematical analytics, and in a doctrine of elements *à la* Empedocles. But over against this he places the way knowledge is gained by means of definitions and syllogisms based on abstract concepts of type and class. In *Physics* I and *De Caelo* I, c.1-3 & III Aristotle has not yet reached awareness of the primary importance of this second method.

In his search for the first elements Aristotle remains very conscious of the intrinsic nature of every genus in reality: all mathematical magnitudes he reduces to linear and circular figures, all motion to three simple motions, all bodies to three simple *somata*. A reduction to another genus is not permissible: 'The principles of derivation ought to belong to the same *genus* as does that which is derived from it'.[171] These principles of derivation Aristotle discovers by the application of diaeresis: the 'element' is defined as 'that which is found after diaeresis of other (complex) *somata*, but which is not itself susceptible to diaeresis in the sense that eidetically different entities result'. As indicated earlier, *Physics* I, c.1 completely concurs with this.

Meanwhile an interesting problem resides here: if knowledge is to be understood as knowledge of the primary components of something, as *De Caelo* III, c.3 claims, to what extent can there be any talk of gaining knowledge of these principles? The implication could be that no scientific knowledge of these principles is possible, but then it would immediately follow that all knowledge is based on scientifically

---

[171] III, c.7, 306a9-11 δεῖ γὰρ ... εἶναι τὰς ἀρχὰς ... ὁμογενεῖς τοῖς ὑποκειμένοις. Compare my interpretation of I, c.1, 268b1, Chapter Four ,A.

unknowable entities. In the area of physical bodies this would mean that knowledge of all complex entities arises by diaeresis of primary components; but the elements themselves cannot be known in the same sense, even though they are sensorily perceptible.[172] It is tempting to compare these implications with the anonymous theory expounded by Socrates in Plato's *Theaetetus* 201d8 ff. Everything complex, according to this theory, is knowable, nameable and – no less important – definable. The elements of the composition, however, are called ἄλογα, ἄγνωστα, but αἰσθητά (202b6; 202d10; 205c). Apparently a theory is at issue in which *aisthesis* is given priority relative to *logos*. Evidently the *logos* can work only with the materials gathered by perception. Aristotle, however, makes no mention of the problem indicated[173].

In *De Caelo* I, c.1-3 & III and *Physics* I Aristotle diaeretically distinguishes three levels:

a. concrete things,[174]

b. the elements, the simple bodies,[175]

c. the *hyle*, the first substrate.[176]

Physics I, c.1, 184a16 ff. shows that Aristotle considered the route from level a) to c) to be the proper way of scientific inquiry. According to this passage level a) is better known to man in everyday experience, but on level c) τὰ σαφέστερα τῇ φύσει καὶ γνωριμώτερα are to be found. The train of thought leads to this: if philosophy is the search for 'the truth and *physis* of all that exists', then the ultimate goal is the 'primary substrate' out of which everything originates and to which all things at last return. It seems as if Aristotle has indeed drawn this conclusion.[177]

---

[172] For the contemporary relevance of this problem see L. Wittgenstein, *Philosophical Investigations*, Oxford: 1963, p. 21.

[173] It seems probable that Aristotle had already reached the view that theoretical knowledge is built on knowledge by experience. *Gnosis* (III, c.3, 302a11), understood as (theoretical) knowledge, could then be placed next to acquaintance with things in every-day practice. In *Anal. Post* I, c.3; II, c.19 Aristotle elaborates this systematically.

[174] *Physics* I, c.1, 184a22; c.8, 191a25; c.6, 189a27.

[175] *De Caelo* I, c.2, 268b27; III, c.3, 302a15.

[176] *Physics* I, c.9, 192a31; *De Caelo* III, c.8, 306b16-20.

[177] *Physics* I, c.9, 192a29-31: ὑποκεῖσθαι τι δεῖ πρῶτον ἐξ οὗ ἐνυπάρχοντος (ἐγίγνετο ἄν)· τοῦτο δ'ἐστὶν αὐτὴ ἡ φύσις. The position of the study 'On the Elements' after *Physics* I, in which the principles, including the *hypokeimenon*, are discussed, is probably also motivated by the fact that *Physics* I penetrates to a still deeper layer of reality.

In *De Generatione et Corruptione* II analysis has progressed. The στοιχεῖα are no longer the ultimate components. Frequent use of the addition 'so-called' to the word 'element' is striking.[178] *Hyle* as ἀρχή is primary; secondary are the contrasting qualities (warm-cold, dry-moist), and then we have the physical *somata*.[179] There is here an advanced stage of analysis and abstraction regarding the concept *hyle*. Once again it cannot be said that this development runs counter to the older teaching of the ὑποκείμενον found in *Physics* I. Rather, problems occasioned by the old scheme have received consistent attention. To be sure, in some matters a shift of emphasis resulted, such that it is highly unlikely that *De Caelo* III, c.3, for instance, was written at the time *De Generatione et Corruptione* was composed.[180] In view of the many references to late Aristotelian works, the repeated use of the word entelechy, and the evident hylomorphistic character of *De Generatione et Corruptione*, a considerable temporal distance must be assumed during which time Aristotle could have gone through this evolution.

3. A Difficulty in this Method

In the epistemological views of the early Aristotle there is a hiatus by reason of the fact that the *proton soma* cannot be reduced to the common substrate of the four earthly elements. *Hyle* is that which lies at the basis of all becoming and passing-away; but by definition the first element is excluded from this. Knowledge concerning the first element, therefore, will not be of the same kind as knowledge in the area of the other elements. It is not by chance that Aristotle explicitly limits his investigation to the realm of γένεσις and φθορά in *Physics* I (c.7, 191a3; 189b30). The early Aristotle's tendency to unification does not yet embrace the whole of reality. It appears that an important motive of his later thinking is the attempt to bridge this gap.

---

[178] I, c.6, 322b1; II, c.1, 328b31; 329a16; b26; cf. W. D. Ross on *Physics* I, c.4, 187a26. H. H. Joachim, *On Coming-to-be and Passing-away*, p. 137.

[179] II, c.1, 329a33-36. Attention is fixed less on the four *somata* than on the four qualities to which all *differentiae* may be reduced.

[180] F. Solmsen, *Aristotle's System*, p. 365, has been properly sensitive to the difference between *De Caelo* III and *De Generatione et Corruptione*.

CHAPTER FIVE

EVALUATION OF THE SYSTEMATIC VIEW
IN *DE CAELO* I, c.1-3 & III

In the previous chapter the most important matters dealt with in *De Caelo* I, c.1-3 & III have been reviewed. I intend to gather up as many data as possible relevant for a more precise determination of this small treatise's place among the philosopher's works. A number of characteristic traits of 'the Aristotelian philosophy' are not found in this part of *De Caelo* – a fact not without significance. I will, therefore, first continue the inquiry in that direction, and subsequently also attempt placement in a positive sense.

A. NO HYLOMORPHISM

1. The eleven chapters which together form the object of our investigation do not contain the term μορφή. The one instance in which the word ἄμορφος is used (III, c.8, 306b17) is a direct reference to Plato's *Timaeus* (51a, in which place it is a predicate of χώρα).

The term ὕλη, on the other hand, does occur in a systematic-philosophic meaning (I, c.1, 268a22; c.3, 270a24; III, c.7, 305b5; c.8, 306b20). Its theoretical scope, however, has not progressed beyond the conclusion of *Physics* I, c.9, 191b31, at the end of the study of the three *archai*: '*hyle* is the πρῶτον ὑποκείμενον'. It is precisely the *hypokeimenon* which, according to Aristotle in *Physics* I, guarantees the reality and continuity of things. In that book he even calls the *hypokeimenon* ἀρχή, since, as substrate, it is the condition for every predication.[1] The part played by *hyle* and *hypokeimenon* respectively in Aristotle's teaching concerning principia in *Physics* I (and presupposed in *De Caelo* I, c.1-3 & III) is far greater than it is in those works where every being is analyzed in terms of a form-principle and a matter-principle (in which antithesis it is the form-principle which receives primacy). In agreement with this is the fact that Aristotle values the *soma* highly enough to feel justified in calling

---

[1] C.6, 189a31; cf. c.9, 192a6, 30.

it 'perfect'. In connection with this non-hylomorphism: H. E. Runner, in his study of the conception in *Physics* I concludes (*op. cit.* pp. 104, 107) that those passages in *Physics* I where a specifically Aristotelian use of the concept *morphe* is found[2], are recognizable on external grounds as results of a later revision, and that in the older part of *Physics* I the word occurs in quotations of Plato only.[3]

2. With respect to the sections I, c.4-II, c.14 & IV of *De Caelo*: the term *morphe* occurs in I, c.7, 275b28. Context and the reference to *Physics* VIII, c.10 (according to Stocks, Guthrie, Tricot, Moraux, Elders and Longo) in 275b21-2 indicate a late date. The term also occurs in I, c.9, 277b32; 278a2; 14, 15 (*morphe kai eidos*!) a24; I, c.10, 280a14.[4]

B. THE TERM ἐντελέχεια IS NOT USED

1. A second point worthy of note is the fact that the term *entelecheia* is not used in the part under investigation. This technical-philosophical term is probably coined by Aristotle himself,[5] and its occurence would be an additional chronological indication – if the date of coining could be determined.

I cannot, however, agree entirely with Ross when he says: 'the commonness of the word in the *Physics*, the *De Generatione et Corruptione*, the *De Anima* and the *Metaphysics*, and its great rarity in the other works suggest that these four works belong to one period of his life, and there is little doubt that the period is a fairly late one.'[6] One could accept this statement only if the works concerned were,

---

[2] C.7, 190b20 and 191a10, 11.

[3] C.9, 192a13. In *Categories* c.8, 10a11 ff. also, *morphe* is not yet used in a late-Aristotelian sense. Its meaning is limited to the 'mathematical form': a biotic qualification is not involved.

[4] O. Longo, *De Caelo*, p. 380.

[5] Cf. Sir David Ross, *Aristotle, De Anima*, p. 15; G. A. Blair, 'Energeia and Entelecheia', p. 102, presents a review of the occurrence of the terms mentioned in the title. He holds that 'entelecheia' is introduced to replace 'energeia' after Aristotle had completely worked out his hylomorphism, pp. 112, 116. Cf. I. Düring, *Reconstruction*, p. 245. Also R. Hirzel, 'Entelechie'. He considers the entelechy to have been introduced after the period of the dialogues, p. 201, and defends the thesis that 'ἐντελέχεια nicht ein von Natur selbständiger Wort ist, sondern eine Umbildung die erst Aristoteles mit der ἐνδελέχεια vorgenommen hat', p. 208.

[6] On *De Anima* I, c.1, 402a26.

in one piece, composed during a limited span of time. But Ross also recognizes that works such as the *Physics* and the *Metaphysics* contain material from widely different dates. But if this is so, the term *entelecheia* can be a chronological indicator for only that portion in which it occurs, and which forms a unified whole, *and* as *terminus post quem* for the latest revision of the *Physics* as a whole. I would therefore readily agree with Ross with respect to *De Anima* and *De Generatione et Corruptione*. The frequent use of the word in the latter work, which displays so much similarity to *De Caelo* III, forces us, notwithstanding this similarity, to date it appreciably later than *De Caelo* I, c.1-3 & III. But the one single instance that *entelecheia* is found in *Physics* I certainly is not sufficient reason to assign a late date to this book as a whole.[7]

It seems reasonable to suppose that Aristotle introduced the term *entelecheia* once he had reached the hylomorphistic phase of his philosophical evolution. The frequent use of the word in *De Anima* and the *Metaphysics* leads me to believe that this new word dates from after 335 BC. Only an accurate analysis of the whole of Aristotle's development will allow a definitive statement.

2. While the term is absent in *De Caelo* I, c.1-3 & III, it is found in *De Caelo* I, c.12, 283a26 and IV, c.3, 311a4,5.[8]

C. THE THEORY OF AN UNMOVED MOVER DOES NOT OCCUR

1. After the publication of the studies by H. Von Arnim and W. K. C. Guthrie (cf. chapter One) many scholars have concurred in saying that the theory of the unmoved prime mover resulted from a later

---

[7] *Physics* I, c.2, 186a3; cf. already Ross himself, *Aristotle, De Anima*, p. 11: 'a single use of the word in a work of Aristotle is of no significance for our present purpose, since it may be a late addition'. H. E. Runner, *Development Illustrated*, who speaks of five later additions in *Physics* I, leaves this passage out of consideration.

[8] O. Longo, *De Caelo*, p. 371. L. Elders, *Aristotle's Cosmology*, pp. 167, 169, 171 considers I, c.12 'not very early', because 'it shows a considerable development of doctrine and there are parallels with ... *Phys.* VIII, c.8, and *Metaph.* IX, c.4. On p. 68 he therefore places this chapter in phase III. The references to *Physics* VIII, c.4 in 311a11 (thus St.; G.; Tr.; Lo.; Mo.), which cannot be taken out of the context, and the use of the broad *metabole*-concept (see Chapter Five F, below) argue for a late date for IV, c.3, which represents Aristotle's own revised theory concerning the properties light and heavy.

development in Aristotle's thought, and that it is not yet present in the original composition of *De Caelo*.[9] The circles described by the heavenly bodies are credited to the motion inherent in these bodies with so much emphasis in *De Caelo*, that it seems impossible that Aristotle should simultaneously already have developed an explication of that motion by means of an ὄρεξις localized in the astral souls and directed towards a transcendent cause of motion. Passages that nevertheless appear to be written on the basis of this latter view were held to be later additions.

It is significant that these 'later additions' as a matter of fact occur in places outside of I, c.1-3 & III.[10] Most authors assign an early date to *De Caelo* I-III taken together, and it seems that this is certainly defensible for the sections that are the object of this study. On the other hand, those who consider I, c.4-II, c.14 to be of a piece with the rest on the grounds of a 'basic impression' should, to complete their case, prove that these sections cannot be located in a later phase of Aristotle's development. Further, it would be necessary to explain how it is that the multiple references to recognizably later works got into the text. It seems to me that the explanation is simpler if I, c.4-II, c.14 is lifted out and independently investigated as to its chronological data. Would the assignment of an early date still be supported by a sufficient number of convincing arguments if this were done?

2. W. D. Ross believes that the theory of the unmoved mover might be indicated in *De Caelo* I, c.9, 279a20.[11] In II, c.6, 288a34-b7 the

---

[9] Cf. F. Solmsen, *Aristotle's System*, p. 100 (note 23): 'the basic impression which the *De Caelo* conveys is that the physical bodies ... move themselves and do not depend on an outside agency to actualize their motion.' P. Gohlke, *Prinzipienlehre*, p. 71; L. Elders, *Aristotle's Cosmology*, p. 89; A. J. Festugière, *Le Dieu cosmique*, p. 245; H. J. Easterling, 'Homocentric Spheres', p. 153. On the other hand, E. Berti, *La Filosofia*, p. 388, holds that *De Caelo* I, 268b11-270a12 certainly does not imply that the notion of the astral element is autonomous, independent: 'Quando infatti Aristotele afferma che all'etere appartiene per natura il moto circolare, intende attribuire alla natura dell' etere non la produzione del moto, ma la circolarita di esso.' Berti, it seems to me, is driven to this forced interpretation because he holds that the *De Philosophia* already contains the theory of the unmoved mover, and because he placed the dialogue before the *De Caelo*.

[10] See our Chapter One, B and C.

[11] *Metaphysics*, I, p. cxxxiv. H. J. Easterling, 'Homocentric Spheres', p. 150, views this *locus* as 'an almost insoluble problem, though I myself do not believe that it contains definite evidence of the unmoved mover.'

occurrence of the theory cannot be denied (cf. W. K. C. Guthrie *On the Heavens* p. xxiii; H. Von Arnim, *op.cit.* 1931, pp. 20-21; P. Moraux, *a.l.*; L. Elders, *op.cit.*, 1966, p. 211; H. J. Easterling, art. 1961, p. 149, note 5). Determination of the exact length of the inserted section, if indeed one must speak of an insertion, is far from easy.

In II, c.12, 292b4 also, the train of thought can be plausibly explained only with the aid of the theory of the unmoved mover (cf. W. K. C. Guthrie, *On the Heavens*, p. 208 note a; H. J. Easterling, art. 1961, pp. 151-152). In addition one could mention I,c.8, 277b9-12; II, c.6, 288b22-30, and IV, c.3, 311a9-12 (cf. H. J. Easterling, p. 150).

D. THE DISCUSSION IS STILL LIMITED TO THE PRESOCRATICS AND PLATO

1. The fact that in the sections of *De Caelo* under consideration Aristotle, to arrive at his own conception, confronts himself exclusively with the views of the leading Presocratics and Plato may not pass unnoticed. Xenocrates and Speusippus, against whom Aristotle's later attacks are mainly directed, are not yet criticized except insofar as they share those views of Plato with which Aristotle is in disagreement.[12]

Critique of Plato is largely aimed at the *Timaeus*. The derivation of physical bodies from triangles in that work is repeatedly object of a spirited Aristotelian attack. The whole of book III may give the impression that the *Timaeus* was fairly recent and still loomed large in the discussion of the school.

2. In *De Caelo* I, c.4-II, c.14, however, I, c.10, 279b32 ff. contains an Aristotelian attack aimed at an exegesis of the *Timaeus* constituting an attempt to defend Plato against the argument that Plato called the world both 'become' and 'eternal', that is to say, it is a defence against a criticism on the part of Aristotle expressed in *De Philosophia*

---

[12] Thus the refutation of a derivation of the physical *soma* from higher principles in I, c.1 is primarily aimed at Plato, but also holds for some of his pupils. Similarly, the critique on Plato's planes-theory in III, c.1 is perhaps also aimed at Speusippus, who drew the consequences of this theory and defended derivation from points. Cf. P. Moraux, *Aristote Du Ciel*, p. cxxxv. It is not certain, however, to what extent Speusippus and Xenocrates had already published their views at the time Aristotle completed his study 'On the Elements'. H. Cherniss, *Aristotle's Criticism*, pp. 142-144, holds that III, c.5, 304a9-18 is also directed at Xenocrates.

and *De Caelo* I, c.1-3. In agreement with Simplicius, *in De Caelo* 303, 33 (Heib.) it is generally accepted that this defense of Plato's views comes from Xenocrates.[13] Taken by itself, this circumstance is no immediate indication in favour of a late date, but if my hypothesis of two layers within *De Caelo* is correct, then P. Moraux' remark,[14] i.e. that already within a few years of Plato's death the meaning of the *Timaeus* was apparently a source of debate, looses its foundation. Discussion with Xenocrates was probably most intense during the years 339 to 323 BC., when he was scholarch of the Academy. II, c.4, 286b27-32 also does not appear to attack Plato's *Timaeus*,[15] but rather a specific interpretation of Plato's cosmology.

E. *DE PHILOSOPHIA* IS NOT CITED

1. For the sake of completeness it should be mentioned that *De Caelo* I, 1-3 & III contains no quotations from the *De Philosophia*, nor references to that work presupposing its existence. In chapter IV, E, section 3 it was shown that there is reason to think that *De Philosophia* ought to be dated later than *De Caelo* I, c.1-3 & III.

2. *De Caelo* I, c.4-II, c.14 contains, according to many scholars, extensive sections derived from the dialogue.[16] I do believe that this opinion may be correct, but it seems to me that these citations indicate a relatively long distance in time rather than simultaneity.

---

[13] Thus Guthrie, *On the Heavens*, p. 98; L. Elders, *Aristotle's Cosmology*, p. 154; O. Longo, *De Caelo*, p. 312. The text is fr. 54 in R. Heinze, *Xenocrates*. H. Cherniss, *Aristotle's Criticism*, p. 88, considers this to be indeed a defense against criticism by Aristotle.
[14] *Aristote Du Ciel*, p. lxxviii.
[15] Cf. L. Elders, *Aristotle's Cosmology*, p. 198.
[16] Thus R. Walzer, *Dialogorum Fragmenta*, and M. Untersteiner, *Della Filosofia*, understand *De Caelo* I, c.9, 279a17-b3 as fragment 28 (38 respectively) of the *De Philosophia*. Cf. Jaeger, *Aristotle*, p. 301. See also P. Moraux, *Aristote Du Ciel*, p. lxxv (note 1); J. Bernays, *Die Dialoge*, pp. 110 ff.; F. Blass, 'Aristotelisches', pp. 497 ff. In addition, Walzer and Untersteiner take *De Caelo* II, c.1 as a whole to be fragment 29 (23 respectively). Cf. W. Jaeger, *Aristotle*, pp. 303 ff.; P. Moraux, *Aristote Du Ciel*, p. lxxxvi (note 3). In 'Aristotelisches' Blass also indicated the following places that might stem from the *De Philosophia*: II, c.4, 287b14-21; I, c.5, 271b1-16; c.10, 279b4-17 (cf. W. Jaeger, *Aristotle*, p. 303); II, c.12, 291b24-292a22; II, c.5, 287b28-288a2.

1. In chapter Four, B it was noted that motion already represented one of the most important pillars of Aristotle's philosophizing in the early work *De Caelo* I, c.1-3 & III. It is well-known that this concept, in correlation with μεταβολή, continued to play a part throughout Aristotle's life. Von Arnim and Guthrie have already shown how even alterations in his theology are closely related to his teaching regarding motion. With respect to the two concepts *kinesis* and *metabole*, therefore, I should like to add a few observations.

Toward the end of the previous century a discussion ensued between P. Tannery and G. Rodier,[17] occasioned by a thesis advanced by Tannery to the effect that a chronological differentiation between book III & IV and V & VI of the *Physics* could be established on the basis of terminological differences. In *Physics* V, c.1,2 *metabole* means, according to Tannery, 'la notion la plus générale du changement'. Later, in *Physics* III, c.1,2, Aristotle supposedly uses *kinesis* instead, and *metabole* is occasionally used as synonym. There is, on this view, a broadening of the *kinesis*-concept from *Physics* V (species of *metabole*) to *Physics* III (synonymous with *metabole*). G. Rodier has thoroughly criticized this viewpoint. W. D. Ross is equally disinclined to accept Tannery's argument.[18]

This discussion led me to investigate these terms in *De Caelo* as well. In I, c.2, 268b17 φορά is used to refer to 'local *kinesis*'. I, c.3, 270a27 mentions ἀλλοίωσις referring to 'qualitative *kinesis*'. It seems that this latter passage together with III, c.8, 306b20-22 implies that *metabole* is used for change of quality only and hence has a *more limited* meaning than *kinesis*. The same holds for *Categoriae* c.1-9, of which c.8 is absolutely necessary for the interpretation of the terms ἕξις and διάθεσις in *De Caelo* 1, c.3.[19] It appears that there also *metabole* is used only for qualitative change and is virtually synonymous with ἀλλοίωσις.[20] With respect to *Physics* I, which most

---

[17] Tannery, 'La Physique', and G. Rodier, 'La Physique'.
[18] *Physics*, pp. 7-8. Cf. also F. Solmsen, *Aristotle's System*, p. 178 (note 20). J. Zürcher, *Aristoteles*, p. 162, is virtually alone in his support of P. Tannery.
[19] 8b27 ff.; b37.
[20] *Categories*, c.5 and 8 often have μεταβάλλω and μεταβολή. The examples given by Aristotle, however, all remain within the category of quality. It is noteworthy that the *Post-praedicamenta* (c.10-15) make repeated mention of μεταβολὴ κατὰ τόπον (15a13; 17; b3; 5; 11) in addition to μεταβολὴ κατὰ ποιόν. Usually this section is separated from the preceding chapters. Cf. H. P. Cook, *The Categories*, p. 80 (note a).

likely preceded *De Caelo* I, c.1-3 & III, the same conclusion obtains.[21]

These texts, in spite of their limited number, lend support to the conclusion that Aristotle here still uses *kinesis* as the more comprehensive concept, and that φορά, αὔξησις and ἀλλοίωσις, μεταβολή are species of it. With this Aristotle follows his teacher: when Plato admitted motion into his philosophy and paid increasing attention to it, Aristotle's mentor had also conceived of this concept in a comprehensive sense.[22] In *Theaetetus* 181c ff. and *Parmenides* 138b8 it includes local motion and change. Later even growth is conceived of as being a species of *kinesis*, for instance, in the extensive compilation in *Laws* X.[23]

Over against the *limited* concept of *metabole* in *De Caelo* I, c.1-3 & III, *Categoriae* c.1-9 and *Physics* I (i.e. as species of *kinesis*), the later parts of Aristotle's works display a far *broader* meaning: there it encompasses not only φορά, αὔξησις, and ἀλλοίωσις, but also γένεσις and φθορά.[24] An attempt will have to be made to arrive at some insight into this difference of approach. Two remarks to that end. First in the early phase *metabole* was, to be sure, a species of *kinesis*, but at the same time the most important species by reason of the fact that it alone stood for the mutual interchange of the elements as ultimate components of reality.[25] Further, Aristotle probably preferred to

---

[21] *Physics* I, c.3, 186a15-16. C.8, 191b33 is not included in view of the misgivings regarding b27-29 on the part of P. Gohlke, *Prinzipienlehre*, p.7, and H. E. Runner, *Development Illustrated*, part II, chapter 1.

[22] Cf. F. Solmsen, *Aristotle's System*, pp. 25 ff., 30 ff.

[23] 893b-894c; cf. F. Solmsen, *Aristotle's System*, p. 34.

[24] For example in *Physics* V and VI; cf. F. Solmsen, *Aristotle's System* pp. 178-179. Significant support for my view on this point is found in G. R. Morrow, 'Qualitative Change', pp. 160-161, who compares *Physics* I, 190b5-9 and *Physics* V: 'It is tempting to think that here [in *Physics* I] we have Aristotle's earlier view, before he had confined himself within the straitjacket of the classification later expounded in *Physics* V, and when he could still look upon all change alike in accordance with the principles he develops in *Physics* I, as a change of properties in a discernible underlying substratum.' In *Physics* V and VI the broad *metabole*-concept indeed dominates. The mere frequency of its occurrence indicates this. A remarkable exception is book VI, c.1-3 – could this be an older writing against the Eleatics included in the larger whole?

[25] Cf. *De Caelo* III, c.8; *Physics* I, c.7, 190b8: τὰ δὲ ἀλλοιώσει(γίγνεται) οἷον τὰ τρεπόμενα κατὰ τὴν ὕλην. *De Caelo* III, c.7, 305b28; 306a5; c.8, 306b21; cf. E. Frank, *Plato und die sogenannte Pythagoreer*, p. 39.

refer to the change from potential to actual being which he discovered in every area of reality, with the term *metabole* with its biological connotation, rather than '*kinesis*' in which the idea of local motion remains dominant.

It is conceivable that both factors play a role in the development in which '*metabole*' gradually takes on a good deal of the significance Aristotle's philosophy formerly accorded to *kinesis*.

2. While this broader meaning of *metabole* is not found in *De Caelo* I, c.1-3 & III, it does occur in I, c.8.[26] There emphasis is very clearly on the beginning and termination-point[27] of every process in connection with the δυνάμει – ἐντελεχείᾳ-scheme, which is expanded to embrace all categories of reality. Precisely this starting-point and termination-point are more clearly expressed in '*metabole*' than they are in '*kinesis*'. The broader use of the concept *metabole* further occurs in I, c.10, 280a24-26 (cf. Guthrie, p. 100); a13; II, c.8, 289b3; 290a12; c.14, 298a1; IV, c.2, 309b26; c.3, 310a22, 24,27; b20; 25; 27.

G. ARISTOTLE'S TEACHING ON THE MOTION OF THE STARS

The first chapter made clear, I trust, that Aristotle's view as to the motion of the heavenly bodies causes a number of problems. I believe that here too, an incision between I, c.1-3 & III and the remainder of *De Caelo* can lead to an appreciable simplification.

Chapters 1 and 2 of Book I, in which Nature is called the principle of motion and where the astro-kinetic theory defended is opposed to Plato's, do not allow for the conclusion, I think, that the motion of the stars depends on a *psyche*. Circular motion is inherent in the first *soma*, in much the same way that earthly bodies possess their own immanent motion.

One does, however, find the idea of ensouled heavenly bodies in *De Caelo* II, c.2, 285a29; c.12, 292a18-21 and 292b1-2. In those places the soul is indeed understood as principle of motion. It is very

---

[26] 277a12 ff.; cf. IV, c.3, 310a20 ff.
[27] 277a14: ἔκ τινος εἴς τι; cf. Aristotle's careful attention for this aspect in his explanation of the word *metabole* in *Physics* V, c.1, 225a1-2.

tempting to consider this latter view to be 'more Platonic' and closer to Plato's *Phaedrus* 245c5-246a2.[28]

Somewhat wider study of the context in II, c.2 and II, c.12 however makes abundantly clear that here Aristotle follows his teacher merely in terminology. During the years that separate *De Caelo* II from the *Phaedrus* the 'soul as principle of motion' received a widely different and more comprehensive content. The psychology here defended proves to rest on *De Anima* and *De Incessu Animalium* (the latter is cited in II, c.2, 284b13). The concept 'principle of motion' is taken as 'principle of *metabole*', which here also includes growth and change. Hence Aristotle is able in both the *De Anima* and *De Caelo* II, c.2 and 12 to ascribe to plants and animals a soul as principle of motion. As to content this has nothing to do with the above-mentioned passage of Plato's *Phaedrus*.

For purposes of clarification the development may be schematized as follows:

1. Plato's *Phaedrus* 245c-246a – *psyche* is ἀρχὴ κινήσεως

2. Aristotle's *De Caelo* I, c.1-3 & III – *physis* is ἀρχὴ κινήσεως

3. *De Caelo* I, c.4-II, c.14 and *De Anima* – *psyche* is ἀρχὴ κινήσεως in the sense of ἀρχὴ μεταβολῆς

In this regard the early phase of Aristotle may be called 'more Platonic' than the second, since here he still reduces all motion to *self-motion*.[29] Later self-motion, as motion of a κινοῦν κινούμενον (an ἔμψυχον!), occupies a mean between the κινοῦν ἀκίνητον and the κινούμενον. Actually the very fact that it is possible to advance arguments to defend the 'Platonic' character of these two theories –

---

[28] Thus L. Elders, *Aristotle's Cosmology*, pp. 68 (schema), 189, 234-235. This author also relates the principle πᾶν τὸ κινούμενον ὑπό τινος κινεῖται (II, c.6, 288a27) to the *Phaedrus*-passage, notwithstanding the evident shift of meaning in 288a30-b7: here the origin of motion is no longer a self-mover as it is in Plato, but an *unmoved* mover. Cf. H. Von Arnim, *Gotteslehre*, p. 28, who looks upon the dogma πᾶν τὸ κινούμενον ὑπό τινος κινεῖται precisely as the decisive breach with Aristotle's early period, 'denn erst durch ihn wuchs Aristoteles über die hylozoistische, pneumatische Theologie nach Art der Stoa hinaus und wurde ein tiefsinniger spekulativer Theologe.'

[29] W. K. C. Guthrie has correctly strongly emphasized this point ('Aristotle's Theology', p. 162; *On the Heavens*, p. xx).

both diverging from the actual Platonic viewpoint – indicates how dangerous and meaningless such characterizations are.[30]

The teaching that the first heaven and the stars possess souls must belong to the latest phase of Aristotle's development; conclusive evidence is the fact that the doctrine of the unmoved mover (the last phase in Aristotle's theory of motion) implies this ensoulment. The unmoved mover does not cause the universe and everything in it to move in the manner that one body causes another's motion, but rather does so in a supra-physical way, i.e. as object of *eros*![31] But if the first heaven is to be influenced in this way it must, as must the stars, belong to the highest category of ensouled beings.[32] In the period in which Aristotle had not yet developed the theory of the immaterial prime mover, there was no need for a distinct immaterial heavenly soul. The description of the fifth element in I, c.2-3 justifies the conclusion that such a conception is indeed absent. In the view there expounded a soul would be utterly meaningless since it could not be the cause of the motion of the first *soma*.

Since it can be demonstrated that in Aristotle's latest phase the ensoulment of the heavenly sphere and the stars form a necessary part of his system, any attempt to harmonize texts that presuppose such ensoulment with *De Caelo* I, c.1-3 on the basis of their supposed Platonic character, seems quite wrong to me. It would unnecessarily imply inconsistency on the part of Aristotle with respect to a central issue. The fact that W. K. C. Guthrie (Introduction, pp. xxxiv-xxxv)

---

[30] In the case of F. Solmsen, *Aristotle's System*, p. 248, for instance, where *Physics* VIII is still called 'Platonic', the adjective seems to have lost its function of critical distinction. But when the aim is to indicate comparable tendencies in Plato's theories, resemblance with the later Aristotle is more readily defended than with works of his early period: cf. G. E. L. Owen, 'The Platonism of Aristotle', p. 146: 'it is tempting to say that in his metaphysics Aristotle has come back to Platonism rather than moved from it.' But "Platonism", to be sure, is a slippery term', p. 150.

[31] *Metaphysics* Λ, c.7, 1072b3: ὡς ἐρώμενον. Cf. W. D. Ross, *Metaphysics*, p. cxxxv and P. Moraux, *Aristote Du Ciel*, p. xlii: '...ailleurs, par exemple dans la *Métaphysique*, où il présente le premier moteur comme le suprême objet du désir et de l'amour, Aristote pourrait difficilement prêter ce désir et cet amour à des êtres qui ne seraient que de simples masses de matière.'

[32] Cf. *De Caelo* II, c.2, 284b10-20; II, c.8, 290a32. Compare also Theophrast, *Metaphysics* c.2, 5a28-b1. Theophrast significantly rejects the unmoved mover and returns to the principle of the irreducibility of physical motion; cf. E. Grumach, *Physis und Agathon*, pp. 53-58.

97

considers himself forced to do this is simply to be charged to his attempt to explain *De Caelo* I-III in terms of *one* unified whole. Unfortunately F. Solmsen, who does recognize the difficulties occasioned by telescoping the two conceptions together, nevertheless rejects the hypothesis of a chronological distinction (*Aristotle's System*, pp. 233-234). It seems extremely difficult to determine at which point the revision of Aristotle's ideas began; in all probability the theory of the unmoved mover, the ensoulment of the heavenly sphere and astral bodies, and the broader *metabole*-concept belong closely together, and all play a role in Aristotle's later cosmology. A precise determination of the manner in which these doctrines are related can be accomplished only on the basis of an analysis of the antinomies within Aristotle's earliest conception.

H. DETERMINATION OF *DE CAELO* I, c.1-3 & III CONTINUED

1. The Early Date of its Cosmology

There is, then, reason to think that *De Caelo* I, c.1-3 & III represents a very early piece. Distinguishing these parts from the remainder of *De Caelo* I-III relieves one of the necessity to assume that the whole of *Physics* I-VI is already presupposed in (the whole of) *De Caelo*.[33] Aristotle views reality as made up of five elements, and the *soma* plays an especially important role in his conception. Further, it was noted that the theory of natural motion and of the first element is meant to refute and replace Plato's theory of a world-soul. This fact, together with the data derived from the fragments of *De Philosophia*, in which the fifth element is introduced as the substance of the stars *and* of the human soul (cf. chapter Six, D), leads to the conclusion that the theory of the fifth element cannot be made to harmonize with a Platonic soul-theory, although it still does betray its influence.

---

[33] As, for instance, H. Von Arnim, *Gotteslehre*, p. 8; F. Solmsen, *Aristotle's System*, p. 302 (note 47). This seems quite improbable in the case of *Physics* III and IV (H. E. Runner, *Development Illustrated*, suggested the following order: *Physics* VII, I, II, V & VI, III & IV, VIII); but *Physics* V, c.6 is inconceivable without the theory of *De Caelo* I, c.2 and III, c.2 as well. If the *Physics* is largely placed before the *De Caelo* the possibility of gradual elaboration of Aristotle's philosophical conception is virtually excluded.

2. The Philosophical View of *De Caelo* I, c.1-3 & III

A difference of conception, based solely on fragment 21b(R) of the *De Philosophia*, has incorrectly been assumed to exist between *De Caelo* and *De Philosophia*.[34] Much rather, the two works complement each other insofar as they make clear that Aristotle's philosophy comprised an independent early phase with a physicalistic character. There has been a suspicion of the existence of such a phase on the part of several scholars, and at times it was even clearly indicated, but on account of emotional reasons or the vast difference compared with Aristotle's late psychology it has been explained away as much as possible[35]; distortions were the inevitable result. In a brilliant study however, J. Pépin, after an extensive investigation of all the material somehow related to the *De Philosophia*, concludes that most interpretational difficulties will be resolved if it be accepted that in the dialogue, 'le ciel et l'intelligence' are, within the macrocosm, understood as 'l'envers et l'endroit d'une même étoffe divine',[36] and that on the level of the microcosm the soul was said to consist of a fifth element.[37] I am of the opinion that a psychology on the part of the early Aristotle should be accepted without hesitation, in which a special *soma* is conceived of as bearer of the psychical functions. Only those *composita* which possess this element are worthy of the qualification ἔμψυχον in this phase, that is to say, this term can be used only to denote the universe as a whole and man himself.[38] It is impossible

---

[34] Cf. Chapter Four, D, par. 8; E, par. 3 above, and Six, D, below. I would return to the interpretation of this passage which used to be given before the idea of an evolution within Aristotle's thought became current. Thus G. F. Schoemann, in his commentary on Cicero's *De Natura Deorum* II, 16, 44: '... die Kreisbewegung ist dem von ihn sogenannten πρῶτον στοιχεῖον ... von Natur eigen; und aus diesem πρῶτον στοιχεῖον besteht der Himmel und die Gestirne, deren Bewegung in sofern auch *eine natürliche*, dabei aber doch eine *freigewählte* ist.' Cf. R. Hirzel, 'Entelechie', p. 197 and F. Blass, 'Aristotelisches', p. 504. It seems to me that with respect to this point the idea of development has been misleading.

[35] Among others by A. Mansion in his Préface to F. Nuyens, *L'évolution*, pp. xii-xiii; G. Verbeke, 'Comment Aristote', pp. 206-207; *id.*, 'L'évolution', p. 350; P. Moraux, *Aristote Du Ciel*, p. lvi; E. Berti, *La Filosofia*, pp. 394, 396, 400, 556.

[36] *Théologie Cosmique*, p. 220; cf. also his 'Interprétation', pp. 474-487.

[37] *Op. cit.*, pp. 242-243.

[38] The fragments of the *De Philosophia*, I believe, warrant the conclusion that Aristotle did not ascribe the fifth element to plants and animals. Cf. W. D. Ross, *Parva Naturalia*, p. 5: 'In the dialogues, when Aristotle speaks of soul, he is clearly thinking of the human soul.' In his later phase plants and animals do possess a *psyche* (*De Anima*) and the *emphyton pneuma*.

that this fifth element by itself or the astral world separately was called 'ensouled'.

The strongest objection to such a phase within the development of Aristotle's thought, i.e. the consideration that, after the refined Platonic psychology, a 'coarse materialism' in the sense of the Ionian philosophy of nature is no longer possible, rests upon no more than emotional argument and neglects the historical development within the Peripatos and the Stoa. Furthermore, one can hardly speak of 'coarse' materialism: Plato's study of the psychical certainly has left its traces in Aristotle's theory of the fifth element, on account of which it is sharply distinguished from the other four.[39] This very development is the reason why Aristotle cannot emulate the unity of, for instance, the conception of Anaximenes and Diogenes of Apollonia. He can only partially agree with their views, i.e. with those on the area of genesis.

In this early phase the soul is an independent substance; the psychology of the *De Anima*, in which the soul is held to be the entelechy of the body, is as yet nowhere foreshadowed. Once the close relationship with *Physics* I is established, c.2, 185a24 of that work – the *psyche* is referred to as 'substance' parallel to 'man' and 'horse' – will serve as additional proof for this thesis.[40] There is reason to identify this phase with the first of the developmental phases in the theory of the soul found by Nuyens, although his platonizing interpretation will require revision.[41]

3. A Correction to the View of W. Jaeger

It is quite useful to trace the differences of this conception relative

---

[39] Hence it is quite possible in connection with the fifth element to speak of 'une matière à la limite de l'immatérialité', 'une matière presque immatérielle', P. Moraux, *Aristote Du Ciel*, p. lviii (this author makes use of these expressions when describing the theory of the later Peripatetics Critolaus and Diodorus, and rejects a 'psychologie hylozoiste' in Aristotle, *op. cit.*, p. lvi); cf. also his 'Quinta Essentia', cols. 1173, 1249. A comparison with Descartes is interesting: in a discussion with Hobbes Descartes uses 'des matières métaphysiques' for the thinking substance, though in sharp distinction from the matter of 'les corps'; cf. A. Bridoux, *Descartes, Oeuvres et Lettres*, Paris: Pléiade ed., 1952, p. 402.
[40] Cf. F. Nuyens, *Ontwikkelingsmomenten*, p. 107.
[41] In his Preface A. Mansion already made mention of Nuyens' insufficient attention to the *De Philosophia* and to the 'materialistic' tendencies in it pointed out by J. Moreau, *L'Ame du Monde*; cf. also G. Verbeke, 'L'évolution', p. 350.

to the *De Anima*, *Physics* VIII and *Metaphysics* Λ. The reaction against *and* the influence of Plato (still strong) point to Aristotle's first Athenian period. But these differences with the later 'Aristotelian' philosophy and the Platonic influences may not lead to the assumption of *identical* views on the part of Plato and Aristotle.[42] On this score W. Jaeger has missed the mark. After he has sharply indicated the difference between the early and the later Aristotle, the first man to do so, he has incorrectly pictured the Aristotle of the dialogues as a faithful disciple of Plato (*Aristotle*, p. 12 ff.). *Aristotle's development was not: gradual attainment of an independent conception, but rather: evolution from a rough conception of his own, with markedly Platonic characteristics, to another, detailed system in his period as scholarch.*

I believe that a middle position must be taken between Jaeger's view and that of his great adversary, I. Düring who, in many articles, has rejected any Platonic phase, and who himself views Aristotle's work as the result of increasingly clear exposition of his own initial insights; *a position between these opposed views in this sense, that the Platonic phase is rejected, but that an evolution in Aristotle's philosophical views remains accepted.*

J. THE ORIGINAL TITLE OF *DE CAELO* I, c.1-3 & III

1. The Opening Lines of I, c.1

In spite of the intensive attention experts have paid to the opening lines of *De Caelo* I (especially in relation to 298a27-b6 of the first prologue of book III) it may be that not all data these lines offer have been utilized. In his study of the lists of titles of Aristotle's works P. Moraux has emphasized that, lacking a title in the modern sense of the word, the Greeks were wont to refer to a work by its first sentence (or a paraphrase of it).[43] Accordingly, Greek authors often intended programmatic significance with the first words of a book. Now, this work announces itself in the opening lines of book I as aimed at 'knowledge of Nature'. Usually interpreters are satisfied to remark that from this it is once more evident that the subsequent

---

[42] Cf. I. Düring, 'Nature and Reality' p. 38.
[43] *Les listes*, p. 7. Moraux refers to E. Nachmanson, 'Der Griechische Buchtitel; Enige Beobachtungen', pp. 37, 50. For examples in the *Corpus Aristotelicum* see P. Moraux, *Les listes* pp. 56, 66, 238.

four books of Περὶ οὐρανοῦ (a title not used anywhere in the *Corpus*[44]) form part of the physical *'pragmateia'*,[45] the composition of which is analyzed in the first chapter of the *Meteorologica*. The eighteen books of the *Physica*, the *De Caelo*, the *De Generatione et Corruptione*, and the *Meteorologica* are then placed, as a cohering unit, over against other groupings of the *Corpus*.

If however, great parts of *De Caelo*, including also its first chapters, are believed to be early, then, in order to make sense of this opening, one must needs resort to that panacea for every difficulty in the *Corpus Aristotelicum*, i.e. a 'publisher' for the works not published by Aristotle himself, such that the former is credited with the bulk of the introductory and transitional sentences. On principle it would be preferable to find a solution in which the 'publisher' (often simply a projection of the helplessness of the writer who appeals to him[46]) can be dispensed with.

2. The Subject-matter of *De Caelo* I, c.1-3 & III as a Whole

Perhaps one could also approach the issue as follows: *De Caelo* I, c.1-3 & III speaks, as appears from 298b6-8, 'On the elements', about the first element in I, c.1-3, and on the others in book III. Before a definition of the concept 'element' is given in III, c.3, 302a15, and prior to the exposition of the theory as a whole, Aristotle also frequently speaks of 'simple bodies' (I, c.2, 268b27 and *passim*). Knowledge of these primary entities enables one to know all bodies (III, c.3, 302a11-17). Now, I, c.1, 268a1 starts with the thesis that knowledge of *Physis* for the most part[47] deals with bodies and that which pertains to them, but that this does not constitute the whole of its field of investigation. This science should also concern itself with the principia (ἀρχαί) that hold for these bodies.

[44] Cf. H. Bonitz, *Index*, col. 102b30.
[45] Cf. among other places *De Caelo* IV, c. 1, 308a1. O. Longo, *De Caelo* p. xxxi.
[46] L. Elders appeals to this mysterious figure altogether too frequently, as if he were a personal acquaintance. Cf. A. Mansion, 'La Genèse', p. 462 on the weakness of this. Gohlke, *Aristoteles*, p. 17, who studies the entire *Corpus* 'im Vertrauen, in jeder Zeile der überlieferten Schriften echte Zeugnisse aristote-lischen Geistes vor mir zu haben' (cf. *Prinzipienlehre*, pp. 1, 53), and who understands contradictions exclusively as the result of later rewriting or cor-rection by Aristotle himself, seems to me to maintain too extreme a view-point as well, although methodically it is far more fruitful than that of Elders.
[47] ἡ πλείστη must be understood as opposed to ἔτι δὲ περὶ τὰς ἀρχάς (a3). The subordination of lines a3-6 ἔτι δὲ ... εἰσίν could perhaps be expressed by brackets.

3. Similarity with *Physics* I, c.1

This calls to mind the beginning of *Physics* I – knowledge, according to that introduction, aims at the 'principles', the 'causes' and the 'elements' of the field of investigation, beyond which inquiry cannot go. 'Knowledge of Nature' should concern itself with the same three kinds of entities, and accordingly Aristotle begins in *Physics* I with a treatment of the 'first principles'. This seems to offer an acceptable basis for the hypothesis that Aristotle, when he began to write *Physics* I, planned to produce a work entitled Περὶ φύσεως, containing the following parts:

a. Περὶ ἀρχῶν,
b. Περὶ αἰτίων,
c. Περὶ στοιχείων.

This hypothesis is corroborated when the passages in the *Corpus* in which references to τὰ περὶ φύσεως occur, are inspected.[48] According to these the work treats of 'causes',[49] of the mutual metabolism of the *somata*,[50] according to *Metaphysics* M, c.9, 1086a21 it deals with 'first principles, first causes, and the elements', and according to *Metaphysics* A, c.5, 986b30 it contains references to the doctrine of Parmenides (located by W. D. Ross in *Physics* I, c.3). These references are found in works that must, I think, be dated later than the original *'De Natura'*; it furthermore appears from *Metaphysics* A, that also the book now known as *Physics* II was included in τὰ περὶ φύσεως. Its doctrine of the four causes I take to be a later development in Aristotle's thought. Nevertheless, it looks as if the original architecture of *'De Natura'* is maintained, even after Aristotle revised and expanded the work, and it seems that the same topics are still treated and considered the most important subjects of physical inquiry.

4. A Work *'De Natura'* in Three Parts

Book I of the *Physics* announces itself as dealing 'Concerning Principles'. It is very well possible that *De Caelo* I, c.1-3 & III, which I abstracted, constituted a work 'On the Elements'. Hence my hypo-

---

[48] Cf. H. Bonitz, *Index*, col. 102a53 ff.
[49] *Metaphysics* A, c.3, 983a33; c.4, 985a12; c.7, 988a22; cf. the commentary by W. D. Ross.
[50] *Metaphysics* A, c.8, 989a24.

thesis: the core of Aristotle's philosophy during the period that he was still a member of the Academy, could have been worked out in a writing entitled Περὶ φύσεως, divided into three books, subtitled, Περὶ ἀρχῶν, Περὶ αἰτίων, and Περὶ στοιχείων, and to be found in revised form in *Physics* I, *Physics* II, and *De Caelo* I, c.1-3 & III respectively. Stringent proof for this hypothesis will be quite difficult to find. Views as to the value of the bibliographical information handed down to us in their relation to the various parts of the *Corpus* differ rather widely. But the following considerations deserve mention: in his *Vita* Diogenes Laertius presents a list of titles which, according to P. Moraux,[51] dates back to Ariston of Ceos, head of the Peripatos around 200 BC., and according to I. Düring[52] hails from Hermippus. Item number 90 is the title Περὶ φύσεως α'β'γ'. W. D. Ross, *Aristotle*, p. 11, suggested that *Physics* I-IV was denoted by this title. A. Mansion[53] and P. Moraux[54] considered this work limited to *Physics* II-IV. It seems to me that my suggestion, which harmonizes with the opening lines of both *Physics* I and *De Caelo* I is at least equally viable: in that case Περὶ φύσεως would offer a *complete* cosmology. It would then follow the Greek philosophical tradition in which many works were entitled Περὶ φύσεως. Further, it would indeed have consisted of three books and not of four, as in Ross' identification.

Regarding the various parts of the work: it is generally accepted that *Physics* I is denoted by the title *Peri Archon*,[55] and that it formed a separate whole.[56] It has already been shown that *Physics* I is presupposed in *De Caelo* I, c.1-3. According to H. Bonitz, *Index*, τὰ περὶ τὰς ἀρχάς in *De Caelo* I, c.6, 274a21 refers to the 'physicorum pars prior', and according to many others[57] *Physics* III, c.4-8 is meant. This need not count as an objection if my hypothesis that *De Caelo* I, c.4-II, c.14 is a later part is correct. If that be the case it would rather

---

[51] *Les listes*, p. 312.

[52] 'Ariston or Hermippus'.

[53] *Introduction* (1946²), p. 45 (note 19).

[54] *Les listes*, p. 104; cf. P. Gohlke, *Prinzipienlehre*, p. 112; 'Entstehungsgeschichte', p. 292.

[55] A. Mansion, *Introduction*, p. 16. P. Gohlke, 'Entstehungsgeschichte' p. 292. I. Düring, *Aristoteles*, p. 189. Perhaps *Vita Menagiana* refers to this work under no. 21 as περὶ ἀρχῶν ἢ φύσεως α'. Cf. P. Moraux, *Les listes*, p. 105 (note 5). I. Düring, *Biographical Tradition*, p. 83.

[56] Cf. A. Mansion, *loc. cit.*

[57] Cf. W. K. C. Guthrie, J. Tricot, O. Longo, and L. Elders *ad locum*. See also A. Mansion, *Introduction*, p. 50 (note 28).

suggest that Aristotle, when he later worked out his views on time, place, and the void, has introduced these into the original scheme of his *physis*-study, under the heading 'principia', even if this meant that now that word received a more comprehensive meaning than was the case formerly.

In a different part of Diogenes' list, item number 39 mentions a Περὶ στοιχείων α'β'γ'. Concerning the content of this work too, opinions differ. P. Moraux, *op.cit.* p. 81. considers two views: the one assigns this title to *De Generatione et Corruptione* I & II and *Meteorologica* IV, other authors think in terms of *De Caelo* III & IV. Moraux himself holds it to be most likely, considering its place in the list, that somatic στοιχεῖα are not meant here, but three books of the *Topics*. P. Gohlke[58] thought that *De Caelo* I-III and *De Generatione et Corruptione* II are meant.

With respect to this very uncertain issue the following might be worthy of consideration: if an original Περὶ ἀρχῶν of one book did exist (*Physics* I), to which *Physics* III & IV were added later, and if there is reason to think that *De Caelo* I, c.1-3 & III comprised a unified Περὶ στοιχείων of one book, then it is in principle possible that *De Generatione et Corruptione* I & II quite obviously meant to be an improved and expanded version of *De Caelo III*, was later, together with *De Caelo* III, referred to by the same title. It must be considered impossible, however, that *De Caelo* III together with *De Gen. et Corr.* I & II were originally written by Aristotle as a single, coherent treatment of the elements, as P. Gohlke suggests. This would leave the most important *soma* out of consideration![59] At any rate, the difference between *De Caelo* III and *De Gen. et Corr.* is far too great for this.

Identification of *Physics* II with Περὶ αἰτίων causes no great difficulties. I am convinced, however, that *Physics* II in its present form does not belong between *Physics* I and *De Caelo* I, c.1-3 & III (cf. chapter Six, B). The following considerations are relevant: if my hypothesis of an original Aristotelian work entitled Περὶ φύσεως and containing the three parts mentioned, representing his earliest

---

[58] 'Entstehungsgeschichte', p. 292. A. Mansion, *Introduction* 1946², p. 45 (note 19) mentions *De Caelo* III-IV and *De Generatione et Corruptione* II, c.1-8.

[59] This argument also applies to O. Longo, *De Caelo*, p. xxxiv, who holds that *De Caelo* III *only* constitutes the 'De Elementis': cf. also P. Moraux, 'Recherches' p. 182. O. Gigon, *Vom Himmel*, p. 31, correctly considers the original aim of *De Caelo* to be the description of the five elements.

cosmology, is correct, then the very location of those parts in the *Corpus* would justify the conclusion that they have been revised. To be sure, *Physics* I remained located at the beginning of the physical writings, but Runner[60] was able to indicate five later additions. Further, it seems that in *Physics* III & IV, which can also be referred to as 'περὶ τὰς ἀρχάς' it has been expanded.

This study of *De Caelo* has, I think, presented a number of reasons to view *De Caelo* I, c.4-II, c.14 & IV as being a much later expansion and correction of I, c.1-3 & III. In addition it may be noted that it became an independent part of natural science, while investigations concerning motion (*Physics* V-VIII) lodged themselves between *De Causis* and *De Elementis*. It will hardly be surprising then, if it must be concluded that the original *De Causis* is to be found back in *Physics* II, only in a significantly revised form. H. E. Runner, *op.cit.*, pp. 108-125, espies also in this book five interpolations, and, following A. Mansion,[61] considers the whole of c.4-6 to be a later additon as well.

This last point encourages me to return to a thought already put forward in chapter Four, C above. If *Physics* II is indeed a later revision of a more original περὶ αἰτίων, would this not render it possible that the original work *De Causis* was a study treating the *three* causes, i.e. *Physis*, *Techne*, and *Tuche*,[62] the middle book of three, flanked by a book on the three principia and a book concerning the three elements, together meant to treat *Physis* in its entirety? If so, the conclusion would be that O. Longo, who views *De Caelo* as the 'nucleo originario' of Aristotle's physics,[63] turns out to be right to a degree. *Part of De Caelo, I suspect, together with a part of the present Physics in an earlier form, constituted the original Aristotelian cosmology.* The development of the *Physics*, then, must very definitely be seen as a process of growth. It may be compared to the thirty-seven books of Epicurus' *Physics*. These too, according to. E. Bignone, were not composed as one unit, but are the result of repeated preoccupation with the problems of physical reality. Epicurus also, if the views of Bignone

---

[60] *Development Illustrated*, pp. 87-108.

[61] *Introduction*1946², pp. viii, 292, 310.

[62] A side-benefit of this hypothesis is that *hyle* would have been treated in a study on the principles, and not again in a study of the causes (as in the present *Physics* I and II).

[63] *De Caelo*, p. xxxi (note 3).

106

40	41	42	43	44	45	46	47	48	49	50	51	52	53	54	55	56	57	58	59	60	61	62	63	64

Name: ....

Address: ....

Country: ....

Will you please indicate in which subjects you are interested, by placing a cross in the appropriate square? We shall then keep you informed of our latest publications in those fields.

40 ☐ Social History
41 ☐ Classical Studies
42 ☐ History
43 ☐ Ancient Philosophy
44 ☐ Mediaeval Philosophy
45 ☐ Modern Philosophy
46 ☐ Anthropology
47 ☐ Social Sciences/Sociology
48 ☐ Psychology
49 ☐ Economics
50 ☐ History of religion
51 ☐ Christianity
52 ☐ Judaism

53 ☐ English Language and Literature
54 ☐ German Language and Literature
55 ☐ Classical Languages
56 ☐ French Language and Literature
57 ☐ Dutch Language and Literature
58 ☐ Medicine General
59 ☐ Anatomy, Embryology and Histology
60 ☐ Internal Medicine
61 ☐ Neurology and Psychiatry
62 ☐ Ophthalmology
63 ☐ Biology and Botany
64 ☐ Natural Sciences
☐ ....

In which book did you find this card?

....

How was your attention drawn to this book?

By means of:

Review in: ....

Bookshop: ....

Radio/T.V. programme of: ....

Prospectus: ....

Advertisement in: ....

....

ROYAL VANGORCUM LTD.

P.O. BOX 43

ASSEN

NETHERLANDS

VANGORCUM ASSEN/AMSTERDAM

NETHERLANDS

are correct, has in the course of his philosophic activity profoundly revised his insights in this area.[64]

Whenever, therefore, authors from the period prior to Andronicus make use of or quote Aristotle's *Physics* or Περὶ φύσεως, one should ask whether perhaps reference is made to the old tri-partite writing.[65]

---

[64] 'La dottrina' pp. 163, 167 (nt. 16) ff.
[65] When Epicurus, for example, in the περὶ τῶν ἐπιτηδευμάτων ἐπιστολή makes mention of the τὰ περὶ φύσεως of Aristotle; cf. W. Crönert, *Kolotes und Menedemos*, p. 174.

CHAPTER SIX

THE RELATION OF SOME WORKS OF ARISTOTLE
TO *DE CAELO* I, c.1-3 & III

Up till now I referred to other parts of the *Corpus Aristotelicum* only insofar as they aided interpretation of *De Caelo*. It may be helpful to gather these occasional comments relative to a small group of writings and possibly add some points in the context of a discussion of each of these works. This pertains to *Physics* I and II, and to the lost works *Protrepticus* and *De Philosophia*. Remarks concerning these parts of the *opera* of Aristotle, however, will be guided by the discussions of the previous chapters. Focus is on those aspects that may be important in the clarification of the relation of these works to *DeCaelo* I, c.1-3 & III.

A. DE PRINCIPIIS (*PHYSICS* I)

The general consensus is that *Physics* I represents a very early writing. Of the eight books comprising the *Physics* only book VII is considered earlier by some authors (following Jaeger),[1] but this view has met with strong protest,[2] and as yet the issue cannot be said to have been resolved. Book I announces itself as the first part of a study *Peri*

---

[1] W. Jaeger, *Aristotle*, pp. 297 ff.; A. Mansion, 'La Genèse', p. 424; W. D. Ross, *Physics*, pp. 8 ff.; H. E. Runner, *Development Illustrated*, pp. 64-66.

[2] Thus H. Cherniss rejected Jaeger's view that *Physics* VII still subscribed to the doctrine of Ideas in a very critical review of Jaeger's *Aristotle* (*American Journal of Philology* 1935 (56), p. 269). According to H. E. Runner, *Development illustrated*, p. 66, Jaeger's argument is untenable, though he agrees with the conclusion that VII is the oldest book of the *Physics*. I. Düring, *Aristoteles*, p. 291, accepts Jaeger's date, but rejects any presence of the doctrine of Ideas in *Physics* VII. H. Von Arnim stressed the opening sentence of the book and, on its basis, emphasized its connection with the late book VIII. Hence he considered *Physics* VII to be later than I-VI, *De Generatione et Corruptione*, and *Meteorologica*. W. K. C. Guthrie, *On the Heavens*, p. xvii, agrees with Von Arnim. A renewed study of this problem is demanded by F. Solmsen, 'Platonic Influences', p. 233 (note 3); the references noted by Ross, *Physics*, p. 8, in version α, 242b41 (= version β, 242b7) and 247b13, and in version β, 242a6 will have to be taken into consideration as well.

Physeos and, as usual in Greek cosmological writings,[3] this first part treats the 'principia'.[4]

1. The References

The references occurring in this book certainly cannot be taken to indicate that the works referred to were written prior to *Physics* I, but rather argue in favour of the thesis that *Physics* I was subjected to later revision. There are none in the historical review with which Aristotle prefaces his own views (c.1-6). Chapters 7-9 do contain references:

a. After the exposition of his own theory regarding the three principles Aristotle suddenly considers it necessary (c.9, 192a34-b1) to refer to the 'first philosophy' for an 'exact' treatment of the form-principle. W. D. Ross (*Physics*, p. 498) holds that this promise is made good in *Metaphysics* Z and Λ, c.7-9. Both books are very likely quite late. *Metaphysics* Λ contains the last of Aristotle's theological views as recognized by W. K. C. Guthrie. *Metaphysics* Z is part of the unit ZHΘ, the tendency of which, according to W. D. Ross[5] is 'to carry Aristotle away from his earlier doctrine that the sensible individual is "primary substance", to one which identifies primary substance with pure form and with that alone.' The 'earlier doctrine' Ross finds in the *Categoriae*. My view is that the study *De Principiis* is in the spirit of that work.[6]

b. In c.7, 191a19 Aristotle considers his exposition inadequate to determine whether the *eidos* or the *hypokeimenon* should be called *ousia*. But the unprejudiced reader of c.6, 189a27-33[7] will not have any doubts! In the original version of *Physics* I it must have been the *hypokeimenon* which is the basis of all that exists and hence of all knowledge. Hence, 191a19 must be a correction on the part of Aristotle after his transition to the views of *Metaphysics* ZHΘ.

c. In the light of the foregoing the reference in c.8, 191b28 to a more extensive treatment of the concepts *dynamis* and *energeia* is most easily understood as a later addition referring to *Metaphysics*

---

[3] Cf. J. Pépin, *Théologie Cosmique*, pp. 17-18.
[4] *Physics*, I, c.1, 184a10-16; Cf. I. Düring, *Aristoteles*, p. 189.
[5] *Metaphysics* I, p. ci.
[6] Cf. H. E. Runner, *Development Illustrated*, p. 147; P. Gohlke, *Prinzipienlehre*, p. 109.
[7] Cf. c.2, 185a32; c.9, 192a4-6.

Θ as well.[8] In addition to the last sentence of c.2 (*entelecheia*) mentioned above, therefore, it seems preferable to leave the closing parts of chapters 7, 8 and 9 out of consideration;[9] as shown in the case of *De Caelo*, Aristotle often places his additions immediately after the section they are meant to amplify.

2. The Composition

Physics I as a whole displays a closely-knit structure. Chapters 1-6 are completely aimed at the thetical expositions of c.7-9. Just as in the case of the inquiry into the problem of *genesis* of the elements in *De Caelo* III, where Aristotle's own solution is found at the end, in chapter 8, so also the core of his *archai*-theory in *Physics* I is laid down in the last chapter (c.9, 192a25-34). In c. 7-9, after an extensive demonstration of the shortcomings of the *archai*-doctrines of his predecessors, he quite confidently[10] presents his own teaching of the *three archai*, the *hypokeimenon*, the *eidos*, and the *steresis*. Every process of becoming, he is sure, may be explained in terms of these.

3. The Principles Constitute a Triad

In chapter Four, C.3 of this study, I already noted that the number three plays an important role in Aristotle's pattern of thought. *Physics* I, c.9, 192a8-9 shows that in this regard he is in agreement with his teacher and some of the latter's students: they also believed all that has become to be explicable in terms of a triad of principles.[11] But in c.9 he very decidedly rejects their choice and considers far-reaching changes necessary.

[8] Cf. W. D. Ross, *Physics*, p. 496. P. Gohlke, *Prinzipienlehre*, p. 107. Notwithstanding M. Untersteiner, 'Frammenti', p. 7. and *Aristotele, Della Filosofia*, pp. 92-93.

[9] C.7, 190b14-191a22; c.8, 191b27-34; c.9, 192a34-b4. Compare H. E. Runner, *Development Illustrated*, pp. 87 ff., who suspected that the following portions of *Physics* I were subjected to later revision: c.7, 190b10-11; 190b17-23; 191a7-21; c.8, 191b27-29; c.9, 192a31-32. P. Gohlke, *Prinzipienlehre*, pp. 107-110, viewed c.2, 185a8-186a6; c.3, 186b17-31; c.7, 191a19-21; c.8, 191b27-29; c.9, 192a34-b2 as later additions. M. Untersteiner, 'Frammenti', pp. 2-4, considers c.8, 191b19-26; 191b30-34; c.9, 192a34-b4 distinct from the rest of c.8-9.

[10] Cf. ἡμεῖς λέγωμεν c.7, 189b30; φαμέν c.7, 189b31; c.9, 192a3; 17; λέγω c.7, 190a2; c.9, 192a31.

[11] C.4, 187a15; c.5, 189a8; c.6, 189b10-16.

4. Aristotle's Criticism of Plato's Theory of Principles

Closer inspection of the two triads first of all reveals that in *Physics* I only Plato is named as defender of the theory Aristotle rejects (c.4, 187a7), although other members of the Academy may be included in the critique.[12] While Aristotle frequently refers to pre-Platonic thinkers, Speusippus and Xenocrates are not mentioned explicitly. (cf. chapter Five, D, above).

The core of Aristotle's teaching regarding the principles in *Physics* I and simultaneously the central issue in his difference with Plato is the *hypokeimenon* (*hyle*). Here Plato's view, Aristotle believes, is decidedly inadequate.[13] For Plato c.s. *to mega kai to mikron* was, as a *me on*, the absolute opposite of the eidetic principle, *to Hen*.[14] According to Aristotle there is no bridge between the two nor could there be one within the Platonic system. At the very limits of logical analysis Plato had been confronted with two logically contradictory origins and in his attempt to explicate the whole of reality out of these principles he could only become entangled in antinomies. Aristotle shifts the discussion to a different area: the realm of the physical. He introduces the physical *hypokeimenon* and in it he distinguishes a positive and a negative side. In point of fact a real discussion with Plato on this point cannot get started, just as Aristotle himself does not think a discussion with the Eleatics is fruitful, since they work on the basis of different *archai*.[15] Over against the logicistic approach to reality used by Plato in his later years Aristotle seeks the unity of things in the unity of their physical substrate. Thus in c.9, 192a2 he offers a criticism to the effect that Platonists, when speaking of the One, think of an absolute (logical) unity that excludes all complexity or divisibility. Aristotle's universal substrate, on the other hand, is indeed the foundation of all things but may display itself in two distinct aspects.[16] Another very penetrating Aristotelian

---

[12] Cf. c.9, 191b35 ἕτεροι τινές; 36 ὁμολογοῦσιν; 192a1 αὐτοῖς; a6 οἱ δέ; a10 προῆλθον; a11 ποιοῦσιν; a19 τοῖς δέ.

[13] C.9, 191b31: ἡμμένοι... καὶ ἕτεροι τινές εἰσιν αὐτῆς, ἀλλ᾽ οὐχ ἱκανῶς.

[14] C.9, 192a6-8; cf. c.4, 187a18.

[15] C.2, 184b25-185a3. Discussion is possible within the area governed by the principles. Concerning the principles itself it is excluded, on account of the direct connection between the starting-points and the pre-theoretical worldview. On that highest level one can go no further but to point to 'states of affairs'; *Physics* I, c.2, 185a13.

[16] C.7, 190a15-16: εἰ καὶ ἀριθμῷ ἐστιν ἕν, ἀλλ᾽ εἴδει γε οὐχ ἕν.

111

criticism holds that according to the Platonists that which becomes arises out of non-being (c.9, 191b36-192a1) : The One and the *Dyad* of *to mega kai to mikron* serve as principles of all becoming. Aristotle places *to Hen* on a level with his own *eidos*-principle. But he continues by concluding that Plato's dyad must function as both *hypokeimenon* (*hyle*) and *steresis* (i.e. non-being!) at the same time (c.9, 192a6-12), since Plato has failed to distinguish these.[17]

Since, according to Plato, all concrete things in the realm of becoming display a combination of the two principles Aristotle's criticism, i.e. that a combination of contradictory principles must needs lead to the destruction of one of them,[18] is completely legitimate. Viewed from the side of the eidetic principle, *to Hen*, Aristotle was able to posit that *to Hen* has no real reason to come into action, since it does not lack anything.[19] If *to Hen* combines with an opposite principle it is no longer what it was; it therefore relinquishes its own unity in diversity and *eo ipso* looses its own fullness of being. In Aristotle's own words (*De Caelo* I, c.1, 268b3): '*ekbasis* (of *to Hen* from out of itself) is necessarily correlate with a decrease of being' (cf. chapter Four, A, above).

The criticisms aimed at Plato in *Physics* I and *De Caelo* I, c.1-3 & III then, complement each other; in *De Caelo* I, c.1 Aristotle rejects Plato's derivation of the physical *soma* from non-physical entities. Only the *soma* can serve as point of departure and receives the predicate 'complete'. In *Physics* I Aristotle digs deeper still: the physical

---

[17] C.9, 192a12: τὴν γὰρ ἑτέραν παρεῖδεν. The note by W. D. Ross, *Physics*, p. 497: 'The other aspect of the ὑποκειμένη φύσις, viz. privation' seems incorrect. Platonists have concerned themselves rather too much with μὴ ὄν in an absolute sense. Beginning at 192a9 Aristotle for a moment views the principles from the standpoint of the Platonic *Hen* and concludes that the Platonists correctly maintained that a different principle has to serve as substrate for it – ὅτι δεῖ τινὰ ὑποκεῖσθαι φύσιν, but that they accepted only one principle, i.e. the absolute negation of *to Hen* (a10 ταύτην μέντοι μίαν ποιοῦσιν). Over against the *Hen* of the eidetic principle however, *two* principles should have been posited. But Plato failed to see one of these clearly enough (i.e. that which Aristotle calls the *hypokeimenon* and which is only οὐκ ὄν κατὰ συμβεβηκός). (From a quite different point of view, viz. when he opposes *hyle* and *ta enantia*, however, Aristotle is quite able to indicate (in c.4, 187a18) the Great and Small as the *hyle* in Plato's system). W. Charlton, *Aristotle's Physics I, II*, follows Ross. His treatment of 191b36-192a1 (pp. 47; 81) must be rejected.
[18] C.9, 192a19; τοῖς δὲ συμβαίνει τὸ ἐναντίον ὀρέγεσθαι τῆς αὐτοῦ φθορᾶς
[19] C.9, 192a21: διὰ τὸ μὴ εἶναι ἐνδεές.

in its totality must, he thinks, be approached from the physical *hypokeimenon* and not, as Plato tries, from a positive and negative *logical* principle. For this would lead to genesis from non-being (*Physics* I, c.9, 191b36), which is the most fundamental *metabasis eis allo genos*.

5. Becoming, Non-being and the Void

On still another issue *Physics* I and *De Caelo* I, c.1-3 & III are complementary. In *Physics* I, c.9, 191b36 Aristotle attacks the principia theory of Plato c.s. since it implies that they must posit genesis in an absolute sense from non-being. In *De Caelo* III, c.2, 301b31 ff. Aristotle adds another implication: referring to τὰ προειρημένα he explains that genesis in an absolute sense, i.e. without a *hypokeimenon* playing a part, is impossible since it would force one to accept a void. Particularly against the Platonists this is a powerful argument.

6. Does the Conception of *Physics* I allow a Fifth Element?

But if it is once again indicated that *De Caelo* I, c.1-3 & III is in close agreement with the views of *Physics* I, as *De Caelo* I, c.3, 270a17 gives reason to believe, the following question arises: does the principia-theory of *Physics* I leave room for an ungenerated and imperishable element? In this connection it should be noted that *Physics* I deals only with that which is subject to genesis.[20] Hence with respect to *Physics* I the alternative is: either the entire area of visible reality is the realm of becoming or, while Aristotle indeed begins his study of Nature with a doctrine of principles, this is not considered to exhaust *reality in its entirety*. There is, I think, no compelling reason to choose the first possibility.[21] A consequence of the fact that

---

[20] C.7, 189b30; cf. c.5, 188b21-26; c.9, 192a13. In c.7, 191a3 we find αἱ ἀρχαὶ τῶν περὶ γένεσιν φυσικῶν. W. D. Ross, *Physics*, p. 494 explains this as '*ta ourania* being excluded', although he has reservations regarding the text; (cf. also note 9 above).

[21] In spite of H. E. Runner, *Development Illustrated*, p. 86. Runner holds that VII, I, II, V & VI were written before the fifth element was introduced, which results in an unusually late date for *De Philosophia* as well. If W. Jaeger, *Aristotle*, p. 144 (cf. also E. Berti, *La Filosofia*, p. 365, note 173) is right in suggesting that the doctrine of the *Epinomis* contains a weak adaptation of Aristotle's new theory, it would imply certain consequences for the dating of that work as well.

Aristotle, rejecting Plato's intelligible world, brought the contrast of the eternal and the perishable down to within *Physis* is that the *archai* of *Physics* I cannot be the principia for the entire realm of *Physis*, but only for a part of it. The tensions in Plato's thought regarding the relation of the intelligible to the perceptible return in Aristotle in the problems of the relation between the fifth element and the *stoicheia* of the realm of genesis. In spite of the difficulties attendant upon this framework, it is indefensible to say that both parts of this conception mutually excluded each other in Aristotle's eyes. The fifth element cannot do without the world of perishable elements; the world of becoming and passing-away would collapse without the concentration and conservation effected by the heavenly substance.

7. The Terminology of *Physics* I

Some attention should yet be given to the occurrence of three terms in *Physics* I. The concept of *ousia*, except in the passages in c.8,9 indicated in footnote 9, frequently occurs as key-term in Aristotle's thought, and exclusively means 'substance', 'subject of predication'. There is a very strong link with the *Categoriae* regarding the *ousia*-doctrine. This supports my view that in *De Caelo* I, c.1-3 & III *ousia* probably does not yet mean 'essence'.[22] The term *metabole* in c.3, 186a16 is closely related to *alloiosis*.[23] Finally, the concept *morphe* is found in c.9, 192a13 in a passage connected with Plato's *Timaeus* 50b-51b.[24]

8. The Distinct Kinds of Genesis

In *Physics* I Aristotle rejects absolute genesis. The genesis which does take place, on the basis of a substrate, he analyzes into various kinds (c.7, 190b5-9):

1. *metaschematisis*
2. *prosthesis* – in case of growth

---

[22] Cf. Chapter Four, D, par. 5 above. It is likely that the expression *quinta essentia* for the astral element represents Aristotle's original intention less accurately than *quinta substantia* or *quinta natura* do.
[23] C.8, 191b33, on the other hand, contains the much broader meaning indicated in Chapter Five, F, above; cf. 191a7.
[24] W. D. Ross, *Physics*, p. 497. In addition, this concept is found in c.7, 190b20; 191a10,11.

3. *aphaeresis* – for instance, in the case of a statue hewn from a marble block
4. *synthesis* – in building a house
5. *alloiosis* – in cases where a *trope* of the *hyle* occurs.

A sharp distinction must be made between variants 1-4 and 5: in c.4, 188a15 Aristotle explicitly says that in the building of a house out of stones which later, when the house is torn down, reappear in their original state, there is a genesis quite different from, say, the air that originates from water and *vice versa*. It was already noted that in *De Caelo* I, c.3, 270a30-31 even growth is considered a lower form of genesis than *alloiosis*. Hence it can be said that the kinds of change listed under 1-4 occur at the level of complex things. Genesis of elements, however, may not be linked with quantitative differences, but with a qualitative change down to the very core (the *hyle*) only.

9. *Physis* Identical with Truth

Two passages indicate that also in the early *De Principiis* Aristotle did not seek true, dependable knowledge in a world behind or beyond *Physis*, but in *Physis* itself. In c.8, 191a25 the *Physis* of things is identified with truth. This *aletheia* is in c.5, 188b30 personified in the same way as was *Physis* in *De Caelo* I, c.1, 268a19.

B. 'DE CAUSIS' (*PHYSICS* II)

Upon reading *Physics* I in its early form, especially its first chapter, one expects, in a study 'concerning causes', a treatment of the forces that start and sustain the process of genesis, as *Philia* and *Neikos* do in the system of Empedocles, and the earlier pre-Platonists' contrasting qualities, which (in I, c.5, 188b33-35) Aristotle refers to as the αἰτίαι τῆς γενέσεως.

1. Two Theories of Causes

Physics II begins with a section that completely answers to these expectations (192b8-193a28): everything that exists and becomes is divided into two main groups: that which has come to be by virtue of Nature, and that which originated through other causes without direct activity on the part of Nature (192b8,13). An extremely important part of the second category is that which (human) formative activity *(techne)* has realized.[25] This is not to say that *techne* and *physis* are on a par. *Physis* remains primary, and human intervention can take place only within the bounds *Physis* provides for.

Agreement of this section of *Physics* II and the abstracted parts of *Physics* I and *De Caelo* is complete. *Physis* is the force manifested in the *hypokeimenon* and these two together with the *ousia* (here also exclusively meant in the sense of 'substance', 'bearer of properties'[26]), constitute the core of Aristotle's thought. The concept *morphe* plays no part. The discussion of Antiphon's views leads to the belief that Aristotle disqualifies the external appearance, alternately called *'rhuthmos'* (cf. c.1, 193a11), *'diathesis'* or *'eidos'* (as in *Physics* I), on account of its impermanence, and reserves the name for the really real, the *ousia*, only for that which constitutes the durable basis of the process of formation and change.[27] If the question were asked whether within this Aristotelian view still more causes are conceivable on a level with *Physis* and *techne*, the most obvious suggestion is that, next to the intentional formative action on the part of man, another power might exist, in which this intentionality plays no (evident) role; the power always referred to by the Greeks as *Tyche*.[28] In contrast, the four causes Aristotle discusses in *Physics* II c. 3, 7, and ever since understood as *the* Aristotelian *causae*, are definitely not on a level with *physis* and *techne* as explicated in c. 1, 192b8-193a28!

---

[25] C.1, 192b18; 30 χειρόκμητα; 28 τὰ ποιούμενα.
[26] II, c.1, 192b33; 193a10, 16, 20, 25.
[27] C.1, 193a14-20. W. K. C. Guthrie, 'Notes', pp. 70-72, shows very clearly how Aristotle overcomes the 'sophistic argument' of Antiphon with the help of his *morphe*-doctrine (in 193b6-12). We must remember that this does not mean that Aristotle was never tempted by the argument. It seems that Aristotle is close to Antiphon's view in the doctrine of principles of *Physics* I, where the *hypokeimenon*, that which endures and in which reality is anchored, is defended against all transformation of the *eide*.
[28] In a diaeretic scheme:

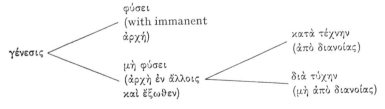

2. The Theory of the Four Causes Does Not Stem From Aristotle's Early Period

To begin with, it should be noted that in chapter 7 this doctrine of the four causes is linked to the theory of an unmoved prime mover.[29] This obliges us to either assign a late date to the whole book or to accept that a revision has taken place such as in the case of *Physics* I and the *De Caelo*. The references to *De Philosophia* and the *Metaphysics* Λ, c.6-10 in c.2, 194a35 point in the same direction. Here too, however, the question is whether bracketing a number of brief passages is sufficient.[30] It is quite possible that other parts of Aristotle's theory are closely connected to the conception of the bracketed passages. The teaching of the four causes, therefore, must be compared with the material that has probably been written early.

One is immediately struck by the sudden introduction of the theory. An introduction, as in *Physics* I, c.1-6 for the theory of the three principles, is not given.[31] I further note that this theory occurs nowhere in the abstracted parts of *Physics* I and *De Caelo* I, c.1-3 & III. This alone is an indication that the generally current early date given to *Physics* II may well require reconsideration. This chronological placement is coupled to that of *Metaphysics* A, which embraces the entire history of philosophy prior to Aristotle in the framework of the doctrine of the four causes for which doctrine it refers to *Physics* II.[32] And this dating of *Metaphysics* A is one of the keys in Jaeger's treatment of Aristotle's philosophical development. He noted the two versions of the criticism of Plato's Idea-doctrine in *Metaphysics* A, c.9 and M, c.4,5, and proceeded to lay special stress on the fact that in those parallel parts of *Metaphysics* M the third person plural is used for the adherents of the doctrine of Ideas, while *Metaphysics* A

---

[29] C.7, 198a27-31 and 198a36-b4. F. Solmsen, *Aristotle's System*, p. 113, therefore points to 198a32 ff. as being a later addition. I. Düring, *Aristoteles*, p. 241, is able to refute this only on the basis of his conviction, 'dasz die Lehre vom Ersten Beweger von Anfang an zur Grundkonzeption des Aristoteles gehört.'

[30] A. Mansion, *Introduction* 1946², pp. viii, 95 (note 5), 292, 310 ff. places c.4-6 separately. H. E. Runner, *Development Illustrated*, pp. 108 ff. agrees and points out additional interpolations: c.2, 194a27-33; 194a35-6; 194b12-15; c.3, 195a12-26; c.7, 198a36-b4; c.8, 199b23-4.

[31] Cf. W. D. Ross, *Physics*, p. 37: 'We do not know how Aristotle arrived at the doctrine of the four causes; where we find the doctrine in him, we find it not argued for but presented as selfevident.' *Metaphysics* I, p. 126. F. Dirlmeier, *Eudemische Ethik*, p. 296.

[32] *Metaphysics* A, c.3, 983a34; c.4, 985a11; c.7, 988a21; c.10, 993a11.

makes use of the pronoun 'we'.[33] From this Jaeger concludes that in *Metaphysics* A, in spite of his criticism, Aristotle still counts himself among the 'Platonists', while in *Metaphysics* M a great distance had come between him and the Academy. On the basis of *Metaphysics* A, c.9, 992a21,22 he believes that Plato has already died. Hence the date of book A can, in his opinion, be determined quite accurately in the years immediately following 347 BC, that is to say, in the same period as *De Caelo* or (more precisely) shortly before *De Philosophia*.[34]

At first sight, Jaeger's argument is attractive and has convinced many authors. A. Mansion (article 1927, p. 441) judges this date 'peut-être ce qu'il y a de plus solide' in the entire work. Other scholars, however, have objected to this point in various ways. In a 1928 review of recent studies P. Gohlke remarks that philological criteria must be subordinated to philosophical ones.[35] Since he judges the doctrine of the four causes to be a later development in Aristotle's thought he suggests that *Metaphysics* A, c.1-2 and 8-9 be dated in the period of Aristotle's stay in Assos, but that c.3-7 be placed in a later phase where, in his view, *Physics* II also belongs.[36] But against this division Jaeger correctly objects that c.8-9 also contains the doctrine of the four causes.[37]

In an extensive review[38] another staunch Jaeger-opponent, H. Von Arnim, remarks that *Metaphysics* A presupposes the first books of the *Physics*; but on the basis of the quotation in *Physics* II, c.2, 194a34 *De Philosophia* would, contrary to Jaeger's suggestion, have been written before *Metaphysics* A.

Too early a date for *Physics* II and *Metaphysics* A leaves insufficient room for a further development in Aristotle's thought. Hence Von Arnim checks the various 'we'-passages in places other than *Metaphysics* A and believes he is justified in concluding that B, c.2, 997b3 and c.6, 1002b14, M, c.10, 1086b16 and N, c.4, 1091a32 need not refer to 'Platonists' exclusively, but that views are meant which

---

[33] *Aristotle*, p. 171; cf. W. D. Ross, *Metaphysics* I, pp. 190-191. In addition to the parallel section (990b9, 11, 16, 19, 23, 991b7) the comparable passages in 992a11, 25, 27, 28, 31; B, 997b3; 1002b14; M, 1086b19; N, 1091a32 stand out.
[34] *Ibid.*, pp. 172, 173; cf. W. D. Ross, *Metaphysics* I, p. 203.
[35] 'Ueberblick', pp. 82-83.
[36] *Loc. cit.*, p. 84.
[37] In *Gnomon* (1928) 4, p. 635; cf. *Metaphysics* A, c.8, 989b22-4; c.9, 992a24-32.
[38] 'Zu Jaeger', pp. 2,6.

Aristotle shared with Plato.[39] To accommodate the places in A, c.9 Von Arnim suggests this solution: c.8 & 9 are added by an editor who derived them from one of the dialogues in which Aristotle repeatedly discussed the doctrine of Ideas. In a dialogue in Platonic *milieu* the use of 'we' would be quite understandable. Von Arnim supposes that the second book of *De Philosophia* was the source.[40] His conclusion is 'dasz wie *Metaphysik* A so überhaupt der ganze uns erhaltene Torso der *Metaphysik*, mit Ausnahme wahrscheinlich des K und des Λ und vielleicht auch des N, erst den athenischen Meisterjahren des Philosophen angehören dürfte.'[41]

Equally critical of Jaeger's results is H. Cherniss in his review of the English edition: 'One of the chief weaknesses of Jaeger's theory lies in the fact that by making the first books of the *Metaphysics* go back to the sojourn in Assos he [Jaeger] is forced to say that the early books of the *Physics* were originally composed in Aristotle's 'Platonic period', that is ... while Aristotle still, according to Jaeger, held to the Ideas.'[42] In Appendix II of his *Aristotle's Criticism of Plato and the Academy* (pp. 488-494) he considers *Metaphysics* A, c.9 to be a résumé of an earlier writing. E. De Stryker believed that this suggestion merited further investigation.[43] At approximately the same time P. Wilpert published his book *Zwei Aristotelische Frühschriften über die Ideenlehre*, in which he concludes, on the basis of an analysis of the data concerning *De Ideis*, that *Metaphysics* A is an extract from that dialogue.[44]

In order to date *Metaphysics* A therefore, new arguments will have to be presented.[45] This means at the same time that it is not

---

[39] *Loc. cit.*, pp. 14-17. For the passage in N, c.4 Von Arnim incorrectly refers to a21 (pp. 16-17); cf. also E. Frank, 'Fundamental Opposition', pp. 180-185; H. Cherniss, *Aristotle's Criticism*, p. 493.

[40] *Loc. cit.*, p. 24. Also F. Blass, 'Aristotelisches', p. 491.

[41] *Loc. cit.*, p. 30.

[42] In *American Journal of Philology* 56 (1935), p. 265.

[43] 'Aristote, critique de Platon', translated reprint p. 198.

[44] *Op. cit.* p. 36. 'Stellung', p. 157; Cf. E. Berti, *La Filosofia*, p. 241.

[45] Cf. Ch. Lefèvre, 'Du Platonisme', p. 247. The fact that *Physics* I and *Metaphysics* A agree remarkably as to arrangement supports the acceptance of a considerable distance in time between the two. Just as Aristotle in *Physics* I treats his predecessors in the framework of his own *archai*-doctrine, so also in *Metaphysics* A he presents a new historical review, but in the wider scope of the theory of the four causes; cf. W. Theiler, 'Entstehung', p. 97. In addition to the argument Jaeger derived from the 'we-passages', there was another motive

certain that the doctrine of the four causes belongs to Aristotle's earliest conception. The question remains legitimate: is it possible that Aristotle had already introduced the four causes as ultimate points of orientation for all scientific inquiry in the phase during which he wrote *De Principiis* and *De Elementis*? I believe that this question must be answered negatively. The change in *Physics* II, c.3,7 compared to the earlier stage of Aristotle's thought is expressed in the distinction between the *causa materialis* and the *causa efficiens*. This division implies a far greater degree of abstraction relative to the matter-principle than Aristotle had reached in *Physics* I. The *prote hyle* of Physics II, c.1, 193a29 differs from the *proton hypokeimenon* in *Physics* I, c.9, 192b31, not only because it lacks any eidetic determination, but also because it does not possess a kinetic qualification. Hence the cause of motion must be sought outside of *hyle* (in the biological form, the *morphe*, or in some other external agent). The biotic is abstracted from its physical substrate and rendered independent in the *morphe*-concept. (The central problem in this view now becomes the ὄρεξις which must be present in *hyle* so that it may be explained how it is that *hyle* can develop itself towards its entelechy!)[46] The teaching of the unmoved mover may be understood as the result of this division between the matter-principle and motion. This

that led him to an early date for *Metaphysics* A, briefly pointed out in Chapter One, A, above. According to him there is a noticeable difference in Aristotle's view of Being and of 'first philosophy' in A-E., c.1 and ZH of the *Metaphysics* (*Aristotle*, pp. 218-219). J. Owens, *Doctrine of Being*, has criticised this thesis in an extensive analysis of the *Metaphysics*, and concluded that 'exactly the same notion of Being and of the Science of Entities is found in ZH as in AE1' (p. 396; cf. pp. 471-473); According to Owens the entire *Metaphysics* was written from the viewpoint that the first philosophy is directed to transcendent being, but is at the same time the most universal science since each mode of being is related to the divine-immaterial being. Owens' refutation of Jaeger's theory of an early Aristotelian *Metaphysics* and Düring's criticism of the view that at one time Aristotle had taken over Plato's transcendent Ideas constitute powerful arguments for thinking that Aristotle's earliest philosophy concentrated περὶ φύσεως, and that the design of a metaphysics is late.

[46] P. Wilpert, *Frühschriften*, p. 132, points out that the doctrine of the four causes has not yet come within the horizon of Aristotle's philosophy in the *Protrepticus* and *Physics* I. H. D. Hantz, *Motivation*, pp. 17, 31-32, 40-41, presents reasons for believing that Aristotle's teaching of the four causes resulted from his biological investigations, which took place especially between 347 and 336 BC.

change is also related to the shift in Aristotle's philosophy from the *hypokeimenon* to the *morphe*-principle.[47]

This transition is clearly demonstrated in II, c.1, 193a28 ff. Although at first sight the text leads one to expect that the preceding and the sequel are concerned with two equal views of *physis* that lend themselves to combination within one and the same conception, F. Solmsen is quite right when he remarks that 'historical analysis reveals that the two concepts are quite different in origin and that Aristotle's procedure is eminently *synthetic*' (italics mine).[48]

If in view of all this the doctrine of the four causes should be understood as a later phase of Aristotle's thought than was reached in *De Principiis* and *De Elementis*, then precisely this discontinuity of the composition of *Physics* II (as compared, for instance, with *Metaphysics* A) may be an argument in favour of an earlier core in *Physics* II from a study *De Causis*.[49] This nucleus must have been formed by an analysis of the concepts *physis*, *techne*, and *tyche*, and particularly those passages in *Physics* II which were repeatedly pointed to as being related to Aristotle's *Protrepticus* and Plato's *Laws* X are linked with this.[50]

3. Self-movement in *Physics* II, c.1, 193a29-b21

If a large part of *Physics* II should stem from a later period than the original core does, the question could be entertained whether c.1, 193a29-b21 perhaps contains a view of self-motion such that it does not occur until on the level of the biotic. With respect to *De Caelo* it was noted that II, c.2, 284b32 must have been written against a background quite different from *De Caelo* I, c.2, 268b16, III, c.2, 301b17, since there the possession of self-motion is ascribed only to

---

[47] Cf. P. Gohlke, *Prinzipienlehre*, p. 43. His view is accepted by M. Wundt, *Untersuchungen*, pp. 44-45; 64-65.

[48] *Aristotle's System*, p. 96; 'Platonic Influences', p. 224.

[49] R. A. Gauthier and J. Y. Jolif, *L'Éthique*, p. 45, note that precisely books V-VII of the *Eth. Nic*, which are a revision of *Eth. Eud.* IV-VI, are extremely disjointed.

[50] C.8, 199a15-20; c.2, 194a21; cf. W. Jaeger, *Aristotle*, p. 74. I. Düring, *Aristoteles*, p. 242 (note 398) suspects that Plato's *Laws* X, 888e ff. was written after *Physics* II, and even believes that it contains an oblique reference to that work of Aristotle in X, 889d; cf. 'Nature and Reality' p. 41 on the relation of *Physics* II and the *Protrepticus*.

all that is 'ensouled' and since the theory of three kinds of soul as found in *De Anima* is presupposed. In this passage of Physics II the 'self-movers' owe their principle of motion and *metabole*[51] to a biotically qualified *morphe*[52] as teleological cause. Motion therefore, is no longer inherent to the *soma* as such, as it was in the early period. Thus it is understandable why Aristotle is especially concerned with matters such as flesh, bone, wood, man, and pays no attention to simple bodies.[53]

C. THE *PROTREPTICUS*

Finally, I should like to devote a few remarks to the fragmentary remains of two important writings, i.e. the *Protrepticus* and the *De Philosophia*. Grateful use is made of the editions of the fragments published during the last decade and of significant studies devoted to the same subject.[54] Once again, I would limit myself to indicating links with the material presented in the preceding chapters.

1. The *Protrepticus* and *De Philosophia* in relation to the *Physics* and *De Caelo*

It was noted that the places in which *De Philosophia* is quoted do not enable us to conclude that the dialogue was written prior to *De Caelo* and the *Physics*, in spite of the current opinion. This pillar of the inquiry into Aristotle's early period cannot be retained.

The chronology of the *Protrepticus* relative to the extant works

---

[51] 193a30. The expansion with the concept *metabole* is significant here.

[52] Since this *morphe* is called *physis* here it may readily be connected with φύομαι (193b17); cf. W. D. Ross, *Physics*, p. 505. In the *physis*-notion of the original 'De Natura' this association does not come to the fore.

[53] F. Nuyens, *Ontwikkelingsmomenten*, p. 111 (note 116) (French ed. p. 122), already noted that lines 193b5-6 provide an argument for a later date for this book. But he thinks that this passage was probably added by someone other than Aristotle (p. 69, note 217). Even if these lines are authentic, Nuyens believes, the dating of book II should not be based on this datum alone. C.1, 192b9-14 does connect motion with simple bodies.

[54] I. Düring, *Reconstruction*. M. Untersteiner, *Della Filosofia*. Cf. E. Berti, *La Filosofia*, pp. 317-409, 453-543; J. Pépin, *Théologie Cosmique*, passim., B. Effe, *Studien*.

mentioned is also far from certain. At best, hypothetical lines of development on the basis of philosophical similarities or differences with other Aristotelian works may lead to statements as to its relation to the *Physics* and *De Caelo*. But the difficulties encountered here are characterized by the fact that, while W. G. Rabinowitz[55] feels justified to say that we possess next to no dependable information on Aristotle's *Protrepticus*, W. D. Ross assigns thirty pages to this work in his edition of the selected fragments.[56]

The general consensus is that Aristotle's dialogues[57] were written before the extant works, and deviations from the views defended in the *Corpus* are ususally understood to be typically early Aristotelian; if possible, Platonizing tendencies are pointed out. But there exists no trustworthy criterion to determine whether the text actually does stem from the early Aristotle, and if so, whether it is uncontaminated. If, however, it be permitted to accept that from the extant physical work a unit of early date can be derived, as I have tried to show, then a number of things would change. In that case the fragments can indeed be verified and checked by comparing them to that early Aristotelian cosmology. For, if a consistent philosophical conception is found, clearly distinguishable from the late-Aristotelian view on the one hand, and from the late-Platonic theory on the other, would it make any sense to suppose that yet a third Aristotelian conception could be found in the dialogues?

2. The *Protrepticus* and *De Philosophia*

As to the chronological sequence of the *Protrepticus* and *De Philosophia*: here there are but few dependable data as well. The *Protrepticus* was usually treated before the dialogue, but as early as 1924 W. Theiler already claimed that the *Protrepticus* displayed a more elab-

---

[55] *Aristotle's Protrepticus I.*
[56] *Aristotelis Fragmenta Selecta*, pp. 26-56.
[57] Including the *Protrepticus* and excluding the *Alexander*. Concerning the question whether the *Protrepticus* was a dialogue or a continuous discourse, cf. I. Düring, *Reconstruction*, pp. 29-32; 'Problems', p. 147. On the basis of a comparison with Augustine, *Contra Academicos* and the fragments of Cicero's *Hortensius*, both of which are meant as 'Exhortation to Philosophy', P. Valentin, 'Un protreptique', pp. 97-117, holds that Aristotle's *Protrepticus* also was partly dialogue and partly *oratio perpetua*.

orate conception.[58] In recent studies I. Düring and E. Berti[59] also assign a later date to the *Protrepticus*.

I am, however, primarily concerned with the philosophical relation of the two works to 'De Natura', and less with a determination of their mutual chronology. Further, there are some links between the *Protrepticus* and the Isocratic school, which imply that it may well have been written toward the end of the fifth decade of the fourth century BC. Third, the only explicit chronological indication we possess regarding *De Philosophia*[60] leads to a date subsequent to 347 BC. In view of all this, I will follow the sequence of the collections of fragments by R. Walzer and W. D. Ross.

3. Are There Traces of the Theory of Ideas in the *Protrepticus*?

Discussion concerning the *Protrepticus* has for a long time turned on the problem whether this work is 'Platonic' or 'non-Platonic' in character. Ever since Jaeger's book of 1923 many scholars have thought that Aristotle here still reveals his adherence to Plato's theory of Ideas. But especially I. Düring has insistently opposed this interpretation of the fragments.[61] According to him they contain absolutely no trace of an Idea-doctrine; rather, they evince the conception found in the writings of the extant *Corpus*. (This does not, however, cause him not to call this view 'Platonic' since, in his opinion, Aristotle remained a 'Platonist' throughout his life.[62])

My inquiry into *De Caelo* led to the conclusion that this work contains no trace of a realm of Ideas in the Platonic sense. Its *physis-*

---

[58] *Naturbetrachtung*, pp. 83-88. On the basis of chapter Four, D, par. 8, I must reject his argument that the *physis*-concept in the *Protrepticus* is closer to the late-Aristotelian view than *De Philosophia* fr. 21b (R). E. Berti, *La Filosofia*, p. 368, also objects.

[59] I. Düring, 'Aristotle and Plato', p. 119; *Reconstruction*, pp. 287-288; *Aristoteles*, p. 400. E. Berti, *La Filosofia*, devotes chapter IV to the *De Philosophia* and chapter VI to the *Protrepticus*.

[60] Fragment 6b (R). The chronological position of the *De Philosophia* may be at greater distance from Aristotle's earliest period if it need no longer be assumed to have been written prior to the *De Caelo* and the *Physics*.

[61] For instance in *Reconstruction*, pp. 184, 205, 212 ff.; cf. E. Berti, *La Filosofia*, pp. 453-463; 528 (note 280).

[62] I. Düring, *Reconstruction*, p. 283. E. Berti, *La Filosofia*, pp. 328, 423, joins Düring in this quest to retain, in spite of fundamental differences, for Aristotle the predicate 'Platonic'.

doctrine constituted an important reason for this conclusion. The *Protrepticus*, therefore, should be checked on the same point.

4. *Physis* in the *Protrepticus*

The view of *Physis* very clearly revealed here agrees completely with that of *De Caelo* I, c.1-3 & III. *Physis* stands for the totality of all that exists. Knowledge of Nature is closely connected with knowledge of the truth.[63] The divine nature of *Physis* may also be noted here.[64] This *Physis* is not the chaotic figure presented in Plato's *Laws* X, but rather a model of rational activity and productivity. The human craftsman with his *techne* can only humbly seek to emulate the great example of meaningful formation on the part of Nature. In virtue of the clear parallel Aristotle notes between the two ways of production he can picture *Physis* as the great demiurge. This view of Nature as rational operative principle is possible only because it is viewed as law-full, ordered, and as possessing its own laws and principles of order.[65]

To be sure, it is worthwhile to trace and refer to the similarities between this *Physis* and the world-soul and demiurge in Plato's dialogues.[66] But one should keep in mind that this relation does not rest on identity of conception, for in that case one could not explain how it is that Aristotle defends a terminologically clearly distinct entity, functioning as ultimate source of meaning in his conception. Why not maintain his teacher's choice of words?[67] Aristotle's criticism is, as was shown, certainly not aimed at insignificant matters, but at issues touching the very heart of the world-view current in the Aca-

---

[63] Cf. I. Düring, *Reconstruction*, B 47 (R: fr. 13); B 44 (R: fr. 12b); B 32 (R: fr. 5b).

[64] *Reconstruction*, B 50 (R: 13); B 18 (R: 11). In his commentary on B 18 Düring remarks: 'I think it safe to say that like certain writers in the *Corpus Hippocraticum* he identifies θεός with the physical processes. To the medical writer and to him the Divine (or God) was nothing supernatural but symbolized the order of nature'; and on p. 222: 'it is noteworthy that φύσις is identified with the divine only in the *De Caelo* and the *Protrepticus*, in two works belonging to the same period.'

[65] Cf. especially fr. 13. Following I. Düring, *Reconstruction*, pp. 44-48, I think that the ὅροι, αὐτὰ τὰ ἀκριβῆ and αὐτὰ τὰ πρῶτα must be understood as immanent laws or values; cf. E. Berti, *La Filosofia*, p. 528, with the references in note 280.

[66] Thus E. Berti, *op. cit.*, pp. 509-510.

[67] Cf. J. Pépin, 'L'interprétation', pp. 447-448.

demy. Aristotle's doctrine of *Physis* also differs importantly from Plato's views regarding the world-soul and the demiurge. The most significant difference is, it seems to me, that in this phase *Physis* is always both subject and object simultaneously, just as for the Stoa τὸ ποιοῦν and τὸ πάσχον constituted two inseparable sides of the one *Physis*. In Plato, on the contrary, the world-soul or the demiurge is exclusively subject, and exclusively object is that which is formed into 'world'.

5. Plato's *Laws* X, 888e ff.

If the views of 'De Natura', as reconstructed from *De Caelo* and *Physics* I, II, in which all emphasis is placed on the physical *soma* and a special *soma* is even posited for the divine stars, are now compared with Plato's last dialogues, it seems reasonable to conclude that Aristotle's explication of reality must have impressed Plato as 'earthly', 'materialistic'. Since the dialogues after the *Parmenides* contain reproaches against the 'materialists', therefore, the question arises whether perhaps the criticism includes Plato's own pupil already as well. This was already pointed out in chapter Four A,5 of this study. In *Laws* X, 888e ff. this thought can hardly be avoided.[68] The conception there attacked hinges on a theory of three causes, *physis*, *tyche*, and *techne*, which is strongly reminiscent of that found in *Protrepticus* fragment 11 (R) and *Physics* II, in which *Physis* occupies the leading place and in which only *somata* and their mutual action and reaction are considered, and not in addition a world-soul or demiurge. In the characterization of the theory criticised, however, Plato's own views of *Physis* intrude, and make it appear as if Plato's opponents saw a close connection between *physis* and *tyche*. To Plato's mind a parallel between *physis* and handcraft is impossible, since for him *physis* is exclusively object. But he does mention that to his opponent the value (and the truth) of the sciences depend on the measure in which they relate their own δυνάμεις to those of *Physis* (889d). There are indeed some texts in the *Corpus Hippocraticum* that point in the direction of such a theory. But in its concrete

---

[68] W. Jaeger, *Aristotle*, p. 74 (note 1). I. Düring, 'Aristotle in the *Protrepticus*', p. 84. In his 'Aristotle and Plato', Düring has correctly pointed out that not only should Platonic influences on Aristotle be traced, but also Aristotelian influence on Plato from the *Parmenides* onward.

form this theory cannot be credited to any pre-Socratic philosopher, even though some take it that Heraclitus, others that Democritus is attacked in this passage. I believe that the analysis of 'De Elementis' lends support to the view that the criticism is aimed at Aristotle. It is important to note that if one read only this fragment 11 of the *Protrepticus* one would certainly not derive a doctrine of causes along the lines of *Physics* II, c.3,7. I. Düring goes too far when he states: 'Aristotle had already developed a doctrine of causation similar to that found in *Physics* II, c.3, even if he had not yet formulated the so-called four causes.'[69] I do think the emphasis already placed on *telos* and its connection with the *agathon* a very important element, which increasingly gains in importance in Aristotle's later philosophy. But there is not a single indication that Aristotle has already divided the *causa materialis* and the *causa efficiens* as rigorously as he would do in *Physics* II, c.3,7.

6. Τὰ πρῶτα

Various remarks in the fragments show that also in the *Protrepticus* Aristotle held that the task of theory is to reach for 'the first things',[70] whether the case be an analysis of physical reality or an inquiry into the relation of different *technai* or their purposes. The Platonic scheme of the genus that differentiates into a number of species, but endows these species with unity and *ousia* and as such has ontological priority, is still very much – be it with corrections – in evidence.[71] This may also be observed in Aristotle's *Categories* and in his book 'De Principiis'. Just as in *Physics* I, c.1, Aristotle defends the view that everything which possesses logical priority is for that reason more knowable,[72] although the distinction 'more knowable for man in his everyday experience' and 'more knowable by nature' is not mentioned. Theoretical knowledge of complex things is considered possible only on the basis of the primary entities.[73] The same view was noted to occur in *De Caelo* III, c.3.

---

[69] 'Aristotle in the *Protrepticus*', p. 84.
[70] Fr. 13 (R) = B 48 (D); fr. 5b (R) = B 35 (D).
[71] Cf. fr. 5b (R) = B33 (D). This fragment was discussed in Chapter Four, A, par. 4; cf. also E. Berti, *La Filosofia*, p. 482.
[72] Fr. 5b (R) = B 33 (D).
[73] Fr. B 36 (D).

7. Knowledge of Nature and Ethics

The *Protrepticus* surveys a broader area than 'De Natura'. Matters such as justice, right action and happiness are discussed, but next to all this there is a good deal of attention to cosmology. Physics and ethics make up the two unbreakably connected parts of philosophical activity.[74] Since *De Caelo* I, c.1-3 & III leads me to conclude that this early period contains no metaphysics it seems that E. Berti[75] shows lack of care when he reads an 'unità di fisica e metafysica' into the *Protrepticus*. This view is acceptable only if 'metaphysics' is used in an extremely loose sense. Fragment 12a (R)[76] evinces a high assessment of the 'cognitio et scientia naturae' also in the area of ethics. It is the basis for happiness and the sole activity of the gods who, unlike man, are not encumbered by 'necessities' such as the concern for food and the like, but whose free choice of will makes them constant 'spectators of Nature'.[77]

Knowledge of nature plays yet another role in the area of human activity: the very important fragment 13(R) says that the norms applied by the politician, by which he is enabled to evaluate every decision in terms of its justice, beauty and usefulness, should be derived from Nature itself. The philosopher is the best counsellor in the design of laws and the determination of action, since he plots his course 'looking toward Nature and the Divine'.[78] There is then, no hint of pre-existent knowledge of the Idea of justice. On this point in his teaching concerning *physis* also, Aristotle moves in directions other than Plato had done. It is clear that for the cognition of nature sensory perception is point of departure,[79] and not the intellectual contemplation of Ideas. The problems concerning perception of universal values and laws in a concrete world of experience are not touched upon in this work; they will be the constant concern of Aristotle's later theory of knowledge.

[74] Fr. B 32 (D); cf. E. De Strycker, 'Fr. 5A'. I. Düring, 'Aristotle in the *Protrepticus*', p. 89; *Reconstruction*, p. 199.

[75] *La Filosofia*, p. 477.

[76] Fr. C 43 : 5 (D). The contrast *necessitas/voluntas* here used seems valuable for understanding *De Philosophia* fr. 21b. Within the human *physis* an area of *Anangke* and one of free will can be distinguished. Similarly, Aristotle held that this contrast exists within the macrocosmic *physis*.

[77] Cf. fr. 12b (R) = B 44 (D); fr. 11 (R) = B 18 (D).

[78] Fr. 13 (R) = B 47 and 49-50 (D); cf. fr. 14 (R) = B 85 (D).

[79] In this connection it is remarkable that Aristotle, according to fr. 24 (R) of the *De Philosophia* ascribed vision and hearing to τὰ οὐράνια.

8. 'Here' and 'Hereafter'

In closing I add a comment concerning fragment 15(R). Regarding the last six lines of this passage I. Düring[80] says: 'an unprejudiced reader of fr. 15 as it now stands in Walzer's or Ross' collection will see immediately that this sentence is an excerpt from another context than the preceding paragraphs. The language is different, and in the first part of the sentence the Greek is bad; what the text says is strange. Neither Plato nor Aristotle can have written anything like this.' I must confess that I fail to see the non-Aristotelian character of this text. As to the unnaturalness of the composition of the elements that make up man: this is supported in fragment 10b (R), where it is compared to the Etrurian custom of tying prisoners to corpses, and in fragment 19b (R) of *De Philosophia*.[81] ἐνταῦθα reminds one of *De Caelo* I, c.2, 269a31 and b16; there a higher mode of being is correlated with a greater distance from 'the things around us' as well. Even a return 'to the place from whence we came' easily fits in the early philosophical views of Aristotle: fragment 27 (R) of *De Philosophia* speaks of the return of the human soul to the realm of the imperishable stars and gods to whom they are related. This return, of course, has the significance of quitting this vale of tears, the world of passing-away, to exchange it for the indestructible world. This highest good for mortals is urgently commended in fragment 6 of the *Eudemus*.[82]

The anthropologies of the *Eudemus*, the *Protrepticus*, and the *De Philosophia* then, contain the very same primary opposition also found in the doctrine of elements of *De Caelo* I, c.1-3 & III.

D. *DE PHILOSOPHIA*

1. The Chronology

In this study I have repeatedly mentioned fragments of the *De Philosophia* and spoken of numerous problems connected with some

---

[80] *Reconstruction*, p. 257. S. Mansion, 'Contemplation', p. 67, also considers it impossible to accept παρὰ φύσιν in this closing section as authentic fragment. C. J. de Vogel, 'Transcendent Ideas', p. 274, on the other hand, finds 'hardly anything unacceptable in this passage.' cf. p. 289.

[81] Cf. also *De Philosophia* fr. 12 a (R): τὴν ἴδιον ἀπολαβοῦσα φύσιν.

[82] Compare ἀπιτέον ἐντεῦθεν of fr. 10c (R) of the *Protrepticus*.

of them.[83] The great similarity with parts of *De Caelo* has been the occasion for many investigators to place the two works closely together; the 'encyclical' writings, cited in *De Caelo* I, c.9, 279a30, usually identified with *De Philosophia*, together with the remarkable characteristics of sections of I, c.9 and II, c.1, which give rise to the belief that they stem from this dialogue – have caused the general conviction to be that *De Philosophia* is chronologically prior.[84]

The same holds for the relation of *De Philosophia* to *Physics* II, the passage c.2, 194a27-36 of which is identified as a fragment of the dialogue by R. Walzer, W. D. Ross and M. Untersteiner. As shown earlier, this argument fails if in *De Caelo* and *Physics* II parts of different date may be distinguished and if it may be considered likely that these references occur in the later parts. My arguments for dating *De Philosophia* later than 'De Natura' may be summarized as follows:

a. If Aristotle, while writing *Physics* I, c.2, 185a2-3 and *De Caelo* III, c.1, 298b20 and 299a1-2, planned to compose a broad study which was to include the *archai*-theories of his predecessors, these passages would be more readily understandable than would be the case if *De Philosophia* had already carried out this program.

b. The fragments reveal that, among other things, three important parts of Aristotle's 'De Natura' were under consideration:

1. his teaching on the principia of *Physics* I,
2. his theory of *Physis* as cause of motion, and
3. his doctrine of the fifth element.[85]

---

[83] Cf. Chapter Four, B, par. 3; D, par. 8; E, par. 3; Five, E.

[84] Cf. J. Moreau, *L'Ame du Monde*, p. 115: 'Le De Caelo, oeuvre relativement peu postérieure au περὶ φιλοσοφίας'. F. Solmsen, *Aristotle's System*, p. 287.

[85] For 1, cf. fr. 6c (R); for 2, cf. fr. 9 (R), 19b (R) and 21b (R); for 3, cf. 21c (R), fr. 27a, d, e (R). E. Berti, however, considers it doubtful that fr. 6c and 9 in fact belong to the *De Philosophia*. But other places, 19b (R) for example, show that in the *De Philosophia* the doctrine of natural motions is presupposed. J. Pépin, 'L'interprétation', pp. 448-452, has, following W. Theiler, *Naturbetrachtung*, pp. 84-85, questioned the presence of this *physis*-doctrine. This leads him to interpret expressions such as κατὰ φύσιν, παρὰ φύσιν and τὴν φυσικὴν τοῦ πυρὸς κίνησιν in fr. 17 and 19b as 'simples façons de parler', which, in view of *De Caelo* I, c.2-3, sounds quite unlikely. Pépin embarks upon this because he holds that his (correct) view that the ether is not only astral element, but at the same time the demiurgic world-soul, is difficult to reconcile with the *physis*-doctrine. It seems to me that here he overlooks the fact that the creative, demiurgic principle need not exclusively be ascribed to the ether, as world-

In view of the fact that in 'De Natura' Aristotle does not hesitate to refer to previously written studies it seems more probable that the first exposition of these theories occurred in 'De Natura' rather than that the dialogue is first.

Apparently Plato himself is introduced in *De Philosophia* as one of the speakers,[86] which could indicate that he was already deceased: in this period of Greek literature it was not customary to let living persons take the part of discussion-partners in a dialogue.[87] It seems that W. Jaeger correctly concludes the same in connection with fragment 6b (R).[88] Not until other reasons establish the contrary should one doubt the interpretation this fragment at first sight forces upon us.[89] Accordingly I assign *De Philosophia* to a place between 'De Natura' and the late works of the *Corpus*. This also means that, in spite of the important agreements noted between this literary work and 'De Natura', the possibility remains that *De Philosophia* already takes a middle-position also philosophically between the two extreme poles of Aristotle's career, and that a number of thoughts of 'De Natura' have already been developed in a direction pointing to his latest views.

soul or world-reason, but may simultaneously apply to *Physis*-as-a-whole, in the same way as the *Protrepticus* ascribes rational action to man as a whole, but especially to the specifically rational part of man. I must remark that as point of departure for my study of the *De Philosophia* I accepted the texts as given by W. D. Ross; in his selection Ross has been very careful: Walzer and Untersteiner publish a larger collection. B. Effe has recently published a clever study. He criticizes the relation to the *De Philosophia* of fragments 6c, 8b, 12b, 13a,b, 19a, 21b, c, 25, 27b and c, selected by Ross, and points out more than fifteen texts of diverse origin as new fragments of the dialogue. His results, rather than giving the impression of offering a basis for a renewed *communis opinio*, more readily lead to scepticism with respect to the possibility of a reconstruction of the dialogue.

[86] M. Untersteiner, *Della Filosofia*, p. xxi; J. Pépin, 'L'interprétation', p. 458.
[87] Cf. E. Berti, *La Filosofia*, p. 412, who quotes V. Rose, *Aristoteles Pseudepigraphus*, Leipzig: 1863, pp. 52-57. B. Effe, *Studien*, pp. 6, 117, accepts a date subsequent to 347 BC.
[88] *Aristotle*, p. 136. With I. Düring, 'Aristotle and Plato', p. 119, I reject Jaeger's argument to the effect that Aristotle did not criticize Plato before the latter's death.
[89] As for instance F. Nuyens, *Ontwikkelingsmomenten*, pp. 95-96, who supposes influence of Hermippus in this fragment. E. Berti, *La Filosofia*, pp. 403-407; J. Pépin, 'L'interprétation', p. 457.

2. Aristotle's Theory of Principles Compared to That of His Predecessors

In the context of an inquiry into the evolution of the concept 'sophia'[90] Aristotle has probably compared his own principia of reality as a whole to those of the most important pre-Socratics and, next, to those of Plato and Parmenides.[91] It is clear, I trust, that I do not believe it possible to maintain that the refutation of Plato in *De Philosophia* concerns only the Ideal Numbers,[92] and not yet the whole of the the background-doctrine. Even though it is true that, strictly speaking, no fragments make explicit mention of Aristotle's critique of the Ideas,[93] this circumstance is no more than the weakest of bases for the thesis that the doctrine of the Ideas was indeed adhered to. One could in the case of *Physics* I defend in the same way that its refutation of the *De Bono*-theory does not exclude Aristotle's possible adherence to views of the *Republic*. At any rate, fragment 11 (R) makes clear that the critique of Plato as in *Physics* I, c.9 and *De Caelo* I, c.1 also played an important part in *De Philosophia*. In addition, it shows that, while Aristotle in these passages only debates Plato's philosophical starting-points insofar as this serves to elucidate his own position, *De Philosophia* II presented an extensive and well-argued refutation of Plato's deduction-theory. Perhaps he was already able to base himself on an older monograph *De Ideis*.[94]

The famous comparison in fragment 13a (R), about men who 'are brought to the light', [95]clearly reveals the anti-metaphysical character of Aristotle's thought in this phase. Here too, there is a striking lack of positive proof for Aristotle's 'Platonism' in the sense of adherence to the Ideas, over against all sorts of indications of the contrary. There is every reason to think that this 'Platonistic period' is doggedly defended[96] because Platonism is generally considered

---

[90] Fr. 8; 6a, c (R).

[91] In view of *De Caelo* III, c.1, 298b14-24 it does not seem impossible that Parmenides and Plato are considered together, on account of their non-physical approach to reality. Hence R. Walzer correctly counts fr. 9 (R) to belong to the second book; cf. fr. 11a. M. Untersteiner, 'Peri Philosophias', p. 349, rejects this division.

[92] Fr. 11 (R). P. Wilpert, 'Stellung', p. 161.

[93] J. Pépin, *Théologie Cosmique*, p. 499; cf. his 'L'interprétation', pp. 453-456.

[94] Cf. E. Berti, *La Filosofia*, p. 340.

[95] Cf. the etymology of 'sophia' in fr. 8b (R).

[96] P. Wilpert, 'Stellung', p. 159. C. J. de Vogel, who agrees with the hypothesis of a Platonic period in the early years, does accept a critical attitude regarding

132

to represent the zenith of Greek philosophy. My analysis of 'De Natura', however, could indicate that this kind of platonistic phase is not likely.

In his 1959 article M. Untersteiner suggested that the criticism aimed at Plato in *Physics* I, c.9 is a restatement from the earlier *De Philosophia*, and in his edition of the fragments he includes almost all of chapters 8-9.[97] None of the eight arguments he advances, however, is decisive.[98] In agreement with E. Berti I would go no further than to note a close relation between 'De Natura' and *De Philosophia*, also in regard to Aristotle's critique of his teacher.

3. The Highest Deity

The third book of the dialogue probably contained important discussions 'on the gods', 'on the eternity of the gods', and, connected with this 'on the divinity of the cosmos'.[99] Every one of

---

Plato's theory of Ideas in the *De Philosophia*: 'Legend', pp. 248-251; *Greek Philosophy II*, p. 30. In her 'Transcendent Ideas' she changes her view in this sense that in the *De Philosophia* only the ideal numbers are criticized; as to content the dialogue is closer to the *Eudemus* than to the later (ca. 347) *Protrepticus*, pp. 290-293. She admits that there exists no proof for the thesis that Aristotle maintained the Idea-theory for 15 years or so, but retains a 'Platonic phase' in this sense that for some time at least, Aristotle did not criticize the doctrine of Ideas, p. 295.

[97] 'Frammenti', pp. 1-23 and *Della Filosofia*, pp. 8-12.

[98] Cf. the criticism by E. Berti, *La Filosofia*, pp. 343, 331.

1. The view that *Metaphysics* A, *Physics* I and *De Philosophia* belong to the same period may be current, but is nevertheless doubtful. Furthermore, simultaneity would be a reason *not* immediately to view relationships between the works as derivations.

2. W. Theiler's view that *Physics* I, c.8, 191b29 must necessarily refer to the *De Philosophia* on account of a parallel with *Eth. Eud.* 1249b16 is difficult to prove by way of this vague indication.

3. To assign *Physics* I, c.9, 192a25-34 to the *De Philosophia* on the basis of Philoponus' commentary on *De Caelo* I, c.9, 279a28-30 (supposedly related to *Metaphysics* Λ, 1072b13-14 and the *De Philosophia*) is too far-fetched. Too many steps in the argument are uncertain.

4. The distinction made by Untersteiner between c.8-9 and c.7 on the basis of terminological differences, is far less clear if one considers *hyle* in c.4, 187a18, 19 and *hypokeimenon* in c.9, 192a31.

5. Regarding Untersteiner's arguments 6, 7 and 8: relationship does not always imply derivation.

[99] a) 'De natura deorum', cf. fr. 14a; b) 'De aeternitate Dei', cf. fr. 16; c) 'De aeternitate mundi', cf. fr. 18, 19, 20.

these is a topic that profoundly influenced later philosophical literature. Treatment of these subjects by the Stoa are clearly influenced by this Aristotelian dialogue. The significance of a correct interpretation of the available fragments, therefore, cannot be questioned. On the other hand, very few pieces of Greek philosophy are as hotly debated. Battle among scholars has not only raged with respect to details such as the term *voluntarius* in fragment 21b (R) and *replicatione quadam* in fragment 26 (R); the very conception of *De Philosophia* is interpreted in so many widely divergent ways that the possibility of one party persuading the others seems excluded. But this does not mean that one should give up the attempt to place *De Philosophia* correctly within the development of Aristotle's thought and Greek philosophy.

The main problem demanding attention first is the question as to how Aristotle here conceived of the highest deity. Once again W. Jaeger is the *auctor quaestionis*: he dated the *De Philosophia* shortly after 347, but placed *Metaphysics* Λ in the same period, and hence was able to say that in the dialogue the same theology was adhered to, i.e. that of an unmoved prime mover.

In chapter One B and C, I mentioned that this dating of *Metaphysics* Λ was quite quickly attacked by A. Mansion, followed by criticisms on the part of W. K. C. Guthrie and H. Von Arnim[100]. These authors ascribed the idea of an immaterial deity who leads cosmic events as *causa finalis* to the latest stage of Aristotle's development. By reason of the fact that they had dated *De Philosophia* early, they considered the theory excluded here.[101] The chronological place of *Metaphysics* Λ remained a bone of contention and various scholars once again place it at the beginning of Aristotle's career, except in some cases for later additions.[102] This made it possible once again that *De Philosophia* be interpreted along the same lines.[103]

The present study of *De Caelo* if its results prove to be depend-

---

[100] Cf. F. Nuyens, *Ontwikkelingsmomenten*, pp. 164-167, who places *Metaphysics* Λ after *De Anima* in view of the psychology adhered to.

[101] Thus also J. Moreau, *L'Ame du Monde*, p. 118; P. Moraux, 'L'évolution', p. 23.

[102] M. Untersteiner, 'Peri Philosophias', pp. 337, 158, 131; I. Düring, *Reconstruction*, p. 287; *Aristoteles*, p. 241 (note 386); E. Berti, *La Filosofia*, p. 73. This view has been criticized again by W. Pötscher, *Strukturprobleme* pp. 71-74.

[103] H. Cherniss, *Aristotle's Criticism*, p. 595; E. Berti, *La Filosofia*, pp. 355-357; M. Untersteiner, *Della Filosofia*, pp. 173-175.

able, can serve as additional argument for the thesis that Aristotle, in a specific, early phase, had not yet developed the theory of the unmoved mover.[104] If so, it seems impossible to maintain that the theory belonged to the lifelong framework of Arisotle's thought.

The great question still is whether *De Philosophia* is closer to the early period or to the later one. The decisive fact seems to me that the Stoa, which used *De Philosophia* copiously, and in so many issues attached itself to the cosmology of the early Aristotle, nowhere reveals any awareness of this late-Aristotelian conception.[105]

How then is the highest deity pictured in this dialogue? Its most important qualifications turn out to be 'demiurge' and '*technites*'.[106] It strikes me as very artificial that E. Berti and M. Untersteiner[107] find reason to hold that this god is demiurge of visible reality *as final cause*! The *techne* of this demiurge, which is the outstanding feature on the basis of which he is compared to an astute general, an experienced helmsman (fr. 12b R), and a talented architect (fr. 13b R), would become a very abstract concept indeed. In that case one would hardly expect the comparison of the cosmos to a ship and its helmsman who safely pilots it into the right harbour, but be more inclined to think of remote control. The metaphors and ter-

---

[104] E. Berti, *op. cit.*, pp. 388, 400, criticizes Von Arnim c.s. with the remark that in *De Caelo* I, c.2-3 only the circular movement belongs 'by nature' to the *proton soma*, but that this does not exclude a transcendent cause of motion. *De Caelo* I, c.2, 268b16 does not seem to support this interpretation; cf. J. Pépin, 'L'interprétation', p. 452.

[105] Cf. J. Pépin, *Théologie Cosmique*, p. 198. W. K. C. Guthrie, *On the Heavens*, p. xx, argues with respect to *De Caelo* that it seems highly unlikely that as central a datum of Aristotle's thought as the unmoved mover could have been kept in the background to the extent that it is in great parts of the work, if the theory had indeed been already developed. The same argument applies to the *De Philosophia*: there too not a single prooftext for a transcendent mover is unambiguous or undebated.

[106] fr. 12b τὸν δημιουργὸν τῆς διακοσμήσεως

    13b ὁ τοῦδε τοῦ παντὸς δημιουργός –

    τὸν θεὸν ... τὸν τεχνίτην.

    19c τὰ τοῦ θεοῦ ,ἅτε τελειοτάτῃ τέχνῃ καὶ ἐπιστήμῃ δημιουργηθέντα –

    τεχνίτης

    13c ὑπό τινος δημιουργοῦ κοσμοποιοῦ

[107] E. Berti, *La Filosofia*, p. 357; M. Untersteiner, *Della Filosofia*, pp. 221, 223 therefore would credit fr. 19c (R) to Plato as discussion-partner; similarly in the case of fr. 13b-d and 27e. Cf. against this J. Pépin, 'L'interprétation', pp. 459-464.

minology actually used give the impression that the deity is conceived in a markedly anthropomorphic way, much closer to Plato's *Timaeus* – which this work is meant to replace – than to the later Aristotle. In this connection may be mentioned that Aristotle named two causes for the awareness of the existence of gods, i.e. the phenomenon of divination and those in the astral world (fr. 12 a R). Apparently the divine is manifested especially in the soul when – while asleep or just before death – it has detached itself from the body and in so doing regains its own nature,[108] and in the astral world, the divine character of which is emphatically expressed in 'De Natura'. The ordered character of the world of the stars would be clear to a Greek who understood the regularity of the planetary orbits. But precisely these astronomical phenomena witness least to the idea that these movements should ultimately be directed towards a higher principle in the sense of Aristotle's unmoved mover. Aristotle only arrives at this later, by way of his investigations in the area of biology, by elevating the teleological directedness there noted to a universally valid principle to which all phenomena, including non-biotic ones, are considered to be subject. The very combination of human soul and astral world as the two areas in which the divine reveals itself most manifestly indicates that also in the *De Philosophia* the divine is directly related to the fifth element which, as will be seen, is the substance of both in *De Philosophia*.

The same passage also leads to the thought that Aristotle, in his picture of the universe, follows the well-known pattern of the parallelism between macrocosm and microcosm. Just as in the *Protrepticus* he expressly pictured the rational part of the soul as the essential and dominating in man as a whole,[109] so also the rational part of

---

[108] Fr. 12a (R) ὅταν ... καθ' αὑτὴν γένηται ἡ ψυχή, τότε τὴν ἴδιον ἀπολαβοῦσα φύσιν. It does not seem correct to me to place the 'positive' approach to the sensible world in the *De Philosophia* over against the 'negative', 'pessimistic' one of the *Eudemus*, as is done by M. Untersteiner, *Della Filosofia*, p. 188, and J. Pépin 'L'interprétation', p. 458. In spite of the value of the *physis* as source of knowledge, both dialogues and the *Protrepticus* show that the soul is not 'at home' here: not until it has been freed from its perishable cloak (*De Philosophia*, fr. 8; 27c and d) will it attain to 'contemplation of Nature' in the manner of the gods.

[109] *Protrepticus*, fr. 6 (R): τὸ λόγον ἔχον is ἀρχικώτερον and ἡγεμονικόν which implies: ἤτοι μόνον ἢ μάλιστα ἡμεῖς ἐσμεν τὸ μόριον τοῦτο. Compare Clemens Alexandrinus, *Protrepticus*, V, 66, 4 éd. C. Mondésert, Paris: 1949² ὁ γε τῆς αἱρέσεως πατήρ ... τὸν καλούμενον 'ὕπατον' ψυχὴν εἶναι τοῦ παντὸς οἴεται· τουτέστιν

136

Physis as a whole, correlative as it is to the fifth element, is the leading, guiding and ordering principle within the macrocosm.

In chapter Five, H it was pointed out that in his study of the relation of Greek and Christian views on the cosmos J. Pépin concludes that 'le ciel et l'intelligence' are to be seen 'comme l'envers et l'endroit d'une même étoffe'![110] According to him the contrast between 'divinités matérielles' and 'divinités spirituelles' in *De Philosophia* disappears if the role of the fifth element, 'qui forme l'étoffe des unes comme des autres' is seen in the proper light (*op. cit.* p. 243). This author is keenly aware of the important consequences this approach implies relative to the evaluation of chapters 1-3 of the first book of *De Caelo* (*loc. cit.* p. 245). The comparisons in fragment 12a and 12b (R), and fragments 17, 13c and 19c (R) lead to the conclusion that according to Aristotle the most important function of the deity was purposeful ordering, '*taxis*'. I recall that in *De Caelo* I, c1-3&III *taxis* seemed inherent in *Physis* as a whole. *Physis* was also encountered as law-*giver* and dispenser of order to reality.[111] The problem hidden in this *physis*-conception was noted, i.e. that which is subject to *taxis* is simultaneously principle of order. The fragments of *De Philosophia* could reveal that Aristotle came to locate the ordering-principle, the νομοθέτης behind the νόμοι, less in *physis* as a whole and more in its rational part. The dialectic tension originally hidden in this *physis*-conception is then pushed back to only the realm of the fifth element. Thus the entire area of the four elements could be understood as object for the deity.[112] This view leaves room for the idea of knowledge concerning the world of perishable things

τοῦ κόσμου τὴν ψυχὴν θεὸν ὑπολαμβάνων αὐτὸς αὐτῷ περιπείρεται. Quoted by L. Alfonsi, 'Traces du jeune Aristote', p. 71. J. Pépin, *Théologie Cosmique*, p. 143 reduces the criticism of this passage by Clemens to an Epicurean example and thus arrives at a connection, via Cicero, *De Natura Deorum* I, 13, 33 with Aristotle's *De Philosophia*. Mondésert's reference to *De Mundo* 397b52 could be confusing.

[110] *Théologie Cosmique*, p. 220; 'L'interprétation', p. 465; *Idées Grecques*, pp. 332, 361-363; cf. J. Moreau, *L'Ame du Monde*, p. 120.

[111] Cf. *De Philosophia*, fr. 13c (R).

[112] Cf. fr. 27e (R): quintum elementum ... illum indicans qui in unum quatuor elementa conjungens mundum fecerit. M. Untersteiner, 'Peri Philosophias', p. 147, must necessarily reject this fragment, since he cannot conceive of a truly demiurgic deity in the *De Philosophia*. Compare, however, also Ps. Justinus, *Cohortatio*, c.5: αὐτοῦ γὰρ Ἀριστοτέλους θεὸν καὶ ὕλην ἀρχὰς τῶν πάντων εἰρηκότος quoted by L. Alfonsi, 'Traces du jeune Aristote', p. 70.

on the part of god (cf. the ἐπιστημονικώτατον in fragment 12a1 (R), and for divine care for this world (fr. 13c). It seems more correct to admit to this possibility in Aristotle's early conception, rather than to credit its every trace to the account of falsifiers of history, as P. Moraux does.[113]

4. The Fifth Element in the Psychology of *De Philosophia*

The problem of the link between the heavenly element and the highest deity in Aristotle's cosmology returns on microcosmic level in his views on the fifth element as basis of the human soul. There are some data with respect to this thought, disappointingly few of them, which nevertheless may not be neglected.

In the psychology of the *De Philosophia* a 'fifth element' did play a part. This is indicated by fragments 27a,b,c, and d (R), concerning which J. Pépin has quite correctly remarked that their strength lies in their lucidity and their weakness in the circumstance that all of them derive from Cicero.[114] To be sure, the fact that a certain datum concerning Aristotle's lost works occurs in only one author has never as such been a reason not to make use of that information, any more than in the case of fragments from other thinkers. But a great many objections have been raised against the content of Cicero's information, which is considered incompatible with the early Aristotelian doctrine. Hence it is indeed regrettable that this side of the dialogue's philosophy did not come to us via additional sources.

Fragment 21c (R) reveals that *De Philosophia* discussed a '*quintum corpus*' described as '*aethereum et quod fertur in circulo*'. The '*quintum*' and '*aethereum*' of this text need not cause one to think of doctrinal differences with *De Caelo* I, c.1-3 & III. The parts of fragment 27 (R) mentioned provides the connection with anthropology. There is talk of a '*quintum genus e quo essent astra mentesque, singulare eorumque quattuor quae supra dixi dissimile*' (fr. 27a R). Elsewhere Cicero speaks of a '*quinta quaedam natura*' of which he says: '*haec et deorum est et animorum*' (fr. 27d R), '*e qua sit mens*' (fr. 27b R) and '*est animus*' (fr. 27e R). It appears in fragment 27b and d that '*quinta*

---

[113] *D'Aristote à Bessarion*, pp. 10, 41 ff. Against his point of view cf. C. J. de Vogel, 'Transcendent Ideas', p. 293.

[114] J. Pépin, *Théologie Cosmique*, p. 229. For the objections brought against the Ciceronian testimonia and a critical analysis of them, see 'L'interprétation', pp. 473-488.

natura' can be replaced by '*quintum genus*'. Aristotle seems to have connected all psychical and logical functions with that substance.[115] Now, the difficulty in discussions concerning *De Philosophia* is: did Aristotle mean one and the same substance in both *De Caelo* I, c.2-3 (*proton soma*) and in the Cicero fragments (*quinta natura*), or did he present here two utterly different theories but in a misleading use of terminological similarity, or are Cicero's data perhaps unreliable? In the course of the years a whole range of solutions has been proposed.

When discussing the problems concerning the highest deity in paragraph 3 above, I noted that one can derive from the continuity of Greek philosophy as a whole an argument for the thesis that we are here confronted with a very refined 'hylozoism'.[116] This holds also for the present problem. *De Philosophia* has greatly influenced the Stoa and this school's views on the ether display great similarity to those of Aristotle interpreted in this way.[117] J. Moreau's study on the World-soul in classical Greek philosophy has been an important break-through in the direction of such an interpretation. His conclusion[118] is that there is every reason to believe 'qu'Aristote professait dans le *De Philosophia* un veritable hylozoisme' and he is not at all inclined to disqualify the testimonies by Cicero as useless through 'stoicizing contamination'.[119] The work of J. Pépin also merits agreement when

---

[115] Fr. 27b (R): cogitare, providere, discere, docere, invenire aliquid, meminisse, amare, odisse, cupere, timere, angi, laetari; 27d: memoria, mens, cogitatio.

[116] Once again I emphasize the difference between this view and 'materialism'. Cf. J. Pépin, *Théologie Cosmique*, p. 246, and his very good exposition in 'L'interprétation', p. 487.

[117] With this important difference, that the Stoa would erase the wide gap between the *proton soma* and the other elements, in favour of the 'sympatheia' which permeates the All; cf. J. Pépin, *Théologie Cosmique*, p. 237 (note 1). For the continuity of early Aristotelian and Stoic philosophy cf. E. Von Ivanka, 'Seelenlehre', p. 223; L. Alfonsi, 'Traces du jeune Aristote', p. 76.

[118] *L'Ame du Monde*, pp. 121 ff. This author describes Aristotle's philosophy of this period as the bridge between Diogenes of Apollonia and the Stoa, p. 143. Cf. L'être et l'essence', p. 195. Further cf. J. Bidez, *Un singulier naufrage*, pp. 33 ff.; L. Alfonsi, 'Traces du jeune Aristote', p. 72; A. J. Festugière, *La Révélation* II pp. 247 ff.

[119] Contamination of the tradition is supposed by P. Moraux, 'L'évolution', p. 34; *Aristote du Ciel*, pp. liii-liv; A. Mansion, in Préface to F. Nuyens, pp. xii ff., and 'L'immortalité' p. 447; W. Theiler, 'Aristoteleszeugnis',p. 131; G. Verbeke, 'Comment Aristote', p. 207, considers the tradition in Cicero 'inconciliable ... avec l'esprit général de la pensée aristotélicienne'. Ch. Lefèvre, 'Quinta Natura', has recently presented a careful and often convincing refutation of the arguments used by these authors.

he claims (pp. 242-5) that more problems are solved if the identity of *proton soma* and soul-substance is accepted than would be the case if one followed S. Mariotti's theory that the *quintum genus* and the *quinta natura* of fragment 27 do not refer to a *soma*, but rather to an a-somatic entity, and that these fragments should preferably be assigned to the *Eudemus*.[120]

It is to be regretted that also W. Pötscher, in his recent work concerning the theology of Aristotle and Theophrastus, is of the opinion that Aristotle, at the time of writing *De Caelo* (and *De Philosophia*) already distinguished between ether and a still higher deity, and proceeds to prove this on the basis of *De Caelo* I, c.9, 279a 8ff.[121]! It is incorrect that an interpretation of Aristotle's early works along the lines of J. Moreau and J. Pépin be brushed aside with the observation that such a 'decline' of psychology after Plato is inconceivable. Much rather, with this theory Aristotle was concerned to solve an overwhelming problem in his master's system, i.e. the issue as to how an a-somatic soul could possibly exert any influence on the *soma*. The fact that his own solution called forth new problems may never be used to prove the thesis that Aristotle cannot possibly have looked in this direction only to shift his course later. And especially if my arguments in favour of dating the *De Philosophia* subsequent to *De Caelo* I, c.1-3 & III are valid, the possibility of assuming a 'more Platonic' conception in the *De Philosophia* than is expressed in the teaching of the *proton soma* is completely excluded.[122]

---

[120] S. Mariotti, 'Quinta Essentia', pp. 179-189; cf. chapter One E, (note 7) above.

[121] W. Pötscher, *Strukturprobleme*, p. 15 (note 2).

[122] The same would hold for the *Eudemus* if fr. 27 of *De Philosophia* ought to be assigned to it, O. Gigon, 'Prolegomena', p. 23. This in view of the fact that fr. 7 of the *Eudemus* seems to presuppose the doctrine of the principles of *Physics* I.

CONCLUSION

In view of the results gained in this study it seems to me that the following themes are of importance for a comprehensive analysis of the development of Aristotle's thought:

1. The development of the concept φύσις to the concept τὸ ὂν ᾗ ὄν.

2. The evolution of the teaching concerning the deity, which was originally conceived of as an immanent, somatically qualified ether-deity with demiurgic characteristics, and in the later phase as unmoved prime mover, not actively involved with the cosmos, whose very thinking is no longer directed to the *Physis*, but to himself.

3. The gradual replacement of the ὑποκείμενον-concept by the idea of the πρώτη ὕλη.

4. The refinement of Aristotle's psychology which, from an early 'hylozoistic' conception in which psychical and logical functions were barely distinguished, led to a theory of an immanent, immaterial *psyche* on the one hand, and a transcendent νοῦς on the other.

BIBLIOGRAPHY

L. Alfonsi, 'Traces du jeune Aristote dans la *Cohortatio ad Gentiles* faussement attribuée à Justin'; *Vigiliae Christianae* 2, (1948), pp. 65-88.

D. J. Allan, *The Philosophy of Aristotle*; Oxford: 1952 (1970²).

Aristotle *Posterior Analytics* by H. Tredennick; *Topica* by E. S. Forster. Loeb Cl. L. London: 1966².

Aristotle's Prior and Posterior Analytics. A revised text with introd. and comm. by W. D. Ross, Oxford: 1949.

Aristotle, *De Anima*, with transl., introd. and notes by R. D. Hicks, Cambridge U.P.: 1907.

Aristotle *De Anima*, edited with introd. and comm. by Sir David Ross; Oxford: 1961.

Aristotelis De Caelo libri quattuor; recogn. brevique adnot. critica instruxit D. J. Allan; Oxford: 1936 (1961³).

Aristotele, *De Caelo*; Introd., testo critico, trad. e note di O. Longo; Firenze: 1962.

Aristotele, *De Caelo*; traduzione di M. Fausta Cini Guerri; Napoli: Ist. editoriale del Mezzogiorno, 1967.

Aristotelis De Caelo et De Generatione et Corruptione; rec. C. Prantl (bibl. Teubn.), Leipzig: 1881.

Aristotle, *The Categories*; *On Interpretation* by H. P. Cook; *Prior Analytics* by H. Tredennick. Loeb. Cl. L., London 1938 (1962⁴).

Aristote, *Traité du Ciel suivi du Traité pseudo-aristotélicien Du Monde.* Trad. et notes par J. Tricot; Paris: 1949.

Aristote, *Du Ciel*; texte établi et trad. par P. Moraux; Paris: 'Les Belles Lettres', 1965.

Aristotle *On Coming-to-be and Passing-away*; a revised Text with Introd. and Comm. by H. H. Joachim; Oxford: 1922.

Aristote, *L'Éthique à Nicomaque*; Introd. trad. et comm. par R. A. Gauthier et J. Y. Jolif; III t. Louvain: 1958-9.

Aristotele, *Della Filosofia*; Introd., testo, traduzione e comm. esegetico a cura di M. Untersteiner; Roma: 1963.

Aristotelis Dialogorum Fragmenta, in usum scholarum selegit R. Walzer; Firenze, 1934 (Hildesheim, 1963²).

Aristotelis Fragmenta Selecta; recogn. brevique adnot. crit. instruxit W. D. Ross, Oxford: 1955 (1964³).

Aristote, *De la Génération et de la Corruption*; texte établi et trad. par Charles Mugler; Paris: 'Les Belles Lettres', 1966.

Aristotle, *On the Heavens*, transl. by W. K. C. Guthrie; Loeb Cl. L. London: 1939 (1960⁴).

Aristoteles' Vier Bücher über das Himmelgebäude und zwei Bücher über Ent-

stehen und Vergehen; Griechisch und Deutsch und mit sacherklärenden Anmerkungen, herausg. von C. Prantl, Leipzig, 1857.:

Aristoteles, *Vom Himmel, von der Seele, von der Dichtkunst*; eingeleitet und neu übertragen von O. Gigon, Zürich: 1950.

Aristote, *Histoire des Animaux*; texte établi et traduit par Pierre Louis; Paris, 'Les Belles Lettres', t. I (livres I-IV), 1964; t. II (livres V-VII), 1968; t. III (livres VIII-X) 1969.

Aristotelis, *De Insomniis et De Divinatione per Somnum*; A new edition of the Greek text with the Latin translations by H. J. Drossaart Lulofs II vols.; Leiden: 1947.

Aristoteles, *Die Lehrschriften* herausgegeben übertragen und in ihrer Entstehung erläutert von Dr. Paul Gohlke. no. 6. *Über den Himmel*; *Vom Werden und Vergehen*; Paderborn: 1958.

Aristotle's Metaphysics, a revised Text with Introd. and Commentary by W. D. Ross, II vols. Oxford: 1924 (1958⁴).

Aristotle, *Meteorologica* with English transl. by H. D. P. Lee; Loeb Cl. L. London: 1962².

Aristotle, *Parva Naturalia*; A revised Text with Introd. and Comm. by Sir David Ross; Oxford: 1955.

Aristotle's Physics: A revised Text with Introd. and Comm. by W. D. Ross; Oxford: 1936 (1960³).

Aristotle's Physics I, II. Transl. with Introd. and Notes by W. Charlton. Oxford: 1970.

Aristoteles *Protrepticus*. Einleitung, Uebersetzung und Komm. von I. Düring (Quellen der Philos. 9). Frankfurt a/M: 1969.

Aristoteles, Werke in deutscher übersetzung, herausgegeben von E. Grumach Bd. 7. *Eudemische Ethik*, übersetzt von F. Dirlmeier; Darmstadt: 1962.

Aristotle, The Works of Aristotle transl. into English under the editorship of of W. D. Ross; Vol. II *Physica* (R. P. Hardie and R. K. Gaye); *De Caelo* (J. L. Stocks); *De Generatione et Corruptione* (H. H. Joachim). Oxford: 1930 (1962⁴).

Aristotle On Dialectic; *The Topics*. Proceedings of the Third Sympos. Aristotelicum edit. by G. E. L. Owen, Oxford: 1968.

Aristoteles in der neueren Forschung; herausgeg. von Paul Moraux (Wege der Forschung, 61), Darmstadt: 1968.

Aristotle and Plato in the Mid-Fourth Century (Papers of the Symp. Aristot. held at Oxford 1957). ed. by I. Düring and G. E. L. Owen; Göteborg: 1960.

Aristote et les Problèmes de Méthode, in Aristote: Traductions et Etudes, collection publiée par l'Institut Supérieur de Philosophie de l'Université de Louvain: 1961.

Naturphilosophie bei Aristoteles und Theophrast. (Verhandl. des 4. Symp. Arist., veranstaltet in Göteborg (1966) Hrsg. von I. Düring, Heidelberg: 1969.

A. H. Armstrong, *The Cambridge History of later Greek and early Medieval Philosophy*; Cambridge: 1967 (1970²).

H. von Arnim, 'Zu W. Jaegers Grundlegung der Entwicklungsgeschichte des Aristoteles'; in *Wiener Studien*, 46, (1928), pp. 1-48.

– 'Die Entstehung der Gotteslehre des Aristoteles'; in *Sitzungsberichte der Akademie der Wissenschaften*, 212Bd 5, Wien, 1931.

143

A. W. Begemann, *Plato's Lysis*; *Onderzoek naar de plaats van den dialoog in het oeuvre*; diss. V.U.; Amsterdam: 1960.

J. Bernays, *Die Dialoge des Aristoteles in ihrem Verhältnis zu seinen übrigen Werken*; Berlin: 1863.

E. Berti, *La Filosofia del primo Aristotele*; Padova; ed. Cedam, 1962.

J. Bidez, *Un singulier naufrage littéraire dans l'Antiquité*; *à la recherche des épaves de l'Aristote perdu*. Bruxelles: 1943.

E. Bignone, *L'Aristotele perduto e la formazione filosofica di Epicuro*; II t. in Collect. 'Il pensiero classico' IV, Firenze, 1936.

– 'La dottrina epicurea del clinamen', in: *Atene e Roma* 8, (1940), pp. 159-198.

G. A. Blair, 'The meaning of 'Energeia' and 'Entelecheia' in Aristotle'; in *Intern. Philosoph. Quarterly* 7, (1967), pp. 101-117.

F. Blass, 'Aristotelisches'; in *Rhein. Museum für Philol.* 30 (1875) pp. 481-505.

H. Bonitz, *Index Aristotelicus*; Ausgabe der Werke des Aristoteles, herausg. von der königlichen preussischen Akad. der Wiss. Bd. V, Berlin: 1870.

C. A. Bos, *Interpretatie Vaderschap en Datering van de Alcibiades Maior*; diss. V.U. Culemborg: 1970.

J. Burnet, *Early Greek Philosophy*; London: 1930[4].

Th. Case, 'Aristotle', in *Encyclopaedia Britannica*, vol. II, p. 501-22; Cambridge, 1910.

H. Cherniss, *Aristotle's Criticism of Plato and the Academy*; Baltimore: 1944.

– *The Riddle of the early Academy*; Baltimore: 1945.

A. H. Chroust, 'The miraculous disappearance and recovery of the Corpus Aristotelicum'; in *Class. et Mediaev.* 23, (1962), pp. 50-67.

– 'The first thirty years of modern Aristotelian scholarship (1912-1942)'; in *Class. et Mediaev.* 24, (1963), pp. 27-57. Revised and reprinted in *Aristoteles in der neueren Forschung*, pp. 95-143.

– *Aristotle, Protrepticus, A Reconstruction*; Notre Dame: 1964.

– 'The probable date of Aristotle's lost Dialogue On Philosophy'; in *Journ. Hist. Philos.* 4, (1966), pp. 284-91.

– 'Eudemus or On the Soul'; in *Mnemosyne*, 19 N.S., (1966), pp. 17-30.

– 'Aristotle leaves the Academy'; in *Greece and Rome*, 14, (1967), pp. 39-43.

– 'The probable date of some of Aristotle's Lost works'; in *Riv. crit. Stor. Filos.* 22 (1967), pp. 3-23.

– 'W. Jaeger and the Reconstruction of Aristotle's lost Works'; in *Symbolae Osloenses*, 42, (1968), pp. 7-43.

G. S. Claghorn, *Aristotle's Criticism of Plato's Timaeus*; The Hague: 1954.

F. M. Cornford, *Plato's Cosmology*; *The Timaeus of Plato, translated with a running comm.* London: 1937 (1956[4]).

W. Crönert, *Kolotes und Menedemos* (Studien zur Paläographie und Papyruskunde VI), Leipzig: 1906.

F. Dirlmeier, 'Aristoteles'; in *Jahrbuch für das Bistum Mainz*, 1950 (Festschrift Dr. Albert Stohr), p. 161-171; reprinted in *Aristoteles in der neueren Forschung*, pp. 144-157.

– *Aristoteles Eudemische Ethik*, Darmstadt: 1962.

144

H. Dooyeweerd, *A New Critique of Theoretical Thought*, IV vols. Amsterdam/ Philadelphia: 1955.

I. Düring, 'Von Aristoteles bis Leibniz'; in *Antike und Abendland*, Bd. 4, pp. 118-154, Hamburg: 1954. Reprinted in *Ar. in der neueren Forschung*, pp. 250-313.

- 'Problems in Aristotle's Protrepticus'; in *Eranos*, 52 (1954), pp. 139-171.
- 'Aristotle in the Protrepticus'; in *Autour d'Aristote*; Louvain: 1955, pp. 81-98.
- 'Aristotle and Plato in de Mid-Fourth century'; in *Eranos*, 54, (1956), pp. 109-120.
- 'Ariston or Hermippus? a Note on the Catalogue of Aristotle's writings, Diog. Laertius, V, 22;' in *Class. et Mediaev.* 17, (1956), pp. 11-21.
- *Aristotle in the ancient biographical tradition*; Acta Univ. Gothoburgensis, vol. 53, no. 2; Göteborg, 1957.
- 'Aristotle on ultimate principles from 'Nature and Reality''; in *Ar. and Pl. in the Mid-Fourth century*, pp. 33-55.
- *Aristotle's Protrepticus, An Attempt at Reconstruction*, Göteborg: 1961.
- 'Aristotle and the Heritage from Plato'; in *Eranos*, 62, (1964), pp. 84-99. Transl. and reprinted in *Ar. in der neueren Forschung*, pp. 232-249.
- 'Did Aristotle ever accept Plato's theory of transcendent Ideas?' in *Archiv. f. Gesch. der Philos.* 48, (1966), pp. 312-316.
- *Aristoteles; Darstellung und Interpretation seines Denken*; Heidelberg, 1966.
- 'Aristotle's Use of Examples in the *Topics*; in *Ar. On Dialectic*, pp. 202-229.

H. J. Easterling, 'Homocentric Spheres in *De Caelo*; in *Phronesis* 6, (1961), pp. 138-153.
- 'Quinta Natura'; in *Museum Helveticum*, 21, (1964), pp. 73-85.

B. Effe, *Studien zur Kosmologie und Theologie der Aristotelischen Schrift 'Ueber die Philosophie'*. (Zetemata 50), München; 1970.

L. Elders, *Aristotle's Theory of the One, a Commentary on book X of the Metaphysics*; Assen, 1961.
- *Aristotle's Cosmology, a Commentary on the De Caelo*; Assen, 1966.
- 'The *Topics* and the Platonic Theory of Principles of Being' in *Aristotle On Dialectic*, pp. 126-137.

A. J. Festugière, La Révélation d'Hermès Trismégiste; t. II, *Le Dieu Cosmique*; Paris, 1949.

E. Frank, *Plato und die sogenannte Pythagoreer*; Halle, 1923.
- 'The fundamental Opposition of Plato and Aristotle'; in *American Journal of Philol.* 61, (1940), pp. 34-53; pp. 166-185.

H. G. Gadamer, 'Der aristotelische Protreptikos und die entwicklungsgeschichtliche Betrachtung der aristotelischen Ethik'; in *Hermes*, 63, (1928), pp. 138-164.

O. Gigon, 'Aristoteles-Studien I'; in *Museum Helveticum* 9, (1952), pp. 111-136.
- 'Prolegomena to an Edition of the Eudemus'; in *Ar. and Pl. in the Mid-Fourth century*, pp. 19-33.
- 'Die Struktur des ersten Buches der aristotelischen Physik (184a10-187b7)'; in *Museum Helveticum*, 23, (1966), pp. 129-54.

145

P. Gohlke, 'Die Entstehungsgeschichte der naturwissenschaftlichen Schriften des Aristoteles'; in *Hermes*, 59, (1924), pp. 274-306.

- 'Überblick über die Literatur zu Aristoteles (bis 1925)'; in *Jahresbericht über die Fortschritte der klassischen Altertumswissenschaft* 54, (1928), pp. 65-110.

- *Aristoteles und sein Werk*; Paderborn, 1952².

- *Die Entstehung der Aristotelischen Prinzipienlehre*; Tübingen, 1954.

E. Grumach, *Physis und Agathon in der Alten Stoa* (Problemata VI), Berlin: 1932.

M. Gueroult, 'Le Xe livre des Lois et la dernière forme de la physique platonicienne'; in *Revue des Et. Grecques*, 37, (1924), pp. 27-78.

W. K. C. Guthrie, 'The Development of Aristotle's Theology'; in *Class. Quart.* 27 (1933), pp. 162-172, 28, (1934), pp. 90-98.

- 'Notes on some Passages in the Second Book of Aristotle's Physics'; in *Class. Quart.* 40, (1946), pp. 70-76.

- 'Aristotle as a historian of philosophy'; in *Journ. of Hellen. Studies*, 77, (1957), pp. 35-41. Transl. and reprinted in *Ar. in der neueren Forschung*, pp. 212-231.

H. D. Hantz, *The Biological Motivation in Aristotle*; New York, 1939.

M. Heidegger, 'Von Wezen und Begriff der Φύσις. Aristoteles, Physik B, 1.'; in *Il Pensiero* 3, (1958), pp. 131-156, 266-289.

R. Heinze, *Xenocrates, Darstellung der Lehre und Sammlung der Fragmente*; Leipzig, 1892.

R. Hirzel, 'Über Entelechie und Endelechie'; in *Rhein, Museum für Philologie*, 39, (1884), pp. 169-208.

D. Holwerda, *Commentatio de vocis quae est ΦΥΣΙΣ vi atque usu, praesertim in Graecitate Aristotele anteriore*. Groningae, 1955.

E. v. Ivanka, 'Zur Problematik der Aristotelischen Seelenlehre'; in *Autour d'Aristote*, pp. 245-254.

- 'Die Seelenlehre des Aristoteles und des hl. Thomas'; in *Aristote et St. Thomas d'Aquin*; Louvain, 1957, pp. 221-228.

W. W. Jaeger, *Studien zur Entwicklungsgeschichte der Metaphysik des Aristoteles*; Berlin, 1912.

- 'Das Pneuma im Lykeion'; in *Hermes*, 48, (1913), pp. 29-74.

- Aristoteles, *Grundlegung einer Geschichte seiner Entwicklung*. Berlin: 1923. English ed.: *Aristotle, Fundamentals of the History of His Development*, transl. R. Robinson. Oxford: U.P. 1948².

H. J. Krämer, *Arete bei Platon und Aristoteles; Zum Wesen und zur Geschichte der platonischen Ontologie*; Heidelberg, 1959.

- 'Retraktationen zum Problem des esoterischen Plato'; in *Museum Helveticum* 21, (1964), pp. 137-167.

146

P. Lang, *De Speusippi Academici Scriptis*; *Accedunt Fragmenta*; Bonn, 1911.

Ch. Lefèvre, 'Du Platonisme à l'Aristotélisme; à l'occasion d'une publication récente'; in *Rev. Phil. de Louvain* 59, (1961), pp. 197-248.

- 'Travaux intéressant l'Aristotélisme'; *ibid.* 68, (1970), pp. 79-94,242-259.
- 'Quinta Natura et la psychologie aristotélicienne'; *ibid.*, 69, (1971), pp. 5-43.

O. Longo, *Struttura e composizione del 'De Caelo' di Aristotele*. In preparazione per i tipi dell'Editrice Antenore in Padova; 197.

A. Mansion, *Introduction à la Physique Aristotélicienne*; Louvain, 1913; 2ème éd., revue et augmentée, 1946.

- 'La genèse de l'oeuvre d'Aristote d'après les travaux récents'; in *Rev. néoscholastique de Phil.* 29, (1927), pp. 307-341; 423-466. Abridged reprint in *Ar. in der neueren Forschung*, pp. 1-66.
- 'L'immortalité de l'âme et de l'intellect d'après Aristote'; in *Rev. philos. de Louvain*, 51, (1953), pp. 444-472.
- 'Het Aristotelisme in het historisch perspectief; Platonisme-Aristotelisme-neo-Platonisme'; in *Meded. van de Kon. Vlaamse Akad. voor Wetensch.*, 1954, no. 3. Brussel.
- *Autour d'Aristote. Recueil d'études de philosophie ancienne et médiévale offert à A. Mansion*; Louvain, 1955.

S. Mansion, 'Contemplation and Action in Aristotle's Protrepticus'; in *Ar. and Plato in the Mid-Fourth century*, pp. 56-75.

S. Mariotti, 'La 'quinta essentia' nell'Aristotele perduto e nell' Accademia'; in *Riv. di Filol.* N.S. 18 (1940) pp. 179-189.

Ph. Merlan, *From Platonism to neo-Platonism*; The Hague, 1960² (1969³).

- 'Metaphysik: Name und Gegenstand'; in *Journal of Hellen. Studies*, 77, (1957), pp. 87-92.
- 'War Platons Vorlesung 'Das Gute' einmalig?' in *Hermes* 96, (1968-9), pp. 705-709.

P. Moraux, 'Einige Bemerkungen über den Aufbau von Aristoteles' Schrift De Caelo'; in *Museum Helv.* 6, (1949), pp. 157-165.

- 'Recherches sur le De Caelo d'Aristote; objet et structure de l'ouvrage'; in *Revue Thomiste*, 51, (1951), pp. 170-196.
- *Les Listes anciennes des Ouvrages d'Aristote*; Louvain, 1951.
- 'Notes sur la tradition indirecte du 'De Caelo' d'Aristote'; in *Hermes*, 82, (1954), pp. 145-182.
- 'L'évolution d'Aristote'; in *Aristote et St. Thomas d'Aquin*, 1957, pp. 9-41. Transl. and reprinted in *Ar. in der neueren Forschung*, pp. 67-94.
- 'From the Protrepticus to the Dialogue On Justice'; in *Ar. and Pl. in the Mid-Fourth century*, pp. 113-132.
- 'La méthode d'Aristote dans l'étude du ciel'; in *Ar. et les problèmes de méthode*, pp. 173-194.
- 'Kritisch-Exegetisches zu Aristoteles'; in *Archiv. f. Gesch. der Philos.* 43, (1961), pp. 15-40.
- 'Quinta Essentia'; in *Pauly-Wissowa R.E.*, 47 Halbband, 1963, kol. 1171-1263.
- *D'Aristote à Bessarion*; *Trois exposés sur l'histoire et la transmission de l'Aristotélisme Grec*; Québec, 1970.

147

J. Moreau, *L'Ame du Monde de Platon aux Stoiciens*; Paris, 1939.

- 'L'être et l'essence dans la philosophie d'Aristote'; in *Autour d'Aristote*, pp. 181-204.
- *Aristote et son école*; Collection 'les grands penseurs'; Paris, 1962.

G. R. Morrow, 'Qualitative Change in Aristotle's Physics'; in *Naturphilosophie bei Ar. und Theophr.* pp. 154-167.

E. Nachmanson, 'Der griechische Buchtitel. Einige Beobachtungen'; in *Göteborgs Högskolas Årsskrift* XLVII, (1941), no. 19, pp. 1-52.

F. J. C. J. Nuyens, *Ontwikkelingsmomenten in de Zielkunde van Aristoteles*; Utrecht-Nijmegen, 1939 (Fr. ed. *L'évolution de la Psychologie d'Aristote*, Louvain, 1948).

- 'Aristoteles' persoonlijkheid in zijn werk'; in *Autour d'Aristote*, pp. 69-80.

G. E. L. Owen, 'The Platonism of Aristotle'; in *Proceedings of the British Academy* (Dawes Hicks Lecture in Philosophy), Vol. LI; London: 1965, pp. 125-150.

J. Owens, *The Doctrine of Being in the Aristotelian Metaphysics. A Study in the Greek Background of Mediaeval Thought*; Toronto (1951), 1963².

J. Pépin, 'La philosophie d'Aristote, ses premières expressions et sa postérité'; in *Etudes philos.* 18, (1963) pp. 429-438.

- 'L'interprétation du De Philosophia d'Aristote d'après quelques travaux récents'; in *Revue des Et. Grecques* 77, (1964) pp. 445-488.
- *Théologie cosmique et théologie chrétienne*; (Ambroise, Exam. I, 1, 1-4); Paris, 1964.
- *Idées grecques sur l'homme et sur Dieu*; Paris: 1971.

M. Pohlenz *Die Stoa Geschichte einer geistigen Bewegung.* IIBd. Göttingen, 1959².

W. Pötscher, *Strukturprobleme der aristotelischen und theophrastischen Gottesvorstellung* (Philos. Antiqua XIX) Leiden; 1970.

W. G. Rabinowitz, *Aristotle's Protrepticus and the Sources of its Reconstruction I*; Univ. of Calif. Public. in Class. Philol. Vol. 16, no. 1, Berkeley 1957.

G. Rodier, 'Sur la Composition de la Physique d'Aristote'; in *Archiv f. Gesch. der Philos.* 8, (1895), pp. 455-460 and 9 (1896), pp. 185-189.

W. D. Ross, *Aristotle*, London, 1923. (1964⁵).

- 'The Development of Aristotle's Thought'; in *Ar. and Pl. in the Mid-Fourth century*, pp. 1-14.

H. E. Runner, *The Development of Aristotle, illustrated from the earliest Books of the Physics*; Kampen 1951.

G. Ryle, *Plato's Progress*; Cambridge, 1966.

H. D. Saffrey, *Le περὶ φιλοσοφίας d'Aristote et la théorie platonicienne des idées nombres*; Leiden, 1955.

G. A. Seeck, *Über die Elemente in der Kosmologie des Aristoteles*; *Untersuchungen zu De Generatione et Corruptione und De Caelo*; (Zetemata, Hft. 34) München, 1964.

148

Simplicii in Aristotelis De Caelo Commentaria consilio et auctoritate Acad. Litt. Regiae Borussicae ed. I. L. Heiberg, (C.C.A.G. Vol. VII), Berolini, 1894.

J. B. Skemp, *The Theory of Motion in Plato's later Dialogues*; enlarged ed. Amsterdam, 1967.

F. Solmsen, 'Die Entwicklung der aristotelischen Logik und Rhetorik'; in *Neue Philol. Untersuchungen*, Heft 4; Berlin: 1929.

- 'Aristotle and Presocratic Cosmogony'; in *Harvard Studies in Class. Philol.* 63 (1958), pp. 265-282. Translated and reprinted in *Ar. in der neueren Forschung*, pp. 168-192.

- 'Platonic Influences in the Formation of Aristotle's Physical System'; in *Ar. and Pl. in the Mid-Fourth century*, pp. 213-235.

- *Aristotle's System of the Physical World*; a Comparison with his Predecessors; Ithaca, 1960.

P. Steinmetz, 'Ansatzpunkte der Elementenlehre Theophrasts im Werk des Aristoteles'; in *Naturphilos. bei Ar. und Theophr.* 1969, pp. 224-249.

J. Stenzel, *Zahl und Gestalt bei Platon und Aristoteles*; Berlin 1924 (Darmstadt 1959³).

E. de Strycker, 'On the first Section of fr. 5a of the Protrepticus; Its logical Structure and the Platonic character of its doctrine'; in *Ar. and Plato in the Mid-Fourth century*, pp. 76-104.

- 'Aristote, critique de Platon'; in *L'Antiq. Class.*, 18 (1949), pp. 95-107. Translated reprint in *Ar. in der neueren Forschung*, 1968, p. 198.

P. Tannery, 'Sur la composition de la Physique d'Aristote'; in *Archiv f. Gesch. der Philos.* 7, (1894), pp. 224-229 and 9, (1896), pp. 115-119.

W. Theiler, *Zur Geschichte der teleologischen Naturbetrachtung bis auf Aristoteles*; Zürich, 1924.

- 'Ein vergessenes Aristoteleszeugnis'; in *Journal of Hellen. Studies* 77, (1957) pp. 127-131.

- 'Die Entstehung der Metaphysik des Aristoteles mit einem Anhang über Theophrasts Metaphysik'; in *Museum Helveticum* 15 (1958) pp. 85-105

Theophrastus, *Metaphysics*: with transl., comm. and introd. by W. D. Ross and F. H. Fobes; Oxford: 1929 (Hildesheim 1967²).

M. Untersteiner, 'Aristotele Phys. I, 8-9. Frammenti del περὶ φιλοσοφίας; in *Riv. di Filol. e d'istruzione classica*, 87, (1959), pp. 1-23.

- 'Il περὶ φιλοσοφίας di Aristotele'; in *Riv. di Filol. e d'istruzione classica* 88, (1960), pp. 337-362 and 89 (1961) pp. 121-159.

P. Valentin, 'Un 'protreptique' conservé de l'Antiquité: le Contra Academicos de Saint Augustin'; in *Rev. des Sciences Religieuses* 43, (1969), pp. 1-26; 97-117.

G. Verbeke, 'Comment Aristote conçoit-il l'immatériel?' in *Revue philos. de Louvain*, 44, (1946), pp. 205-236.

- 'L'évolution de la psychologie d'Aristote'; in *Revue philos. de Louvain*, 46, (1948) pp. 335-351.

W. J. Verdenius 'Critical and Exegetical Notes on De Caelo'; in *Naturphilosophie bei Aristoteles und Theophrast*, pp. 268-284.

149

C. J. de Vogel, 'Problems concerning later Platonism'; in *Mnemosyne* (S. IV,2) 1949, pp. 197-216, 299-318.

– 'La théorie de l'ἄπειρον chez Platon et dans la tradition platonicienne'; in *Revue philos. de la France et de l'étranger*, 84, (1959), pp. 21-39.

– 'The Legend of the Platonizing Aristotle'; in *Ar. and Pl. in the Mid-Fourth century*, pp. 248-256.

– *Greek Philosophy*, vol. II; *Aristotle, the early Peripatetic school and the early Academy*. Leiden, 1960².

– 'Did Aristotle ever accept Plato's Theory of Transcendent Ideas? Problems around a new edition of the Protrepticus'; in *Archiv f. Gesch. der Philos.* 47, (1965), pp. 261-298.

D. H. Th. Vollenhoven, 'De Ontwikkelingsgang van Aristoteles I'; in *Philos. Reformata*, 16, (1951), pp. 16-63.

– 'De Ontwikkelingsgang van Aristoteles als zelfstandig denker'; in *Philos. Reform.* 21, (1956), pp. 44-80.

G. J. de Vries, 'Marginalia bij een esoterische Plato'; in *Tijdschr. voor Filos.* 26, (1964), pp. 704-719.

– 'Aristoxenos über περὶ τἀγαθοῦ'; in *Hermes*, 96 (1968), pp. 124-126.

– *A Commentary on the Phaedrus of Plato*; Amsterdam, 1969.

W. Wieland, *Die Aristotelische Physik*; *Untersuchungen über die Grundlegung der Naturwissenschaft und die sprachlichen Bedingungen der Prinzipienforschung bei Aristoteles*; Göttingen, 1970².

P. Wilpert, 'Reste verlorener Aristotelesschriften bei Alexander von Aphrodisias'; in *Hermes*, 75, (1940), pp. 369-396.

– 'Neue Fragmente aus περὶ τἀγαθοῦ'; in *Hermes*, 76, (1941), pp. 225-250.

– 'Die aristotelische Schrift 'Über die Philosophie'', in *Autour d'Aristote*, pp. 99-116.

– *Zwei Aristotelische Frühschriften über die Ideenlehre*; Regensburg, 1949.

– 'Die Stellung der Schrift 'Über die Philosophie' in der Gedankenentwicklung des Aristoteles', in *Journal of Hellenic Studies*, 77, (1957), pp. 155-162.

W. Wundt, *Untersuchungen zur Metaphysik des Aristoteles*; (Tübinger Beiträge zur Altertumswiss. 38), Stuttgart: 1953.

J. Zürcher, *Aristoteles' Werk und Geist*; Paderborn, 1952.

INDEX OF NAMES

Alexander of Aphrodisias: 51 n.61
Alfonsi L.: 137 n.109 n.112, 139 n.117
 n.118
Allan D. J.: 6 n.4, 14 and n.51
Anaxagoras: 53, 71, 72 n.126, 79 n.158
Anaximenes: 100
Andronicus: 107
Antiphon: 116 and n.27
Ariston of Ceos: 104
Armstrong A. H.: 35 n.11, 57 n.78
Atomists: 17 n.76, 53, 64, 70, 72
Atticus: 57
Aristoxonus: 41
Arnim H. von: 1, 10-12, 13, 14, 17
 n.76, 18, 20 n.87, 21 n.89, 23, 28,
 32 n.18, 49, 62, 70 n.120, 89, 91,
 93, 96 n.28, 98 n.33, 108 n.2,
 118, 119 and n. 39, 134, 135 n.104
Augustine: 123 n.57

Begemann A. W.: 70 n.121
Bernays J.: 92 n.16
Berti E.: 5 n.1 n.2, 6 n.6, 55 n.69,
 57 n.79, 64 and n.96, 68 n.115,
 90 n.9, 99 n.35, 113 n.21, 119
 n.144, 122 n.54, 124 and n.58 n.59
 n.62, 125 n.65 n.66, 127 n.71, 128,
 130 n.85, 131 n.87 n.89, 132 n.94,
 133 and n.98, 134 n.102 n.103,
 135 and n.104 n.107.
Bidez J.: 139 n.118
Bignone E.: 17 n.76, 106
Blair G. A.: 88 n.5
Blass F.: 92 n.16, 99 n.34, 119 n.40
Bonitz H.: 58 n.81, 102 n.44, 103 n.48,
 104
Bos C. A.: 80 n.164
Bridoux A.: 100 n.39
Burnet J.: 67 n.111, 74 n.133, 77 n.149

Callippus: 16
Case T.: 5 n.1
Charlton W.: 112 n.17
Cherniss H.: 91 n.12, 92 n.13, 108 n.2,
 119 and n.39, 134 n.103
Chroust A. H.: 55 n.69
Cicero: 12 n.38, 23, 54 n.66, 62, 64,
 83 n.170, 99 n.34, 123 n.57, 137
 n.109, 138 and n.114, 139 and
 n.119
Claghorn G. S.: 54 n.68
Clemens of Alexandria: 136 n.109, 137
 n.109
Clemens (Ps.): 54
Cook, H. P.: 94 n.20
Cornford F. M.: 31 n.14
Critolaus: 100 n.39
Crönert W.: 107 n.65

Diels H.: 76 n.146
Democritus: 37, 48 n.51, 53, 64
Descartes R.: 100 n.39
Diodorus: 100 n.39
Diogenes of Apollonia: 64, 100, 139
 n.118
Diogenes Laërtius: 104, 105
Dooyeweerd H.: 37 n.15
Drossaart Lulofs H. J.: 24 n.4
Düring I.: 7 and n.9, 13 n.45, 29 n.1,
 32 n.17, 44 and n.39, 47 and n.50,
 57 n.78, 63, 76 n.146, 77 n.147,
 78 n.151 n.155, 79 n.158, 83 n.170,
 88 n.5, 101 and n.42, 104 and
 n.55, 108 n.2, 109 n.4, 117 n.29,
 120 n.45, 121 n.50, 122 n.54, 123
 n.57, 124 and n.59 n.62, 125 n.63
 n.64 n.65, 126 n.68, 127, 128 n.74,
 129, 131 n.88, 134 n.102

Easterling H. J.: 17 n.75, 21 n.88, 60 n.85, 90 n.9 n.11, 91
Effe B.: 122 n.54, 131 n.85 n.87
Elders L.: 12, 17, 18-22, 25 n.13, 26 n.16, 29 n.4, 30 n.5 n.9, 35 and n.8, 36 and n.13, 44, 46 n.45, 50 n.56, 58 n.81, 65 n.102, 69, 70 n.120, 72, 75, 88, 89 n.8, 90 n.9, 91, 92 n.13 n.15, 96 n.28, 102 n.46, 104 n.57
Eleatics: 31, 45, 48, 63, 67 and n.113, 68, 94 n.24, 111
Empedocles: 53, 60, 64 n.98, 66 and n.110, 70, 72 n.126, 79 n.158, 84, 115
Epicurus: 64 n.95, 106, 137 n.109
Eusebius: 58 n.80

Festugière A. J.: 57 n.78, 90 n.9, 139 n.118
Frank E.: 7 n.9, 79 n.158, 94 n.25, 119 n.39

Gaiser K.: 18
Gallileo: 55 n.70
Gauthier R. A.: 121 n.49
Gigon O.: 2 n.1, 14 and n.53, 15 and n.57, 17, 24 n.5, 25, 26 n.16, 29 n.1, 33 n.1, 35 n.8, 48 n.51, 56 n.74, 60 n.84, 69 n.119, 78 n.152, 105 n.59, 140 n.122
Gohlke P.: 1, 10 n.20, 14 n.54, 23, 26 n.16, 29 n.2, 30 n.5, 43 n.37, 59 n.81, 79 n.157, 90 n.9, 94 n.21, 102 n.46, 104 n.54 n.55, 105, 109 n.6, 110 n.8 n.9, 118, 121 n.47
Grumach E.: 97 n.32
Guthrie W. K. C.: 1, 12-14, 16, 17 n.76, 20 n.87, 21 n.89, 28, 29 and n.2 n.4, 30, 35, 39, 44, 47 n.48, 49, 61 n.89, 62, 65 n.101, 88, 89 and n.8, 91, 92 n.13, 93, 95, 96 n.29, 97, 104 n.57, 108 n.2, 109, 116 n.27, 134, 135 n.105

Hantz H. D.: 120 n.46
Harder R.: 42 n.34
Heidel W. A.: 77 n.149

Heinze R.: 92 n.13
Heraclitus: 53, 69 n.116, 71, 127
Hermippus: 104 and n.52, 131 n.89
Hesiod: 53, 69 n.116, 71
Hirzel R.: 88 n.5, 99 n.34
Hobbes Th.: 100 n.39
Holwerda D.: 77 n.149

Isocrates: 124
Ivanka E. von: 139 n.117

Jaeger W.: 1, 5-10, 11 n.31, 12, 14, 19 n.79, 21, 23, 24 and n.4, 29 n.1, 44 n.41, 48 n.52, 55 n.69, 56, 57 n.79, 59 n.83, 62, 68, 76 n.146, 83 n.170, 92 n.16, 108 and n.1 n.2, 113 n.21, 117, 118 and n.38, 119 and n.45, 120 n.45, 121 n.50, 124, 126 n.68, 131 and n.88, 134
Joachim H. H.: 86 n.178
Jolif J. Y.: 121 n.49
Justinus (Ps.): 137 n.112

Kraemer H. J.: 18

Lefèvre Ch.: 44 n.39, 119 n.45, 139 n.119
Longo O.: 3 n.14, 15, 16 n.64 n.65, 21 n.89, 24 n.5, 25, 26 n.16 n.17, 29 n.4, 30, 35 n.8, 46 n.45, 58 n.81, 88, 89 n.8, 92 n.13, 102 n.45, 104 n.57, 105 n.59, 106
Longrigg J.: 21 n.88

Mansion A.: 5 n.1, 6 n.4, 8 n.14, 9 n.18, 10 and n.20 n.21, 29 n.1, 78 n.153, 79 n.157 n.158, 99 n.35, 100 n.41, 102 n.46, 104 and n.56 n.57, 105 n.58, 106, 108 n.1, 117 n.30, 118, 129 n.80, 134, 139 n.119
Mariotti S.: 17 and n.75, 140 and n.120
Merlan Ph.: 35 n.11, 42 n.34, 57 n.78
Mondésert C.: 136 n.109, 137 n.109
Moraux P.: 15 n.57 n.63, 16-18, 21 n.89, 23 n.1, 24 n.5, 25 and n.15, 26 n.16 n.17, 30, 35 n.8, 43, 44, 46 n.45, 54 n.67, 55 n.70, 58 n.81,

152

65, 66 n.110, 73 n.130, 88, 89 n.8, 91 and n.12, 92 and n.16, 97 n.31, 99 n.35, 100 n.39, 101 and n.43, 104 and n.55, 105 and n.59, 134 n.101, 138, 139 n.119

Moreau J.: 7 n.8, 17 n.76, 23, 57 n.79, 100 n.41, 130 n.84, 134 n.101, 137 n.110, 139, 140

Morrow G. R.: 94 n.24

Nachmanson E.: 101 n.43

Neo-platonists: 15, 42

Nuyens F.: 1, 5 n.2, 29 n.1, 65 n.102, 99 n.35, 100 and n.40 n.41, 122 n.53, 131 n.89, 134 n.100, 139 n.119

Owen G. E. L.: 6 n.6, 37 n.17, 97 n.30

Owens J.: 9 n.19, 120 n.45

Parmenides: 48 n.51, 51, 67, 69, 71, 103, 132 and n.91

Pépin J.: 7 n.7 n.8, 9 n.17, 17 n.75, 55, 58 n.79 n.80, 60 n.85, 61 n.91, 64 n.97, 68 n.115, 99, 109 n.3, 122 n.54, 125 n.67, 130 n.85, 131 n.86 n. 89, 132 n.93, 135 n.104 n.105 n.107, 136 n.108, 137 and n.109, 138 and n.114, 139 and n.116 n.117, 140

Peripatos: 100, 104

Philolaus: 66 n.104

Philoponus: 133 n.98

Plato: 3, 5, 6, 7, 8 and n.10, 9, 10, 17, 18, 19, 20 n.82, 31 n.14, 32, 34 n.4, 35 and n.11, 36 and n.13, 37 38, 39, 40, 41, 42, 43, 44 and n.40, 45, 46 and n.45, 47 and n.50, 48 n.51 n.52, 49 n.54, 51, 52 and n.63, 54, 56, 57 and n.78, 59, 61 and n.90, 63, 64 and n.95 n.98, 66, 67 n.110 n.111, 68, 69 and n.118, 70, 71, 72, 73, 74, 76, 77 n.146, 79 and n.158, 83 and n.170, 85, 87, 91 n.12, 92, 94, 96, 97 n.30, 98, 100, 101, 111, 112 and n.17, 113, 114, 117, 118, 119, 120 n.45, 121 n.50, 124, 125, 126 and n.68,

128, 129, 131 and n.88, 132 and n.91 n.96, 133, 135 n.107, 136, 140

Plato (Ps.): 80 n.164

Plotinus: 2, 42

Pohlenz M.: 17 n.76

Porphyry: 2

Pötscher W.: 134 n.102, 140 and n.121

Prantl C.: 69 n.116

Presocratics: 36, 78, 132

Ptolemaeus: 43 n.38

Pythagoreans: 34 and n.4, 66 and n.105

Rabinowitz W. G.: 44 n.42, 123

Rodier G.: 93 and n.17

Rose V.: 131 n.87

Ross W. D.: 1, 13 n.45, 14 n.50, 24 n.4, 28, 29 n.2, 32 n.22, 35 and n.10, 44 n.42, 65, 77 n.149, 85 n. 179, 88 and n.5, 89 and n.7, 90, 93, 97 n.31, 99 n.35, 103 n.49, 104, 108 n.1 n.2, 109, 110 n.8, 112 n.17, 113 n.20, 114 n.24, 117 n.31, 118 n.33 n.34, 122 n.52, 123, 124, 129, 130, 131 n.85

Runner H. E.: 5 n.2, 30 n.5, 50 n.57, 88, 89 n.7, 94 n.21, 98 n.33, 106, 108 n.1 n.2, 109 n.6, 110 n.9, 113 n.21, 117 n.30

Ryle G.: 4 n.3

Sceptics: 1

Schoemann G. F.: 99 n.34

Schwyzer H.: 42 n.34

Seeck G. A.: 12, 15 n.57, 17, 24 and n.2 n.7, 25, 26 n.16, 30, 31, 50 n.57, 61 n.88, 72, 73 n.132

Sextus Empiricus: 31 n.12, 48 n.52

Simplicius: 31 n.13, 35 n.8, 40, 43 n. 38, 58 n.81, 66 n.105, 92

Skemp, J. B.: 47 n.50

Socrates: 51, 79 n.158, 85

Solmsen F.: 13 n.45, 17 n.73 n.74, 24 and n.3, 32 n.18, 44 n.41, 47 n.50, 49 n.53, 54 n.67, 57 n.78, 59 n.82, 61 n.88, 64 and n.94, 74 n.134, 79 n.158, 86 n.180, 90 n.9, 93 n.18, 94 n.22, n.23 n.24, 97 n.30,

98 and n.33, 108 n.2, 117 n.29, 121, 130 n.84

Speusippus: 11 n.33, 19, 46, 91 and n.12, 111

Steinmetz P.: 26 n.16

Stenzel J.: 18, 45 n.43

Stoa: 9, 17 n.76, 62, 100, 126, 134, 135, 139 and n.117

Stocks J. L.: 14 and n.50, 35 n.8, 88, 89 n.8

Strycker E. de: 119, 128 n.74

Tannery P.: 93 and n.17 n.18

Theiler W.: 7 n.9, 58 n.80, 119 n.45, 130 n.85, 133 n.98, 139 n.119

Theophrastus: 40 and n.28, 97 n.32, 140

Thomas Aquinas: 15

Thompson, D'Arcy W.: 28

Tredennick H.: 38 n.18

Tricot J.: 14 and n.52, 15, 18, 30, 31 n.12 n.16, 35 n.8, 76 n.145, 88, 89 n.8, 104 n.57

Untersteiner M.: 57 n.79, 62 n.91, 64 n.97, 77 n.146, 110 n.8 n.9, 122

n.54, 130, 131 n.86, 132 n.91, 133 n.98, 134 n.102 n.103, 135 n.107, 136 n.108, 137 n.112

Valentin P.: 123 n.57

Verbeke G.: 99 n.35, 100 n.41, 139 n. 119

Vogel C. J. de: 7 n.9, 57 n.79, 77 n.146, 82 n.171, 129 n.80, 132 n.96, 138 n.113

Vollenhoven D. H. Th.: 1, 37 n.15

Volkmann: 42 n.34

Vries G. J. de: 66 and n.104

Walzer R.: 92 n.16, 124, 129, 130, 131 n.85, 132 n.91

Wieland W.: 23, 79 n.157

Wilpert P.: 6 n.4, 8 n.10, 44, 119, 120 n.46, 132 n.92 n.96

Wittgenstein L.: 85 n.172

Xenocrates: 36 n.13, 46, 91 and n.12, 92, 111

Zeller E.: 29 n.1

Zürcher J.: 93 n.18